T0285307

"I came to know Jesus Christ as my Lord and Savior after having a Bible slapped to my chest by my commanding officer as we boarded ships for an overseas deployment. He told me, 'You need to know your Lord and Savior, read this on the way.' Like a good Marine, I followed orders. For the first time in my life, I read the Bible from cover to cover. It changed my life, forever. In *The Apostate*, Mark Christian describes how he found eternal life. Mark was intent on bringing Islam to America with what he believed were iron-clad arguments. But reading God's word in the holy Bible dismantled Mark's arguments favoring Islam and pointed him to truth: Jesus Christ tells us 'I am the way and the truth and the life. No one comes to the Father except through me.' This great book is a must read!"

—LtCol Oliver L. North USMC (Ret),
bestselling author of *We Didn't Fight for Socialism.*

THE APOSTATE

My Search for Truth

Dr. Mark Christian

FIDELIS
PUBLISHING

FIDELIS PUBLISHING

ISBN: 9781737176305
ISBN (eBook): 9781737176312

The Apostate
My Search for Truth
© 2022 Mark Christian

Cover Design by Diana Lawrence
Interior Design by Xcel Graphic—xcelgraphic.com

For information about special discounts for bulk purchases, please contact Bulk-Books.com, call 1-888-959-5153 or email—cs@bulkbooks.com

Fidelis Publishing, LLC Sterling, VA • Nashville, TN
fidelispublishing.com

Manufactured in the United States of America
10 9 8 7 6 5 4 3 2 1

Fidelis Publishing, LLC
Sterling, VA • Nashville, TN
fidelispublishing.com

CONTENTS

Prologue   v

Chapter 1: Becoming a Bond Slave   1

Chapter 2: Acceptance and Transformation   7

Chapter 3: Forgiveness at Any Cost   17

Chapter 4: Fatherhood and Brotherhood   29

Chapter 5: My Mentor   47

Chapter 6: Meeting a God I Did Not Know   57

Chapter 7: Awakening   67

Chapter 8: The Islamic State Is Born   93

Chapter 9: An Eye Toward the Grave   117

Chapter 10: Sadat Makes Concessions with the West   131

Chapter 11: Of Summits, Trains, and Swords   153

Chapter 12: The Prophet Mohamed   175

Chapter 13: Mecca in History   185

Chapter 14: Origins   199

Chapter 15: The Source of the Quran   209

Chapter 16: The Night Journey   213

Chapter 17: The Jewish Problem   217

Chapter 18: The Christian Problem   229

Chapter 19: Islam the Victorious   243

Chapter 20: The Spread of Islam   253

Chapter 21. The Pilgrimage Problem   259

Chapter 22: Confusion and Challenges   263

Chapter 23: The Safest Person   271

Chapter 24: A Godless World   279

Chapter 25: Love and Marriage   287

Chapter 26: God Is Love   297

Epilogue   305

Notes   307

PROLOGUE

Our separation began in 1992, when my questioning of Islam became too much for this devoted Muslim leader to bear. He refused to entertain my doubts and concerns and was enraged that I would dare challenge Mohamed or Allah or our once shared devotion. As a result, I distanced myself from this man and he from me. He spent many years hoping I would come to my senses and resume my place of honor as a righteous believer. That was never going to happen. He once asked me, "You say Islam is wrong and that it is not the truth. So, what is the truth?"

Oh, how that question tormented me! I had no idea what the truth was or where to find it. I was completely lost. I knew there was a Creator and there was a God somewhere—but where? Who? Finding the meaning of life was the one quest above all others driving me.

I tried many times over the years to reconcile with this religious man. I called him on his birthday, on my birthday, on random occasions, seeking some sort of resolution. I am sure I should have known better. Islam would not allow him to budge so much as an inch. If he had, he believed he would face the judgments of an unforgiving God. I knew that, but I was too persistent not to try.

When I got a phone call instructing me to meet him in the early morning hours of March 29, 2003, I was surprised that for the first time in years he wanted to meet with me—I was exuberant. Perhaps, for the sake of preserving some sort of relationship, he was willing to call a truce. Perhaps he would satisfy himself with an "agree to disagree" détente. I hoped deep in my soul this would be the day we reached our armistice.

I did not want to waste a moment lest he change his mind. I headed out the door that morning, telling my wife, Dina, I would not be long. As I drove to his medical clinic and walked up to his office, I couldn't help but feel hopeful. I hadn't felt hope for a very long time, and it felt good to have a chance to think of the good times, the days of seeing eye to eye with him and meeting man to man.

The door to his office in the clinic was characteristically open. I took this as his overture to indicate we could begin to meet regularly once again. I smiled to myself thinking it would be nice to reach a truce of some sort. I opened the door of the darkened office, walked through the hallway leading to his personal office, and tripped on the rug. I reached out with my hand to break the fall, and my hand triggered what happened next. In that instant, I heard a sound like a rush of wind, and everything before my eyes erupted in flames. Before I could determine what happened, a surge of heat and an intense burning sensation overwhelmed me.

This was one of those out-of-body experiences you read about, the kind in which you feel as if you are looking down on yourself as the scene unfolds around you in slow motion. I couldn't process what was happening and could only think in a disjointed, one-syllable sort of way. Fire. Burns. Hurt. Anger. Why? Looking back at the explosion, I believe tripping probably saved my life.

Gathering myself from the floor, I thought for a second I should rush through the fire to save him from the blaze, but it dawned on me I was the only one in the office. At times, a cloud of smoke blinding our eyes is all our hearts need to see clearly. This was one such time. I ran from the building, out into the street, dazed, confused, and screaming as I rushed headlong toward my car. The words, "Get to the car, get to the car, drive home," circled around and around in my head. I can only imagine what the people on the street must have been thinking as they saw this fire-scarred monster lunge out of the building toward his car, screaming like a wounded animal.

I raced home, not stopping to look at myself in the rearview mirror. To this day, I have no idea how I managed to find my way through Cairo's early rush-hour traffic. As I pushed open the front door, Dina's eyes met mine with a look of horror. "Go to the bathroom, hurry!" she said. "Don't let Alex see you! He will be frightened." Alex, my son, had every reason to be frightened. His grandfather—my father—had just tried to kill me. There was no reason to believe he wouldn't try again.

CHAPTER 1

BECOMING A BOND SLAVE

Allah will use your holy war and jihad to forgive you. Only by the virtue of your jihad, Allah will forgive your past sin and what is to come. That will bear witness to mankind to follow you in Islam and they will join you and fight a holy war for the cause of Islam.

—Quran 48:2 The Conquest*

I was five years old when I first met him, the almighty Allah. On that fateful day, in a dark room, my life began as surely as if I were emerging from the womb. I, Mohammed Abdullah, can never erase that memory, and I'm certain I should *not* try. This day marked the moment I first got to know Allah. On that day I first acknowledged my own status as a Muslim, a status that if neglected merited only one outcome, an eternity of hellfire.

My father yanked my arms backward and tied me by his military-issue belt to the bed. In the creeping darkness, I could still

*When quoting from the Quran throughout this book, I will be using my own Arabic translation skills to convey accurate meaning.

see the dresser, the closet, and the vanity where my mother would put on makeup each day. I should have felt safe in my parents' room. Instead, I was bound, alone, and afraid. I trembled with the fear of what was to come, and my mind raced as the deepening shadows loomed like so many monsters ready to tear me apart.

I could hear my parents just outside the bedroom—my father yelling at my mother, chastising her, she was dissolving in tears, helpless to save me or herself. Only a few hours earlier, my mother and I and her older brother were sitting in a movie theater. I was lost in the thrill of a police chase, all flashing lights and wailing sirens, I had not a care in the world.

Surprisingly, my father was waiting for us when we got home. My mother was frightened to see him. My father was supposed to be at work. He said Allah guided him to swing by the house. "Divine intervention," he called it.

Without saying a word to me, he forcefully took me by the hand and pulled me into the bedroom, tied me up, and left me in the dark to ponder what I did to deserve such a fate. I tried to see what was happening outside the room, but there was only darkness. Mother continued to weep as my father shamed her and her family, especially her brother, who was an accomplice in her sin. A good Muslim man would have stopped her from sinning. He would not have sinned along with her. Once finished scolding my mother, my father stormed into the restroom. I could hear him cleanse himself, just as he would do before performing the *salat*, the ritual Muslim prayer.

When Dad pushed open the bedroom door, I sensed he was about to conduct holy business. I hoped against hope he would remember he was my father and a father should love his son and not harm him. But as I learned over time, it was precisely because he loved his son he had to harm him. As Quran 64:14 reminds us, this was the true Muslim way: *"O you who have believed, indeed, your wives and your children are enemies to you, so beware of them."*

My father sat on the floor beside me and began to teach me the nature of Allah. He explained that mankind was created for one reason—to worship Allah. *"All of Allah's creation is only created for himself. And it is for Allah's creation to totally submit to Allah and worship him,"* he said, quoting from the Quran 51:56. The meaning was clear: if I was not doing good, if my every action was not an act of worship, then I was doing bad and deserved punishment. One can worship Allah through religious rituals, but working hard can be an act of worship as well. So can studying.

"I will beat you," he said solemnly, "so that Allah will see you are being punished for what you did." With those words, he unfolded his prayer rug, faced Mecca, and began praying. I watched in silent wonder, daring not to move or draw his attention away from his prayers. Meanwhile, I was considering his words. Even at such a young age, I acknowledged I deserved to be beaten and readied myself for punishment. I knew I had to be cleansed.

When my father finished his prayers, he stood, folded his rug, pulled out his leather belt, and began raining down blow after blow on my tender flesh. Tears streamed down my face as he recited verses of the Quran, chastising me as fervently as he beat me. He was doing his duty to cleanse the evil out of me and teach me to never make the same mistake again. Somehow, I understood he was right to do what he did.

"You shall not follow anyone blindly in those matters of which you have no knowledge, surely the use of your ears and the eyes— all of these, shall be questioned on the Day of Judgment," he said, quoting Quran 17:36. He continued quoting verses from the Quran, placing curses on my life and lashing me. *"And whoever turns away from my remembrance—indeed, he will have a depressed life, and we will gather him on the day of resurrection blind."*

This was the day my father became my teacher. He was not angry. He was merely doing his duty before Allah, teaching me the correct path. Even at five, I could sense his passion and his righteousness. That day my father helped me understand the depth of my sin. My education had begun. In time, I learned the words the Prophet Mohamed said just before his death, *"Today I have perfected the religion, and completed my favors for you and chosen Islam as a religion for mankind"* (Quran 5:3). The meaning was clear. No other religion mattered. Indeed, nothing that happened before or since mattered. Nothing could be added to or taken away from the scripture. Every essential word regarding how we should live our lives, he expressed therein.

The Prophet also said, *"Every form of amusement which the believer engages in is forbidden, except for three: a man being playful with his wife, a man being playful with his horse, and archery."* Music was forbidden. Prophet Mohamed said those who played or listened deserved to have molten lead poured into their ears. Acting was forbidden. It was only an elevated form of lying. Art in all its forms was forbidden. The scripture told us every painter would go to hell, there to be assigned a personal tormenter to punish him for the sin of creating art. Any entertainment for entertainment's sake was forbidden. The car chase I so enjoyed was forbidden. It was an affront to the Prophet.

My shame was great. My father said that by seeing and hearing things of which Allah would not approve, I dishonored Allah, and he would never, ever, forgive me. Allah would punish me on Earth, he told me, reciting Quranic scripture. He added that if my sin were not dealt with, Allah would punish me beyond the grave and again on the Day of Judgment. The words from the Quran were clear—Allah gives the gift of vision and hearing. If those gifts are not used in worship or to honor Allah, he might as well take them away.

I had an aunt who was blind. In those hours of physical and emotional torture in that darkened room, I thought of her and feared my fate would be the same. Although I did not know the nature of her sin, I assumed we were both sinners unworthy of forgiveness. I was ashamed to have disappointed my father. I was crestfallen at having caused him to deserve a punishment from Allah as well. My dad was my world, and I wanted nothing more than his approval and love. I also wanted him to be favored by Allah and to enjoy heaven ever after. The last thing I wanted was for Allah to turn his wrath on my father because of me. If I needed this cleansing to be worthy of his love, and his own cleansing from the sin I committed, then I would take it as bravely as any child could.

With each blow, my relationship with Allah and my father was being perfected. Through word and deed, my father showed me vividly and accurately the nature of our god. Allah is judgmental. Allah is exacting. Allah would rightfully crush me for my sin. As the man of the house, my father was doing his duty. He was cleansing his family, and thereby himself, of all sin. The cleansing went on for hours. So seriously did my father take his obligation to chastise me he skipped his afternoon work at the clinic, one of the very few times I have known him to do this. I took notice.

That day, I was introduced to what it meant to be a devout Muslim, wholly submitted to Allah. Through my tears and pain, I was learning my place in this world and how I was to live. My life's journey of devotion to Allah started in that dark room. I learned a life-changing lesson that day—Muslims, one and all, are terrified of the wrath of Allah and will do almost anything to escape it. We hope against reason we can hide our sin away so he will not see.

Ultimately, though, Allah will exact his wrath on everyone, even a five-year-old boy. There on the floor, battered, bruised, and awash in my own urine, I signed over my life to Allah. I enlisted in the struggle, the lifelong struggle for forgiveness from Allah for the heavy yoke of sin upon me. I was small, but my will was great. My father, the man who prodded me by belt into the kingdom of Allah and who demanded complete submission from my mother, was instructing us in how to live for Allah. From that day forward, my mother and I were changed.

Islam means submission, and I, Mohamed Abdullah, was learning that submission to Allah comes with a very high price. That price is particularly high when you are the firstborn son of a prominent imam. I was that son. My father was a man whose devotion to Allah mandated he discipline his son even, yes, to the point of death.

CHAPTER 2

ACCEPTANCE AND TRANSFORMATION

The Prophet of Islam said, "Every one of you should be slaves to Allah and to Allah alone should you prostrate yourself. But had it been permissible that a person may prostrate himself before another as he prostrates himself before Allah, I would have ordered that a wife should bow as a slave before her husband."
—Tirmidhi 285

What does it mean to be human? The answer depends on who is being asked. The response of a master will bear no resemblance to that of a slave. The response of a son will bear no resemblance to that of his mother.

Having been shamed for seeing a movie, my mother and I began our journey of transformation and redemption. Our evolution was an upward trajectory for me and a downward spiral for her—same destination, different outcomes. Every Muslim man and woman traveled similar paths. The man's journey elevates, the woman's journey diminishes. In either case, Islam requires total submission. My father, wholly devout and submissive to Allah, understood and, for the sake of our souls, he wanted to make sure we understood as well.

My mother acknowledged her sin before Allah and began with new urgency to cut out still more pieces of her soul. To become the properly observant Muslim wife, she sliced with surgical precision. She began by severing again the bond with her own corrupt, profane family. Yes, again!

Truth be told, Mother began her journey years before by marrying my father. During those early years, she tried diligently to measure up and be a good wife, but it was never easy. To remove the residue of a life ill lived, my father had to take her in hand, shake her, and threaten to beat her like a carpet. To my knowledge, he never did hit her, but the threat was often in the air.

At first, my mother rejected the facts presented to her by my father. She argued that Islam could not possibly teach what my dad was revealing to her and insisted his ideas about Islam were twisted. She thought those ideas might be the fruit of my dad's poor farm life or his harsh religious upbringing.

My father responded by showing her proof. Unconvinced, my mother asked other imams and religious leaders, even her own mother and father, and they all confirmed what her husband was saying was true. Nevertheless, she continued to rebel. She tried every trick she knew to lure my father to change his ways. When that strategy failed, she tried to pretend, tried to just play along, but after her chastisement for attending a movie, the days of pretending were over.

My father judged everything and everyone through the lens of Islam: what Prophet Mohamed said and what the Quran teaches. His faith demanded he remove my mother from her old life in every way—from family ties, from old friends, from old habits that did not reflect Islamic teachings. To compensate, he surrounded her with suitable friends. With the guidance of other women who understood the dictates of Islam and the duties of a Muslim wife, she set about rooting out her free spirit, her personal longings, and all the European or Western influences in her life.

The new women in her life were wives of my father's devout Muslim associates. They helped my mother see a better, more righteous path. Under their tutelage, she began removing "inappropriate" clothing from her closets and learned to wrap a proper hijab. She learned when, where, and for whom her beauty was to be exposed. She understood she would no longer leave the house without the permission of her husband. And she learned to suppress her free spirit until she, too, accepted the devout life as the better way.

It was hard for me to reconcile the woman I knew as my mother with the woman of her youth. Little trace of that younger woman remained. At eighteen, she was beautiful, refined, happy, and intent on studying philosophy in college. She shopped with friends, dined at fine restaurants, went to the theater. She had no concept that seeing a play or watching a movie was wrong. Back then, she had no understanding of Islam.

She learned. By the time she took me to the movies she understood Islam well enough to know it was an act of defiance. She consciously crossed a line into the forbidden. And in Islam there is a price to be paid for every sin. At age five, I committed only one such sin, but, as my father suspected, my mother had committed many. This time she got caught red-handed. My father made sure she understood she could not close her eyes to sin. He had to make her see.

MOM'S EARLY YEARS

My mother's family was Muslim, but not at all devout or properly observant. Her father was a successful, self-made businessman in the construction industry. He had amassed incredible wealth and was able to provide for his family of twelve children in ways unimaginable to my father. Their home and lifestyle were grand, and they lived as lavishly as Europeans if more conservatively in a Middle Eastern way.

Mother attended a prestigious French school in Cairo. Her personal driver took her there every day. She wore the most expensive makeup available and had a stylish wardrobe that did not include a single hijab. Hijabs were for the family's servants, not for my mother and her friends. Forward looking, mother hoped to attend college to study the great thinkers and to immerse herself in her beloved French literature, just as her twin sister would later do. She was a romantic, my mother, a dreamer, and a socialite who thrived on being the center of attention, admired for her beauty and wit.

When my mother was born, Egypt was still a British colony, and Cairo boasted beautiful architecture, a dazzling cultural scene, and a rightful place at the center of the Arabic world. She prospered in Cairo society, then a rival to Paris.

This world was about to change. A 1952 military coup drove the British out and brought the Communists in. In the 1970s, the sleeping giant of Islam once again awoke after a half-century hibernation and started to scatter the Communists. That same giant slowly choked the strength and beauty out of my mother and ultimately enslaved her to Allah.

Mother had nothing in common with a man like my father. Nothing. I believe my father saw her as spoiled, which she was, but he was drawn to her, and she was drawn to him. As it happened, one of my mom's older sisters married my father's older brother, my uncle Ahmed. Three days after the wedding Ahmed was arrested and imprisoned for his association with what the government considered "the wrong people," the Muslim Brotherhood. He spent many years in custody. When my father's family learned that my mom's sister was pregnant, they urged my dad to check on her welfare.

As an Ob-Gyn and young military officer, my father was happy to oblige. He impressed my grandfather with his drive and determination. A self-made man, my father respected the material achievements of a patriarch like my grandfather, but he could not love a man who lacked a singular focus on Islam or, more accurately, lived an Islam of his own making, not the one Prophet Mohamed created. This is why, from the beginning, my father harbored deep contempt for my grandfather's lack of piety.

As for my grandfather's sons—my mom's brothers—my father outright loathed them. The years never softened his assessment of their failings, which under Islam destined them to torment in the grave and a substantial time in hell. He saw them as spoiled, foolish, and unrepentant in their lack of devotion to Allah. If Islam and the words of the Prophet were the standard, mother's family failed in every meaningful way.

Grandfather struggled for many years with heart and other health problems, and my father started attending to his medical care during his visits to check on his sister-in-law's pregnancy. Dad's presence in the home gave my mother many opportunities to admire him from behind doorways and around corners, and my father noticed her as well. How could he not? She was beautiful, free-spirited, and nine years his junior. The attention of this older, handsome man flattered my mother. Although not allowed to spend any time together, their relationship discreetly blossomed.

A WEDDING THAT CHANGED EVERYTHING

In July 1968, my father, twenty-eight-year-old Abdou, married his love and gained the whole world, or so it seemed. Their union brought great blessing, not the least of which was money to build a new medical clinic in a prestigious neighborhood. While my grandfather wanted to donate the money, my dad was too proud to accept it as a gift. He insisted it be a loan. According to sharia law, however, there can be no interest charged on a loan. As Quran 4:160–161 clearly spells out, charging interest on loans is a dirty Jewish heritage. A pure devout Muslim man would never follow such a sinful practice.

Following his wedding, my father moved out of his apartment, a Muslim Brotherhood fraternal dwelling located near the famous Cairo University Medical School, and into my mother's family compound. This was an opulence he could previously only have imagined. My grandfather built this cluster of homes with the singular goal of keeping his family all together. The compound was—and is—in the same neighborhood as the president of Egypt, and my parents' home, furnished as it was with the finest offerings from Europe, looked like it belonged.

My father, who grew up poor, interpreted this 180-degree turn in his life as a sign he was doing right according to Allah. Had he not found favor according to Allah, he would have had nothing but misfortune. My mother was also introduced to a new way of life—a devout Islamic life. The contrast was sudden and shocking. Her marriage, which initially seemed a dream come true, quickly turned nightmarish.

My mother's frustration and sorrow over the transformation required by Allah was obvious to anyone who cared to see. A budding philosopher, she soon learned life was not what she hoped it would be. Little by little, with my dad shaming her every step of the way, Islam was wiping away the thoughts, emotions, and even physical attributes that made her who she was.

As my mom was to learn, a Muslim woman does not have the right to set her own boundaries. Those are for her husband, father, brothers, or other male relatives to set. The law is clear and my father, in his devotion to the words of Allah, made sure he fulfilled his obligations. Allah, he knew, would judge the male and female equally according to their deeds and duties, but the duties and obligations of the male were quite different from those of the female. The male's role was to enforce the law of Allah. The female's role was to obey and to report the sins of other family members to the male. Quran 4:34 reads, *"Men are superior and supreme over women, because Allah has made men to excel over women."*

And "excel" my father did. My mother, used to sitting high on a pedestal, now had to bow at the feet of Allah, represented here on earth by her husband, my father. He patiently instructed her in the ways of Islam, ways as foreign to her as they would be to the average Valley Girl. I believe she tried, in small ways, to regain her freedom by wearing makeup and sneaking off to a movie theater now and then. Eventually, though, she grew to accept her old way of life was not the life Allah willed.

Her sin on the day of my introduction to Allah was threefold: First, she was not obedient to Allah, and her actions were sinful. Second, she was not obedient to my father and went out of the home without his permission. And third, she indulged in entertainment that stirred the senses in ways not honoring Allah. She knew, if caught, there would be a price to pay for what she did.

A *hadith* is a saying of Mohamed. Sahih Al-Bukhari hadith 3.592 reads, *"Every one of you is a shepherd and responsible for your herd. The shepherd is fully responsible for the deeds of his flock. If his flock obeys, the shepherd will be praised. But if the flock disobeys, the shepherd shares in their sin and will likewise be punished."* My father was my mother's shepherd, and he took that responsibility seriously.

DAD HAD A PLAN

Not long after marrying my mom in 1968, my dad developed a family plan he felt would benefit himself, his wife, and any children that would come along later. His dreams were for my mother to go to college and study law. Perhaps she could become a professor, he reasoned. Initially, she followed his directives, but after two semesters she was miserable. Law was too concrete for my mom, and she begged my father to allow her to study philosophy. He wouldn't agree to that idea, however, until she couched her goal in terms of Islamic philosophy. That was a plan he could support.

In the few short years after their marriage, my dad's new medical practice prospered. The fact that everything fell into place was his assurance he was doing right by Allah. Things were not going well on my mother's side of the family however. In 1969, a terrible car crash killed her youngest sister and two brothers-in-law while injuring her mother and one of Mother's nieces.

Then, late in 1970, Anwar Sadat ascended to power and immediately started to build up the military in anticipation of a new war with Israel. Obligatory military contracts paid little, and many other civil government contracts went unreimbursed. This put enormous financial stress on my grandfather's construction business and was compounded by financial mischief and mismanagement of his brothers. With my emotionally-wrought grandfather stretched for money, his sons leaned on my father to repay the interest-free loan my grandfather gave him.

Dad was indignant. He placed all blame for their straitened circumstances squarely at their own feet. "You have never lived righteously under Allah, and your hardship is the penalty for your sin," he told them coldly. To my mom, he justified his refusal to pay the loan back—at least at this time—as a way of awakening her brothers to their own sins and of guiding them all to the path of righteousness and repentance. As further justification, he cited Mohamed's example of raiding the unbelievers' businesses.

When grandfather's health took a dramatic turn for the worse, the brothers began fighting about how best to manage the company and its assets. The infighting got ugly, and my father said he would stand for no more. "Your family and the fighting about their wealth is shameful," he announced to Mom one day. "They do not honor Allah with either their words or actions, and you must remove yourself from their sin. Their failures are solely because they have not followed the words of Allah." With that dictate, my mother had to cease all interaction with her family members, including her twin sister. She felt helpless to save them or herself, and she felt as if my father had torn her in half.

The break with her family was so complete in fact, in July 1971, when my mother was giving birth to me, her own mother and sister could not attend to her. They hovered nearby, mere yards away, but my father would not allow them to assist with the delivery of my mother's first child. Instead, he had his hand-picked "new" friends attend to Mom. I can't imagine how hurtful (devastating) this was to my mother, who undoubtedly felt scared, alone, and abandoned.

Control and bondage are the hallmarks for any properly devout, observant Muslim family; my family was no exception. My father mastered his own life, seized control of my mother's life right down to the womb, and demanded complete submission from his children. That was as Allah willed. Mother struggled every day to live up to what the Quran and my father instructed her to do and what she was to be, and every day she failed. She did not practice the Muslim prayers until she married, and her recitation was clumsy and often incorrect as she struggled with Arabic script. My father saw this as another sign of her family's

As an infant I helped bridge the gap between my mother and her family and opened a small channel of communication. Although my weary grandfather dearly loved me and welcomed my birth as a sign of renewed family fortune, the tension remained. When his heart finally failed in 1973, my mother was not allowed to mourn his death properly. My father justified his rigid decision-making as a way of sharing Allah with my mother and of shaming her family for their lack of righteousness.

failure to raise her as a good Muslim. But incorrectly reciting prayers was the least of my mother's problems.

Here was her greatest problem—my mother's failure to understand marriage was not necessarily monogamous. Her father, my grandfather, had the means to have multiple wives. This would have been acceptable for a religious Muslim man, but he had only one wife for whom he cared deeply his entire life. As a girl, that relationship was what my mother knew. She dreamed of the same for herself, but she ultimately sacrificed that dream—and the loyalty of her husband—on the altar of Islam.

To make sure his goals for our family worked as he planned, my father put my mother on birth control. As anticipated, the pill prevented her from getting pregnant until she completed her university studies. However, the pill did long-term damage to her body. She gave birth to my brother in 1975 when she was in her thirties and found herself in early menopause, unable to have any more children. She longed to have a large family, like her own, but that was not to be. With difficulty, she learned to content herself with me and my younger brother. Eventually, she silenced her sorrow in the knowledge she was obedient to Allah and my father.

CHAPTER 3

FORGIVENESS AT ANY COST

Muslim fathers must instruct and guide their off-spring into the Islamic faith and ensure they grow up Muslims, and into a total submission and obedience to Allah. Those are the only fathers who will ever be rewarded to heaven.

—Quran 52:21

When I came out of that dark room in which my father beat me at age five, my life looked very different. I viewed the world from a new perspective. Totally and radically transformed, I saw everything in a different light. Everything! Islam became for me the only truth, the only way. The walk of faith of my father and my forefathers was the only path to righteousness, success, blessing, and a favorable afterlife. It was my one hope for redemption.

I was terrified. There was only one way to dig myself out of this hole I dug for myself through sin. I would have to become the very best slave to Allah. I would never again invoke his wrath. To embody Quran 66:8 was my desire, *"O ye who believe! Turn to God with sincere repentance, in the hope that your Lord will remove from you your ills and admit you to Gardens beneath which Rivers flow."* Allah demanded sincere and faithful repentance, free from pretense and hypocrisy. This was the first sign of *tawba*, the contrition and hard work leading to redemption. Guilt birthed in me a burning desire to learn the path to righteousness. This meant beginning to observe the five pillars of the faith, which are grounded in the word and law of Allah. If this foundation was not strengthened through strict observance, the weak servant would be punished throughout his life and for eternity after death.

At this very young age, I had to become a new person, and I needed to do it quickly. Fueling this sense of urgency was a mind-numbing fear Allah would strike me deaf and blind for the error of my ways. To find the path of righteousness I began to learn the "appropriate meek and humble" way to petition Allah in prayers.

THE FIVE PILLARS OF ISLAM

The first pillar of Islam is the *shahada*, *"There is no god but Allah, and Mohamed is the seal and the final of all the prophets."* The shahada became the cry of my heart, a constant affirmation of Allah and Mohamed. I pledged the words of shahada would always be on my lips. I uttered them over and over and over each day and fully intended to do so until I drew my last breath on this earth.

The understanding that Allah was to be my Master and I his slave guided my practice of the *salat*, the ritualistic prayer said five times daily and the second pillar of Islam. I came to long for the times of prayer. The prayers are specific, obligatory, and need to be observed in order and at specific times. Prayer for us Muslims was not a petition to Allah but rather an act of total submission of the body and the mind. The words and actions were prescribed and were to be followed without addition or omission. On bended knees with my forehead rubbing the ground, I assumed the position of a slave bowing before his master. I would achieve closeness with Allah I could not otherwise achieve—so the Prophet told us.

As a beginner, I was not yet expected to know the prayers' proper execution, but my dad was diligent in my instruction. A hadith speaks expressly to this matter: "The Apostle of Allah (peace be upon him) said: *Command and order your children to pray throughout their first seven years old and then beat them for missing prayer until they become ten years old.*"[1] After the age of ten the standing order is that as long as the child is under your roof the head of the household is fully responsible for that child's actions and has to do whatever it takes to keep him/her on the straight path and in complete obedience to Allah.

The third pillar deals with the tithe, *zakat*. A Muslim earns money to further Allah's cause on the earth. Money has no other purpose. As an act of worship I was expected to judge the obedience of other Muslims before I handed them my tithe. They had to be worthy of furthering Allah's kingdom in some way. If they were not deemed worthy—or were not a Muslim or not in the process of becoming one—I learned not to share my tithe with them. Although I had no income at the time, I knew tithing would be an important component of the submissive life as it was to my father, and so I committed myself to learning how to judge the worthiness of others. Mohamed said, *"I have been ordered to kill the people until they testify that there is no god except Allah, and that Mohamed is the messenger of Allah, and they establish prayer and pay the Zakat."* Mohamed continued, *"If they do that, their blood and wealth are protected from me save by the rights of Islam. Their reckoning will be with Allah."*

This foundation strengthened me, guided me, and made me a wholly submitted servant. Even as a child, I knew this was enslavement, but it was enslavement at will. I willingly laid aside my own childish desires as much as I could and began to desire only what Allah had for my life. When I drifted and began to look with envy or lust at what my cousins were doing, I quickly reminded myself of the physical pain suffered that day in the dark room and the emotional pain buried in my heart from fear of eternal punishment.

I analyzed my day-to-day activities through an Islamic filter, assessing whether each act was in obedience to Allah. And while I was going through the prescribed motions, I begged Allah for forgiveness of my sins. Each day I ended begging once more for forgiveness so if I died in my sleep, I would be found a faithful servant. I wholeheartedly believed I was not worthy of forgiveness, but Quran 19:71 gave me hope that once I paid my dues in the fires of hell I would one day see heaven.

I considered myself one of the lucky ones. I learned the foundational truths of Islam early on. I did not have time to commit the whole spectrum of sins before I found the correct path. Others were not so lucky. As Quran 6:125 asserts, *"Allah chooses those whose hearts he will open and those whose hearts he will leave closed. All of the chosen come to the same understanding but not at the same time of their lives.*

Some do not open their hearts until, after a lifetime of error, they are confronted with the judgment that waits. Others do not open their hearts until they face the grave and the eternal torments beyond."

Rather than spending my days in play with other kids, I spent my time thinking about sin and how I could achieve some measure of forgiveness. My reflections all led me to one place—the Quran. Within the holy text was the instruction I needed. If I was too young to be held fully accountable, I was old

At an early age I put the puzzle together. It was my father who faithfully helped me assemble the pieces. My creator was Allah, and he alone was my master. I was created to serve him and nothing more. Allah, in his perfect wisdom, judges according to the only acceptable law, sharia, the path Allah has set for us through this life and into paradise. The instructions for navigating Allah's path were clear. Mohammad revealed them to us. There was no room for compromise and no grace. Whether life was just or not was of no consequence. "It is as Allah wills" was an honorable and true answer to any hard question I would ponder in the years to come.

enough to be held to account for sins of impurity, lying, and disobedience, either to Allah or to my parents.

My understanding led me to one conclusion: I must go all-in and become a slave of Allah. I must pledge my allegiance to him above all others, even my parents. The Quran taught me I should obey my parents as long as they obeyed Allah. If they disobeyed Allah and his messenger, Mohammad, they had no right to my obedience. Abu Bakr, the most revered of Mohammad's disciples and his heir to Islamic state leadership, told us, *"Obey me so long as I obey Allah and his messenger. And if I disobey Allah and his messenger, then I have no right to your obedience."*[2]

Not only was I to test my parents' will against that of Allah, but, as a shrewd and obedient Muslim, I would test the will of all those around me. I was a slave and a soldier. I obeyed Allah and made sure others did as well. I was going to be the best child soldier for Allah anyone ever saw.

I gained a great deal of insight into my father and his actions on that day in the dark room. As an act of worship and a sign of obedience to Allah, fathers were to inflict pain upon their children if those children failed in their Islamic duties and especially if they committed sin.

There was, however, a class of sin called *hudud* that demanded severe retribution. These were the acts transgressing the limits Allah set and were specifically proscribed in the Quran or in Mohamed's divine sayings. They included theft from another Muslim, highway robbery of another Muslim, drinking alcohol, illicit sexual intercourse, falsely accusing a Muslim female of being unchaste, murdering a fellow Muslim, or, most grievous of all, apostasy. Since Allah set these laws, no pardon was possible. Divine punishment had to be exacted. If someone were to grievously disobey Allah through an act of apostasy, he was to be killed. If Allah so willed, community, family, or even parents were to be the agents of retribution. This was a truth I learned from the scriptures—Quran 5:38; 24:4, 6; 9:29, 66; 16:106; 5:33–34 among others—and accepted as did every devout Muslim.

In a similar spirit, a mother rightly rejoices when her sons die as martyrs in acts of *jihad* because those sons bring honor to Allah and pave a way to heaven for both mother and son. Allah revealed as much, and none of us was in a position to disagree. Quran 47:4 told us, *"Those who are killed in the way of Allah martyrs fighting in Allah's holy war, Allah will never let their great deeds be lost and they will be rewarded in paradise."*

The Prophet Mohamed specifically reported the seven gifts Allah would grant the *shahid*, the Muslim martyr. These included total forgiveness with the first drop of blood, immunity from the punishments of the grave, and, of course, seventy-two voluptuous young virgins to take as wives. Just as importantly, the shahid would be allowed to intercede on behalf of as many as seventy family members. I accepted these truths from the scriptures as every Muslim must.

Had my sin not been dealt with righteously it would have been a stain on my father's record. Given his responsibility for me, my father would have earned Allah's wrath and jeopardized his own place in heaven had he not dealt with my sin as firmly as he did. The good my brother, mother, and I did tilted the scales of judgment in the right direction. Likewise, the bad we did tilted the scales in the wrong direction. Allah kept a count. "Please, Allah," I begged, "forgive me and forgive my father, who rightly inflicted your judgment on me."

To outsiders looking in—less than devout Muslims or "normal" kids—my behavior didn't make sense, but I didn't care. I did whatever represented pure devotion to Allah and his Prophet. Some called my behavior radical. Others called me weird, a nerd. Others sneered in jealousy when I was called "blessed." But I didn't care. Mohamed said actions like mine were examples of devotion, and that is all that mattered to me. I figured that was all that should matter to any good Muslim seeking Allah's reward. I wanted to be the Muslim the Prophet Mohamed described in this hadith "as a man who says, 'I fear Allah,' a man who gives in charity and hides it, such that his left hand does not know what his right hand gives in charity; and a man who remembered Allah in private and so his eyes shed tears."[3]

In the days and months after my introduction to Allah, I walked around in fear of going blind. I believed I deserved the punishment. In fact, I felt privileged Allah chose to get my attention by showing me my sin. If Allah wanted to make his slave blind, so be it. He knew best. All my senses, even my very life, were on loan to me from Allah. If I used those gifts in a way that did not honor him, it was his right to take them away.

Allah was a just judge, I believed, and Muslims were obligated to be his law enforcers. We imposed sharia law on ourselves first, then on those who belonged to us, and then on those around us. As his soldiers, we were obliged to spread his law to the farthest corners of his ever-expanding kingdom on earth and enforce it. This was and is the heart of Islam, and I sincerely embraced it. Admittedly, this was not normal behavior for a young child. In time, I would make the expansion of Allah's kingdom my life's mission with consequences I could never have foreseen.

For a Muslim, there is a binary quality to life. People are either devout or sinful. They are Muslim or infidel. They are male or female. My dark room experience changed everything. My intimate, personal, painful knowledge of the heavy weight of sin allowed me to see the sin in others. I resolved in my heart I would do *anything* for redemption. In time, that resolve took a very specific form, namely my personal quest to expand Allah's kingdom on earth.

In the meantime, I needed to prepare myself for Allah's justified wrath. With great seriousness, when no one else was around, I closed my eyes tightly and practiced walking around the house, trying to memorize the placement of the furniture. Bruised knees and bumps on my forehead did not deter me from attempting to imagine a potential life of blindness. I also tried to etch the images of my parents' faces in my memory just in case I woke and never had the chance to see them again.

I can personally testify anticipating Allah's wrath took a toll especially since I did not know when it was coming. The punishment my father delivered was immediate. He followed his words with actions, and I got over it. But the Quran taught that Allah would deliver his wrath on his timetable, not mine. The anticipation was agonizing—a never-ending punishment in itself. I learned Allah knew best how to sanctify and purify his followers.

I entertained a childish hope that my dad, being a prominent Islamic teacher, would get me off the hook by telling me what I had to do to be forgiven. But that never happened. It doesn't happen for anyone. All sin requires a penalty be paid, and no one has the power of redemption or forgiveness. All are prey and predator. All are prisoners and prison guards at the same time. All are incarcerated within the walls of Allah's law. His whip was—and is—always at hand. My dreams of redemption faded with the realization my future was bleak unless I took decisive action.

THE 4TH PILLAR – FASTING DURING RAMADAN

The summer I turned six I had an opportunity. The holy month of Ramadan was coming, and everyone around me was excitedly preparing to observe the holy fast from sunrise to sundown. I asked my mother if I too should prepare to fast. "No," she said. "You are much too young. You must wait for your dad, and he will explain."

When I asked, my father explained to me I was not yet obliged to fast. Allah ordained that fasting was not obligatory until puberty. Hearing this, I secretly breathed a sigh of relief, but only for a moment. To be forgiven for my sin, I needed to take a step beyond what was expected of me.

That year the holy month fell in August, and a miserably hot August it was, 110 degrees in the shade, day after day. Although our home had no air conditioning then, I did not worry about my temporal comfort. I worried about my eternal destiny. Fasting, I figured, would get Allah's attention and maybe ease his anger toward me.

Guilt is a remarkably powerful motivator. It crushes like a giant rock placed upon one's chest. I ceaselessly wondered what I did to deserve that weight and how I could get rid of it. To lift the burden of shame from my soul I was willing to do anything—even if I died in the process. Although not as redemptive as martyrdom through jihad, dying while performing a holy ritual would relieve me of a life of guilt and sin. In my mind, it would be a million times better than living as a man condemned.

Guilt is also a powerful weapon in the hands of the soldiers of Allah, who, on all fronts, use it to judge and condemn. Wielding this weapon, they recruit others to become fellow soldiers, and the army swells one Muslim at a time. Little do the recruits suspect they are not so much soldiers as they are slaves to a "controller" and "conqueror," two of the ninety-nine names Mohamed assigned to Allah.

The fast of Ramadan is a month-long journey in which the servant's mind and body are cleansed through submission, suffering, and endurance. It is the fourth pillar, and I wanted badly to participate. Considered the best time of the year, Ramadan gives the faithful Muslim an opportunity to show his master, Allah, the depth of his devotion by denying himself the basic necessities required to sustain life.

My mind was made up. I would fast. The ninth month of the Islamic lunar calendar, Ramadan requires fasting from sunrise to sunset. This meant I would completely abstain from any eating and drinking during this time. I didn't have to, but I could see no other way to show Allah how remorseful I was. Once I headed down that path, there would be no turning back. A promise was binding, and if I promised Allah I was going to perform a ritual, then I had better make good on that promise. I would be severely punished if I didn't.

It is difficult for me to communicate how monumental this decision seemed at the time, but I had to do something about my one sin. One sin, yes, but it was major. Again, it was all black and white. Sins added up. Allah kept a running tally. Upon becoming an adult, every follower of Allah had two angels sitting on his shoulders counting sins. The angels remained until the individual died or was declared insane. Otherwise, the counting continued. I wanted my angels to look at me, say, "One," and then say no more!

On the first day of the holy month, my mother called me to come eat my breakfast. "I am going to fast," I announced. "But you are too young! Didn't your father explain that to you?" she protested. "Yes, he did," I shot back, "and I know, but I want Allah to accept me and look at me with favor." And that was that.

I thought my mother would become angry with me, but she was just the opposite. She called up her mentors, the women who were helping her become a faithful Muslim, and announced proudly I was attempting this feat of holiness. In her mind, it was a beautiful and worshipful act of total obedience, even if I did so at my own peril. Though her mother's heart feared, given my age, fasting might lead to death in the August heat, her Muslim heart, budding with her own obedience to Allah, rejoiced in the knowledge that she, too, would receive a reward for my obedience.

The tremendous heat, coupled with my hunger and thirst, was brutal, and I wondered a time or two if I had clearly thought this through. My stomach rumbled, and my mouth became dry and parched. All I could think about was having a bite to eat with a sip of water. No sooner, however, would an image of food flash through my brain than it would be followed by an image of Allah crushing me. My physical needs that day paled in comparison to my fear of being blinded for life or tormented in hellfire for eternity.

Throughout the stiflingly hot day I would turn on the bathroom faucet and gaze in holy reverence at the water. I didn't drink any—not a drop. I didn't even touch it. But I took comfort in watching the cool water pour out of the faucet and fill the sink. Then I quietly returned to my room and felt sustained, if only for moments.

My mother met my father at the door when he returned from the military hospital. "Mohamed is fasting," she said excitedly. I wish I could have seen his face when she told him. The man who walked into my room that day was not the same man who beat me not long before. This man was smiling, happy, overflowing with praise and wonder. He hugged me, the first hug from my father I can remember.

My father understood my commitment to such an act of worship and obedience committed him to supporting me. That afternoon, to reward me for my efforts and to strengthen me as the fast continued, he took me to the mosque for his teaching.

"Mohamed, did you commit to fast the whole day?" "Yes," I answered. As I spoke those words, my hunger and thirst evaporated, my hope for forgiveness surged. "May Allah bless you," my father said with joy, the pride shining from his eyes. "Go and cleanse yourself and get ready for prayers. We will help each other go through the rest of the day."

And just like that, I became a blessing to my father rather than a burden. I remember sitting at the right side of my father, the leader. I saw the weight of my sin diminishing, the giant rock breaking into a million tiny pieces. Gone was the fearful little boy whose eyes revealed a trembling heart. In his place was a victorious young Muslim filled with a sense of power, boldness, and authority. I stood taller and my eyes exuded the steely strength of a victor. Righteousness is intoxicating. That feeling of being a faithful servant and the boldness flowing from that feeling would soon become addictive.

I did well. I was sure Allah was changing his mind about me. The message I heard was loud and clear—when you do something

I also discovered, as an observant male child, I had power. My relationship with my parents and everyone who knew me changed. Yes, I obeyed my mother, but only when I felt her directives were in accordance with the word of Allah. Never, ever again would she be able to take me to a movie theater and cause me to sin. When I told her, "No," and there were many times over the years I did so, my father praised me. I was walking in righteousness, and she was not. I became her de facto guardian.

extraordinary, Allah, in his ultimate judgment, will perhaps love and care for you, at least not try to crush you. As the weight of my sin lifted from my shoulders, my life began to transform. I learned the secret to the successful Muslim life, and I was never going to forget it!

But the truth is, no Muslim ever feels completely free from his sin. No Muslim is ever forgiven. The stain of all sin remains on the heart for eternity. In the most unexpected times, those demons from the past surface and force a Muslim to question whether or not he was truly safe from Allah's wrath. Sensing this, I knew I needed to walk that extra mile every day in hopes of redemption. Nothing was more important to me than being a devout, upright Muslim.

The Fifth Pillar of Islam is going on Hajj at least once in your lifetime. I will go into that pillar in much more detail later in this book.

The lessons I learned beginning in that dark room and culminating in my Ramadan fast became the foundation of my world. The years ahead, I was certain, were going to be filled with extraordinary feats!

CHAPTER 4

FATHERHOOD AND BROTHERHOOD

I your God Allah will examine you; I will challenge you in your material belonging, your properties, your loved ones and even in your health. Sometimes I will let the Jews and the Christians, my and your fierce enemies harm you, to see how steadfast you will be, but if you show resilience and strong faith, I will make you prevail and stronger and will let you conquer all of them at the right time.

—Quran 3:186

I am, at my core, a product of my father. He was the single greatest influence on who I was, am, and will be. The lessons he taught me weave through my story like threads that cannot be cut out without unraveling my very being. No ordinary man, my father is the pure product of the teachings of Prophet Mohamed, a modern exemplar of what a Muslim should be, the living incarnation of Mohamed's first disciples, Abu Bakr and Umar.

As a doctor specializing in women's health, my father has had to adapt to the times we live in while at the same time defining how women should be protected in Islamic society. He has had to pioneer this path without ever losing sight of how to be a pure Muslim at all stages and at all times. This is what has made him a unique and a much sought-after religious leader.

My father understands what it means to be extraordinary although he would never claim to be. He, above all else, knows Allah requires him to go the extra mile to secure his place in heaven. As a child, I saw him as a giant among men. And yet, he, like every other man, woman, and child under Islam, is consumed by the fear of Allah's wrath. Even the giants tremble and are driven to do greater things for Allah. That is my father.

On the first day of my first Ramadan fast, I walked by his side to the mosque. The repentant son, I looked to my father for guidance. That day, I saw him in action for the first time, a leader and a spiritual guide to many. The minute the salat was over, people gathered around him in a big circle, seeking his counsel. My heart swelled when he beckoned me to stand by his side. No words can describe how I felt upon leaving the crowd and being elevated to the spotlight of righteousness. I soaked up every minute of his pure Islamic preaching as I did for many years to come.

When we left the mosque that day, our relationship was transformed. In some homes, a father beams with pride if his son earns good grades or does well at sports. He may give him a few dollars and tell him to buy a toy or nowadays, a new video game. That kind of pride, however, paled in comparison to what my father felt for me. He was vocal about his pride and reinforced his feelings with Quranic scripture. I was setting out on the path of righteousness and committing my life to serving Allah. For a boy my age, this was major, and my father knew it. He was a grown man before he set out on the same path.

"Do you intend to fast again tomorrow?" he asked as we began the walk home.

"Yes, I am fasting tomorrow and after that," I answered with a newfound sense of confidence. My heart beat a little faster, filled as it was with religious fervor and my excitement at the change in my relationship with my father.

"Then we will come to the mosque tomorrow for the afternoon salat and lecture just as we did today," he replied.

It is said in the Quran 25:47 and Quran 66:6, a father who has brought up a righteous son will have rewards added to his own eternal treasury. My father felt Allah truly blessed him by giving him such a son as I. Could there be a better blessing than to see that son begin the journey and at such a young age?

My father became my hero, and I became my father's hope and his promise for a bright future. As for myself, I felt my singular act to achieve atonement made me a man. As a man, I became his shadow, his constant companion, his closest friend. And as I grew to know my father and to understand intimately what made him the man he was, I stood in awe. In my mind, my father was second only in righteousness to Prophet Mohamed, the perfect man.

I've never met another man quite like my father. Many people liken him to Umar, one of the Prophet's boldest, most trusted associates, an expert Muslim jurist known for his pious and just nature. Umar's piety earned him the nickname "al-Farooq, the one who distinguishes between right and wrong." My father, likewise, was bold. He never bent backward to protect anyone's sensitivities. He spoke plainly, answered clearly, and showed an unwavering commitment to Allah. Some people found his lack of tact off-putting. Others embraced it and knew they could come to him if they wanted an honest, unbiased religious opinion, or *fatwa*. Many of the Muslim men and women who were ignorant of how to handle their daily lives according to sharia law and Islamic teachings would turn to my father. "What a bold Umar-like answer," I heard men say when referring to my dad, or, "Go ask Umar."

His strength of character was undeniable, still is, and I have great respect for his devotion to what he believes to be true. I saw him as unbreakable, unflinching, unapologetic, but always within the bounds of the Quran or the acts of the Prophet. He instilled those values in me. In the process I grew in his likeness a little more every day.

The father I knew was a successful preacher, Muslim leader, physician, Islamic author, businessman, and high-ranking military

officer who helped drive the Jews out of Sinai, but his early life did
not presage such heights.

MY FATHER'S EARLY YEARS

He grew up in what many would call humble surroundings. I'd
call it abject poverty. We used to drive out to the countryside several times a month to visit with his parents. On those hundred-mile
journeys, I soaked up his abundant wisdom on Islam, the Muslim
Brotherhood, and on the experiences that made him the man he
was. For two days every other week, I was privy to insights from
one of the keenest minds in the Islamic world.

As we drew closer to his childhood home, I was always amazed
by the transition. We were only ninety minutes from our comfortable Cairo home, but it felt like another world. All around us were
rundown homes—mud houses really—illuminated by candlelight.
I saw the village residents drawing water from wells. For a bathroom
they used a hole in the ground so primitive I would hold it in until
we got back to "civilization." As I looked at the accomplished man
beside me, I had a hard time squaring who he was with his origins.

My fraternal grandfather was a teacher of Arabic and Islamic
studies, and later a principal in the village school. He was devout,
disciplined, and proud. He didn't have much, but he was not
ashamed of who he was. He did, however, dream of more for his
children. He wanted them to have good educations and opportunities that would take them out of the small village. One look
around and I knew my father's childhood was anything but idyllic.
He and his siblings had to delight in the simple things and in each
other's company. Family mattered. When my dad's younger sister,
Aida, died from tuberculosis, my father was heartsick. That loss
made him decide to become a doctor who would provide hope and
healing to the poor. He dreamed of making a difference and of
pulling himself out of the backward conditions that contributed
to his sister's death. Disease and poverty were the two enemies he
swore to conquer.

I am certain his parents doubted he could make that dream a
reality, but my dad was always a hard worker. People who grow up

with nothing learn to reach for the prize through hard work, wit, and skill. My dad had those qualities and never gave up when told he could not accomplish something. Every time he was knocked down, he got back up again. To this day and even at an advanced age, he still has the heart of a fighter, always pushing toward his goals.

THE MUSLIM BROTHERHOOD

The Brotherhood was always and still is on the lookout for a particular kind of member—ambitious young men who could help the group grow and help Islamic society thrive. My dad and his

My father's uncle, my great-uncle Mohammed Abdel Aal, played a major role in changing my father's life. He was a founding member of an organization of interest to my father and his brother—the Muslim Brotherhood. A major fundraiser and organizer, he was credited with recruiting the third spiritual leader of the Brotherhood, Omar El-Tilmisani who would lead the organization from 1972 to 1986. Under his leadership, the Muslim Brotherhood emerged as the driving force of a global Islamic movement.

brother, who assisted with Brotherhood activities since their school days, fit that profile. A landowner, Uncle Abdel Aal, also worked as stationmaster with the railroad. When my dad was fresh out of high school, his uncle offered him and his older brother farmhand jobs. Not waiting for a response from his sons, my grandfather immediately replied, "Thank you, but no. My sons are going to go to college."

Their refusal to work on the farm alerted my great-uncle to the fact his nephews were looking for a better life. He offered them a vision and would provide them in time with resources and connections in Cairo to bring that vision to life. Even as boys, they saw the appeal of an organization offering lifelong bonds with like-minded individuals who shared a passion for Islam and a desire for professional and material success. Under British colonization, Egypt offered little in the way of Islamic identity and even less in the way of religious education. The Muslim brotherhood saw the void and exploited it.

My dad's immediate older brother quickly pledged allegiance to the group and its mission. My dad weighed his options, just as he did with all major decisions. From the time he was old enough to think for himself, my self-reliant father was cautious about aligning himself with anyone or anything. That said, however, he never wanted to let a good thing pass him by. So he decided he would test the waters a bit to see what membership could offer.

The organization offered a great platform, a bridge to many opportunities my dad hoped would be to his advantage. Eventually, he signed on. To this day, he and his brother are counted among the elder statesmen of this powerful and feared organization. My father's first allegiance, however, was always to Allah. Although he saw the practical value of membership in the Brotherhood, he remained his own man. As I came of age, I met all of the men in my father's circle. They were his closest friends and confidants and played a big part in our daily lives. I heard their stories, learned of their struggles and victories, and saw firsthand their battle for power.

The Brotherhood tested my Uncle Ahmed's mettle. As the collector of dues from fellow members, he possessed a great deal of sensitive information about the group's resources and its membership. To assure he would keep his secrets under duress, members hazed him, beat him, demanded he give up names and the money he collected. But Uncle Ahmed stood his ground. He passed all of their loyalty tests and proved himself to be worthy to become the bookkeeper for his district. His selfless allegiance helped pave the way to a law degree and a successful life in Cairo. Many years later, that allegiance inspired the government to label him a revolutionary and throw him in prison more than once.

Meanwhile, my father performed tasks like selling and handing out Islamic teaching books by Islamic jurists and scholars, including books by the Brotherhood's founder, Hassan al-Banna. Although he agreed with al-Banna's teaching, my father was a true Islamic teacher to the core, a skeptic who was not afraid to voice his opinions.

The Brotherhood favored him in no small part because of Ahmed's dedication to the cause. When my father lacked transportation for the six-mile trek to high school, the Brotherhood gave him a bike. When he needed a place to live in Cairo during medical school, the Brotherhood provided him and his brother with lodging. That's what a brotherhood did—they looked out for one another. Membership opened doors to these two poor young men from the countryside which would otherwise have remained locked tight.

The Muslim Brotherhood, however, was and is much more than a social network. It is a political and spiritual force centered on a return to pure Islam. Its founder, Hassan al-Banna, hoped to recapture the fighting spirit of Islam's first century as a way to recapture the caliphate's early glories. A devout Sunni Muslim, al-Banna was disturbed by the collapse of the Ottoman Empire and the Islamic caliphate following World War I. The League of Nations carved the once grand empire into small, manageable pieces. Western and Christian influences replaced Islamic heritage and culture. The West could not have accomplished this without the help of Turkish sell-out Kamal Ataturk. Ataturk bought wholeheartedly into the West's anti-Islamic efforts and hastened the collapse of a caliphate that existed without interruption from the time of Mohamed. Right before his eyes, al-Banna saw the crumbling of the prophecy that the Islamic state would control the entire world and endure.

WESTERN OCCUPIERS

Not since the fall of the Ottoman Empire in 1924 was there an Islamic dynasty. Nations previously governed by sharia law surrendered their heritage to the British, French, and Italians, who were all too happy to divide the spoils. New maps were drawn up, new countries created, and Islam was relegated to the dustbin of history.

The Western occupiers knew Islamic ideology and theocracy would always be a stumbling block. Their global chess game would only succeed if they modernized formerly Islamic countries and neutralized Islam as a governing authority. Their strategy was to advance their Western and Christian culture by importing Western ideals, one institution at a time. They believed wholeheartedly that Islamic nations were relics of the Dark Ages, mired in religious traditions, less enlightened than their own traditions of individual liberty and religious freedom.

The occupiers dismantled centuries-old ways of doing things in the religious, social, and political order. They replaced Allah's sharia law with a Christian-inspired common law emphasizing equality and justice in full indifference to Allah's word. The idea of universal equality is not even found in Islam. To the degree equality exists, it is only among the brotherhood of the faithful.

MOHAMED'S LAW

In his farewell speech, Mohamed reinforced this point. *"Know for certain that every Muslim is only a brother of another Muslim,"* he said, *"and that all Muslims are brethren. Treat your women well, for they are like domestic animals. If they abstain from evil, they have the right to their food and clothing in accordance with custom, but if they disobey you then God permits you to shut them in separate rooms and to beat them."*[4]

Allah's law is abundantly clear: men and women are not equal; men are dominant. Women are forbidden from seeking education and working outside their homes. They can only venture out with the permission of a guardian. In my mother's case, it was okay for a woman to continue her education as long as it was for the cause of furthering Islam. Muslims and non-Muslims are not equal; Muslims are superior. Christians and Jews are to be disdained and humbled. Atheism and agnosticism are forbidden, and blasphemy against Allah is swiftly punishable by death.

All social activities and entertainment that do not honor Allah are forbidden. Movies, concerts, and other frivolous entertainments are forbidden as is singing by women. According to the Quran, Allah created humanity only to worship him. With regard to commerce, Western-style banking is not allowed. All forms of credit and interest-bearing loans are forbidden. Says Quran, 3:130, *"O you who have believed and became Muslims, do not consume usury, doubled and multiplied, and do not trade with interest, but fear Allah that you may avoid hellfire on the day of judgment."*

These are not mere concepts or cultural standards. These laws of "inequality" are Allah's laws, and every Muslim nation one time observed them religiously. The Western occupiers were subverting traditional cultures and purging the ideals of the past. Worse, non-Muslims were making the demands, which in itself was an affront to everything Muslims held to be good and true.

Mohamed spoke decisively about the status of Muslims in the world. They were to maintain political and economic control over non-Muslims. Period. Islamic law requires non-Muslims to pay the *jizyah*, a limitless yearly tax that, upon payment, allowed them to exist as citizens in a Muslim nation and practice their faith. Places of worship for non-Muslims were highly regulated and monitored if they were allowed to exist at all. Non-Muslims were not allowed to own land or property outside their own enclaves.

A NEW DAWN IN THE MIDDLE EAST

When the Europeans established their control over the Middle East and other Muslim nations, they restructured governments and introduced constitutions. They imposed strict regulations on religious institutions, especially Al-Azhar University, more than a millennia old, the most authoritative and prestigious center of Islamic learning. They restricted Al-Azhar imams in what they could preach, and many simply gave up preaching. Many mosques sat empty. New civil codes and ordinances restricted the imams' freedom to take to the minarets to sing out the call to worship Allah. One by one, formerly Islamic nations surrendered to the Siren song of a new civilization and embraced the liberties the West offered.

This transition hit with cataclysmic force and gave rise to a new kind of Muslim, "nominal Muslims." Years of Western influence caused them to lose sight of proper religious observance or Islamic governance. They had little understanding of Allah, sharia law, and the teachings of the Prophet Mohamed. And worst of all, they took their ideas of what it meant to be Muslim only from friends, neighbors, and coworkers who knew no more than they did. These nominal Muslims no longer sought out the imams who, to them, now seemed archaic. Their faith devolved into a watered-down mishmash of ideas, and they assumed for themselves the right to interpret Islam from their own limited understanding.

New Western-style education systems, universities, and media remade society. In the process these institutions created a professional workforce unfettered by any religious doctrine, especially a restrictive doctrine like Islam. As the barriers of Islamic thought and tradition fell by the wayside, Christian institutions and ministries associated with the West and the colonizing forces saw an opening.

With sharia law no longer blocking their way, Christians penetrated as far east as India, as far west as Mauritania, and as far south as the Horn of Africa. They enjoyed the freedoms offered under the new Western laws in places traditionally identified as Muslim, and this protection allowed them to expand their ministries everywhere. Suddenly, churches and Christian schools and universities became a part of the landscape. The cross appeared on signs that would formerly have featured the star and crescent.

For the first time, women were encouraged to go to school and get an education. The healthcare system was transformed as missionaries ventured into rural areas to offer medical care. Hospitals with Christian names cropped up in city centers. Orphanages were established to provide an avenue for the adoption of children who had no family—a concept ignoring the prohibition of Quran 33:4–5 against a man adopting a son or a daughter for whom he was not the biological father.

A new age dawned in formerly Islamic nations as the old social order was upended. With no fixed point of reference, Muslims lost confidence in a religion they knew little about and unwittingly adopted a Christian-influenced version of Islam. There was no Islamic religious institution to tell them anything different. The imams were muzzled and the voice of Mohamed effectively silenced.

THE BIRTH OF THE MUSLIM BROTHERHOOD

But just when it seemed hopeless, an Islamic grassroots movement sprang up from a seemingly barren landscape. Some traditional imams, who once kept their burning religious convictions to themselves, stealthily began to train their own sons in the proper observance of Islam and sharia. Circumventing Western influences and restrictions, these imams began to include family and friends in small circles of observance. Many of the sons and others newly trained arose to accept the challenge. They did from the inside what the Western occupiers did from the outside: they altered the culture through the primary institutions. These young men, observant Muslims, attended universities to become teachers, doctors, lawyers, and other professionals of influence, all the while maintaining the roots of their faith and teaching it to anyone who would listen.

Eager to keep Islam alive, these young men met with a thirsty audience. They found others who wanted to reclaim their heritage, their faith, and their power. Small pockets of devout Muslims congregated away from traditional religious institutions and mosques. Everywhere groups began to spring up and, once again, the Quran was being discussed at work, in homes, and in settings entirely apart from the traditional mosques.

Hassan al-Banna was one of those men. He received a proper Islamic education at home from his imam father. In the madrassa, he studied the Quran and memorized it. In due time, he earned a professional degree from the university in Cairo. With it, he taught Arabic at a school built by French missionaries near the Suez Canal. He was a smart, polished professional and used every opportunity to preach the values of Islam to a new generation. It wasn't long before he and a group of devout, like-minded professionals in Egypt formed a group to represent their goals—the Muslim Brotherhood. With all the efforts to dim the fire of Islam, the Brotherhood passionately worked to keep an ember burning and to fan the flames of religious fervor throughout the grassroots with the ultimate goal of resurrecting Islam and the spirit and promise of the Prophet Mohamed.

Al-Banna wrestled with the obvious questions. Given that Islam is the most righteous of all faiths, how could the powerful Islamic state be humiliated, subdued, and occupied? How could Muslims fall under the control of the infidel British rulers when Allah said Islam would rule the world? His conclusion: Allah could not have been wrong. The fault could only lie with al-Banna and his fellow Muslims. Muslims, one and all, were to be blamed for their transgressions and must return to their roots, repent, and begin to serve Allah without reservation. If not, they would continue to be punished.

With that unshakable conviction, al-Banna gave birth to a movement. His goal was to awaken the Islamic giant in the hearts and minds of Muslims everywhere and set the Islamic state once again on the path to righteousness. This second caliphate, Allah's kingdom on earth, was to start in Egypt and spread to the rest of the world from there. As a first step, he envisioned overthrowing the king of Egypt and establishing an ever-expanding Islamic monarchy with himself as the head.

Unfortunately for al-Banna, things did not work out as planned. With the blessing of the British colonizing power, the pseudo government of Egypt ordered his assassination right after he returned from fighting the Jews in 1948. The secular authorities were concerned with the Brotherhood's increasing assertiveness and its popularity among the masses. They were equally alarmed by the confirmed intelligence of the Brotherhood and al-Banna's plan to blame the Egyptian government for the military failure that led to the creation of Israel. More troubling, al-Banna and his associates were, in fact, plotting the overthrow of the government. On February 12, 1949, al-Banna and two of his brothers-in-law were shot to death.

Al-Banna's death did not bring an end to the Muslim Brotherhood. It grew stronger and more widespread for one simple reason: its goal of advancing Islam transcended the Brotherhood's founder's vision; it was timeless. The Brotherhood offered a way out of the shadows, spiritual as well as political, to which Muslims had been condemned. The Quran teaches the caliphate existed not for any personal glory, but for Allah's purpose alone. Achieving that goal and restoring the caliphate was a sure sign from Allah that Muslims were on the right path. The truly faithful would not rest until they succeeded.

Like many of the faithful, my dad embraced the Brotherhood's slogan, "Islam Is the Solution." That slogan perfectly summed up his feelings of Muslims in and out of the Brotherhood. "It is the nature of Islam to dominate, not to be dominated," al-Banna said, echoing the words of the Prophet, a sentiment with which all thinking Muslims would agree. My dad believed with his whole heart Islam was *the* answer for everything. He still does.

Throughout the decades, no matter who was in power, the Brotherhood has had a love/hate relationship with Egyptian leaders. The Brotherhood's growing membership thought of most Egyptians as sellouts, secular infidels, agents of the West, even collaborators with the Zionists. The Brotherhood, my father included, blamed these leaders for the delay in Allah's promise of total Islamic dominance.

Whether it was loved or hated by the leadership, however, the Brotherhood could not be denied. The organization continued to grow. It was well financed. Its roots were deep and growing deeper by the day. Its members were—and are—influential in law, medicine, finance, and other fields. My father and uncle became professionals of influence thanks in no small part to the Brotherhood's support.

Egypt is and has historically been a lynchpin of the Middle East and the Muslim world at large. As it goes in Egypt, so it goes throughout the region. It has the largest population, the strongest military, and an exceptionally long history. Since the beginning of time, Egypt has played a central role in world affairs.

NASSER CHANGES EVERYTHING

In 1952 Gamal Abdel Nasser staged a bloodless military coup against the British and Western influences in his country and set the stage for another transformation of the Muslim world. A new order was introduced, and it bore little resemblance to either Muslim governments of the past or the Western-inspired governments established by the occupying European nations. It was revolutionary—a caliphate system, but entirely secular in nature, a counterfeit in every way of what Allah ordered through his prophet Mohamed. Nasser was the architect of a revival movement among former Muslim Arab nations. He planned to unite them under a new banner with himself serving as the secular head of the caliphate.

Under Nasser's anti-religious, anti-Islamic vision and direction, Egypt enhanced the secular mindset and purged all the Western and Christian influences. At the same time, taking advantage of its founder's assassination, Nasser pushed the Brotherhood further underground. Nasser aimed to stamp out all religious influence from Egyptian society and government institutions. In the process, he drew the ire of Islamists throughout the region. His actions violated the words of Quran 5:49: *"Govern only with Islam and not from any earthly desires. Muslims should be fully aware of those who try to seduce them into a different path."*

As an operating principle, Nasser readily adopted the Communist ideology: "No god, state above all." At his invitation, the Soviet Union partnered with him in the transformation of Egypt and surrounding Arab and Muslim nations, infecting them with Communist ideology. Nasser's apprentices read like a who's who of the Middle East: Saddam Hussein in Iraq, Muammar Gaddafi in Libya, and Haffez Assad in Syria as well as leaders in Afghanistan, Pakistan, and other countries.

The twentieth century saw the Middle East and the Muslim world go from Islamic caliphate to Westernization to socialism in remarkably short order. Today vestiges of each era remain. Nasser's Pan-Arabic secular caliphate succeeded in reducing Western and Christian influence and driving pure Islam from the minds and hearts of vast numbers of Egyptian people. In less than two decades, he and his Communist comrades dug the region into a deep pit.

In 1965, Nasser was "reelected" in a sham election and promptly outlawed all opposition. When his second term began with a fake assassination attempt, Nasser placed the blame squarely on the Muslim Brotherhood and its new rising star Sayyid Qutb. His government arrested Qutb and forced others underground. Uncle Ahmed was among those arrested. He served six years of hard labor. Prison was no place for a kind, thoughtful man like my uncle. Nasser's guards routinely beat him and tortured him using techniques learned from the KGB including electric shock and other torments too grotesque to detail.

Despite the torture, the experience only served to solidify my uncle's allegiance to the Brotherhood. For a time, he shared a cell with Sayyid Qutb, one of the Brotherhood's most prominent spiritual leaders. Qutb was an educator, an Islamic theorist, and an author. Most in the West consider him the father of the modern Islamist movement, Qutbism, and the inspiration for jihadist organizations worldwide.

The reality, however, is more complex. Qutb advocated a two-pronged struggle: civilizational jihad in conjunction with terrorizing the enemies of Islam. His goal was to further the cause of Islam and eliminate evil, which, by his definition, was anything Western or non-Muslim. In 1966, Qutb was convicted for allegedly plotting to assassinate Nasser and was hanged. His execution made him a martyr in the eyes of Islamist groups all over the world, and he remains one today.

My dad risked the same dreaded fate as my uncle. It helped that he was shrewder and less fully committed. Still, had it not been for an elaborate plot by fellow Brotherhood members, he would most certainly have been arrested. By that time, Dad was already a doctor and working at a Cairo university. He had a bright future. After Nasser started cracking down, Brotherhood members crafted a plan for my father to join the military as a ploy to distance him, at least publicly, from the group. Given his options, he really had no choice but to resign from his dream job and enlist. The plan worked, and he avoided prosecution, but it was not at all the life my father envisioned. As he would soon learn, Allah had other plans.

DAD SHIFTS GEARS AND AVOIDS PRISON

Dad's enlistment could not have come at a more troubling time. In June of 1967, a surprise attack by Israel wiped out most of the Egyptian Air Force and military in a matter of hours. My father served as the unit doctor and the second in command at a small air base near the Suez Canal. Just he and one other survived.

Only those who have witnessed the carnage of war firsthand understand what it does to a man. My father was shaken and utterly defeated. What made the defeat all the more demoralizing was it came at the hands of Islam's mortal enemies, the Jews. Egypt was in turmoil. Most Egyptians could make no sense of how the tiny state of Israel could have beaten them so soundly. Nor could they grasp why Allah would have allowed the defeat to happen. True Muslims, however, had the answer. They understood that by following the secular path and especially by executing the true Muslim man, Sayyid Qutb, the state turned its back on Allah.

The order came down for all Egyptian troops to surrender, retreat, and return to the base in Cairo. How they were to get there was their problem. Many died of starvation or dehydration en route. Dad just started walking. He hitched a ride on the back of a truck for part of the journey. When the driver asked where he wanted to go, Dad just said, "Home." He needed to go back to his roots, to think, to repent, to throw himself under the feet of his master Allah, to show his servitude to the one who caused all this to happen, both to his country and, more importantly, to himself.

This humbling was my dad's dark room experience. Allah spares no one from his wrath and judgment. Says Quran 14:42,

"Never think that Allah is unaware of what the wrongdoers do. He only delays them for a Day when eyes will stare in horror." That day shaped my father's character as did no other. It played a major role in our relationship in the years to come.

EGYPT IN DESPAIR

Meanwhile, the Egyptian economy was in shambles with no jobs and no opportunity for a future. The people, as a whole, were in a state of hopelessness, and they had no god to bail them out. Egypt looked every bit like the poster child for the failures of Communist ideology. Meanwhile, secularism waged its own war. All kinds of immoral behavior were visible on the streets, including drug abuse, sexual misconduct, and criminal activity. Western-style capitalism had no answers. Communism had no answers. Egypt's leaders failed them, and their way of life failed them. The sense of despair was palpable. Egypt and other Muslims nations were paying the price for disobeying Allah. No one escapes his wrath, no nation either.

Years later, as my father and I stood in his little village, he recounted the details of the story, the agony still alive in his soul. He lost everything. At the time, he saw nothing but darkness around him. The recognition of Egypt's great defeat being punishment from Allah crushed his spirit, and it was righteous punishment at that. Egypt was secular. Hedonistic. Its people were Muslim in name only. Their faith was as foreign to many of them as to the Jews across the border. "We deserved Allah's punishment," my father told me. "*I* deserved Allah's punishment."

I could not imagine a time when my dad was not strong in his faith, but he confessed to me he failed Allah and his failure terrified him. My father displeased the creator of the universe. He was insincere and uncommitted. He treated Islam as more of a duty than a holy submission. He did next to nothing to spare himself Allah's wrath. I understood that feeling only too vividly from my deserved punishment in the lightless room.

For all his tribulations my father survived to live another day, to have another chance. "Why me?" he asked at the time. And then he knew. Allah spared him for a very special purpose—to help others walk in righteousness. True rewards, for himself and for his nation, could only come with repentance, with full submission to Allah. The following verse from Quran 3:179 sprang to his mind:

> *Allah would not leave the believers in that "state" you are in "presently" until he separates the evil from the good. Nor would Allah reveal to you the unseen. But "instead," Allah chooses of his messengers whom he wills, so believe in Allah and his messengers. And if you believe and fear him, then for you is a great reward.*
>
> *And let not those who disbelieve ever think that because we extend their time of enjoyment it is better for them. We only extend it for them so that they may increase in sin, and for them is a humiliating punishment.*

Allah broke my father for a reason. He emerged from the experience a new man, a different man. Allah took everything and tested him in order to get his attention, and it worked. My father has lived every moment since then believing he must be faithful to Allah in all things. If not, he will lose everything and die without securing a place in heaven. The alternative, living the status quo, terrified him. His eyes were opened to the power of an angry god who demanded submission or else.

CHAPTER 5

MY MENTOR

Allah promises you Muslims that if you adhere to his commands, and work hard to fulfill all your Islamic duties and rituals that he Allah himself will grant you victory over all nations, award you all their lands and their treasures. Allah will make you the supreme power and authority over all other religions and political systems.

—Quran 24:55

I believe promises mean something. The words, "I promise," can calm the human spirit, inspire it to greater heights, or cause it to shrink in fear and despair. It all depends on what is being promised and who is doing the promising.

The promises of Allah are many. Some are sweet like honey; others sour like vinegar. No matter the content, Allah's promises motivate every Muslim man, woman, and child. When I came of age as a young man, the promise of seventy-two virgins was a provocative one, but that promise was of no consequence to me as a child and certainly of no consequence to a woman save perhaps as a source of jealousy. There are, however, many promises that apply to everyone. Most notable among them is the failure to submit to Allah means unspeakable punishments in this life and in the life beyond. That is a promise.

Allah promises if one follows "any other religion" or just believes "in doing good deeds," they are in for a grim surprise at life's end and an unpleasant destiny. Hellfire for eternity is the clear promise for these people, including all Christians and Jews. Quran 24:39 tells us, *"Those who disbelieved—their deeds are like a mirage in a lowland which a thirsty one thinks is water until, when he comes to it, he finds it is nothing, but finds Allah before him, and Allah will force him to pay in full his dues; and Allah is swift in account."* Quran 3:85 and Quran 3:19 make the same point.

On the other hand, Allah promises if you bow before him in total submission, he will show you the kingdoms of the world in all their splendor. Jesus, son of Marylsa ibn Marym was taken to the high mountain and promised those kingdoms, but he refused the offer. When Allah offered the same to Mohammad (hadith Muslim: 8/171, Abu Dawod: 4252), he willingly and proudly accepted.

Growing up, I strongly believed Jesus refused that offer only because Jesus knew he was not the chosen one and Mohamed was. I believed Mohamed was above all other prophets and the only one worthy to accept Allah's offer. Mohamed's confirmation is recorded in Sunan Ibn Maājah 4308, *"I am the master of the children of Adam, and it is no boast. I will be the first for whom the earth is split on the Day of Resurrection, and it is no boast. I will be the first to intercede and whose intercession will be accepted, and it is no boast. The banner of praise will be placed in my hand, and it is no boast."* Mohamed set the example, and I believed every Muslim was obliged to toil and struggle to be worthy of calling himself a follower. Faithfulness to Allah, I believed, came with great duties as well as rewards.

ANWAR SADAT CHANGES EVERYTHING

Among those rewards was the ascension of Anwar Sadat to the presidency upon the death of Nasser in 1970. Egypt and most of the Muslim world had lost its way to Western and Christian ideologies, followed by years of secularism and communism under Nasser. The result was grim punishment by Allah and a decisive defeat at the hand of Israel, which created total humiliation and despair among the Muslims. This dark room experience for the Muslim nations resulted in a willingness to repent and return to Allah's path. Many in the Muslim world felt this way, but many others chose to stay blind and in denial of their despair.

Sadat was one of those true Muslims at heart and a Muslim Brotherhood acquaintance and sympathizer since his youth. Sadat was discreet about his affiliation. The Quran 3:28 approves dissembling if it advances Allah's cause. For years, Sadat served as a secret liaison between the Muslim Brotherhood and his predecessor Nasser, going back to 1952. In fact, he recruited the Brotherhood to help Nasser ascend to power, only to witness Nasser betray his friends. Mohamed set the example that every Muslim, Sadat included, should do his best to achieve the promises of prosperity. Faithfulness to Allah comes with great reward.

Sadat knew what needed to be done. As soon as he took office, he started cleaning house. In 1971's aptly named "Corrective Revolution," Sadat sacked the government, threw the Soviets out, and freed the imprisoned Muslim Brotherhood members. Upon opening the prison doors, Sadat said boldly, "I want you to fight for me on every front."

Although my Uncle Ahmed emerged from prison a broken man—even the simple act of driving a car became too much to bear—he never lost faith. He chose a path of the wise and observant recluse. Many faithful Islamic leaders, including those in the Muslim Brotherhood, were released from prison as well. Among those the Brotherhood members released was future al-Qaeda leader Ayman Al Zawahiri, a Brotherhood member. They now had the opportunity for which they waited nearly five decades. They moved freely into all facets of society—political, social, and religious. Eventually, the Muslim Brotherhood became an international movement under the leadership of the first spiritual leader, Umar al-Tilmisani, who my great-uncle hired thirty years earlier.

Islam was making a renewed grand entrance on the world stage, with Egypt front and center. Whether they were devotees of the Muslim Brotherhood or merely loyal to Islamic ideology, the faithful Muslims of Egypt had a new hope. For decades, outsiders told them where to place their trust. Finally, they could grab on to something tangible and traditional. Where before there were only problems, now there was a solution—"Islam is the solution." Egyptians could see how faithfulness to Islam could reap boundless benefits.

Although conceived as a nation state by the United States, Saudi Arabia never bowed to outsiders, including the U.S. By staying faithful to pure Islamic teachings throughout the years, Saudi Arabia showed Muslims everywhere that righteousness paid dividends. I was one of those Muslims.

I grew up during this exciting time when the Islamic Revolution was exploding all around the globe. The Iranian Revolution, the Afghan War, and other conflicts erupted as physical manifestations of the great and powerful Islam reclaiming its place of superiority in the world. It was exhilarating to live in the midst of it all. Islam had been bound and gagged for more than fifty years. When the Brotherhood emerged to revive the word of Allah and the message of the Prophet, imams emerged from the shadows and began to reclaim the land for Allah. Once again, the prophecies of Prophet Mohamed seemed within reach.

Through the years, I heard countless stories from my father and his circle of influential friends about the wild shifts of power in Egypt and in other Muslim countries, and I never ceased to be amazed. I heard their stories and firsthand accounts, but even more than that, I heard their passion for Islam. These men were some of the greatest influences in my life and I was proud to be a Muslim.

ALLAH DELIVERS ON HIS PROMISES

In my experience, Allah always seemed to deliver on his promises, at least to those who submitted to his will. I was a witness to my father's faithfulness and the rewards that came as a result. I saw abundance in the lives of the obedient, and I saw famine and punishment in the lives of the unfaithful. There were always exceptions, but I assumed faithful Muslims would find their reward in heaven, if not on earth. In the here and now, Muslim leaders deliberately trained their followers, me included, to highlight the evidence of how Allah kept his promises. In this way, the leaders kept them striving to be worthy of those promises—money, power, success, virility, prowess, and all the pleasures of the earth. It was all right there in print:

- *"He will open upon them blessings from the heaven and the earth"* (Quran 7:96).
- Mohamed said, *"Allah has shown me the entire earth and told me that the kingdom of my nation will reach and possess all of it. Islam is victorious."*[5]
- *"We will bestow on such believers their reward according to the best of their actions"* (Quran 16:97).
- *"You have the right to wives, multiple, up to four, and those who your right hand possesses from captivity and prisoners"* (Quran 33:50). (In Muhamed's time "right hand" meant any slaves, concubines, or servants. In modern times, some believe servants, maids, and those who work for you are considered among those you possess.)
- *"You are not supposed to have sex with anyone unless in marriage or with whomever your right hand possesses"* (Quran 23:5–6).
- *"He will bestow on them courage and no defeat, no fear and no grief"* (Quran 2:57).

The words of Allah were directed to the faithful Muslim male. The blessings the male received were then to be bestowed upon the obedient, submissive female. No promises were made directly to women anywhere in the Quran or hadiths. But Allah provided that women could receive rewards if they were properly devout to their Muslim guardians. Unlike men, women did not have to be Muslim, but they did have to be submissive to one.

I saw the result of fulfilled promises in my father's life, and in my mother's life by extension. Emerging from his war experience as a man reborn, my father saw his faithfulness rewarded a hundred times over just as Allah promised. He met my mom, married into a wealthy family, and got a beautiful home with all the modern conveniences while his poor native village struggled.

The bounties overflowed. My father began his preaching career. Promotions in military rank came his way as well. In 1975, he resumed his medical practice and opened his first private clinic in the most prestigious neighborhood in Cairo. Just nine years after the war, when my dad lost everything, he got everything back and then some. Anyone could see his submission to Allah changed his life completely. He was gaining all the splendors of the earth. He was successful. He kept company with the then-president of Egypt. He had wealth, comfort, a wife, and children. In 1977, I, his first-born, became one of the faithful. All these signs meant my father was doing Allah's will and was receiving the fruits of the promises. By the time my uncle was released from prison, the power and influence of the Muslim Brotherhood were becoming apparent. The light was shining throughout the Middle East. Everywhere, it seemed, men were waking up to Islam, and a revival began to sweep the region.

A TRUE SLAVE OF ALLAH

As a boy and young man, I *never* met anyone more devoted to Allah than my father. He read the Quran through every three days. He led pilgrimages to Mecca every year and took worshipers on the *umrah*, a brief visit to Mecca, every month. I doubt if anyone on the planet has visited Allah's house in Mecca more times than my dad. His greatest aspiration was and is to draw his last breath there in the hopes of seeing the fulfillment of the hadith that says, "Whoever can die in my city, let him do that, because whoever dies there, I will intercede for him."[6]

I was convinced no better teacher could be found for my Islamic education than my own father. Together we delved into the scriptures, memorizing and reciting them, and edifying one another in the process. As we learned and grew together, he began to relate to me as a man, a companion on a spiritual journey. His expectations for me were great, but he gave me the confidence to reach and then surpass the bar he set for me.

Over the years, my father built an extraordinary library in our home and filled it with books fundamental to the faith: *The Life of Mohamed* by Ben Isihk; *Sahih Bukhari* and *Sahih Muslim*, the primary sources of the teachings and actions of Mohamed; and the preeminent book on sharia, *The Reliance of the Traveler*. These were just a few of his important texts.

Whenever my father was at home, he could be found in his library or in our home *masjid* where we prayed. It was there, surrounded by books on Islam, where he was most content. He and I whiled away hours in deep discussions about the texts surrounding us. One side of the library was devoted to the Quran, the other to Mohamed. These were all original source materials. My dad had no time for the interpretations of scripture offered by modern Islamic scholars. According to the Prophet, my father's approach was correct. Mohamed claimed to have so perfected the religion that no one else could add or subtract from it, and my father agreed wholeheartedly.

In the final analysis, I think my dad has a teaching gene in his DNA, a gene he inherited from his father. Perhaps that gene was Allah's reward. Whatever the source, my father was a very successful teacher and has led thousands in the proper observance of Allah's word and law. His teaching has also fulfilled an essential component of Islam: the obligation to pour resources back into Allah's kingdom to establish a place for oneself in heaven. Dad often said, "I'm building castles for myself in heaven." And, according to the hadith, he was indeed: "The Prophet (peace be upon him) said: '*Whoever builds a Masjid (mosque) for Allah, Allah will build for him likewise in Paradise*'" (Ṣaḥīḥ al-Bukhārī 450, Ṣaḥīḥ Muslim 533).

One of my father's primary mentors was Abdel-Halim Mahmoud, the former head of Al-Azhar University in Cairo. Al-Azhar remains one of only two schools in the world sanctioned to offer certificates for Sunni imams to teach. Sunni imams throughout the world, including the United States, must be licensed by one of these universities. I often accompanied my dad when he went to visit Abdel-Halim Mahmoud. We sat at his feet to drink in his wisdom. My father had many teachers, but this man was the only one he

My father and I were best friends. I spent quality time with this busy man by accompanying him wherever he went: the mosque, the clinic, a military installation, or a Muslim Brotherhood meeting. You can imagine the looks I received from those important people as I knelt or stood awkwardly in the middle of whatever my father was doing, surgeries included. But that was what he wanted, and it was how I learned more about government, history, medicine, and the Brotherhood than I could possibly read in ten books.

trusted and revered. When Mahmoud died in 1978, my father was at his bedside. Several of Mahmoud's books have a prominent place on my father's bookshelves.

Although in many ways unconventional, my father was a passionate and devoted slave to Allah and still is. When my father's name is mentioned in the streets of Cairo, even today, it is with great respect. Likewise, I was anything but conventional. On a mission to secure the blessings of Allah, I took extraordinary measures just as my father did. I sought out additional instruction from different local imams and mentors. I attended extra prayers at the mosque, the only child among fifty men. I memorized, prayed, studied and did it all over again each and every day. My only goal was to please Allah and be spared his wrath.

I was my father's confidant, sounding board, and ally in analyzing, critiquing, and pronouncing judgments. He trusted me with his innermost thoughts and no one else. For me this relationship became normal. I knew no other way of life. Every Tuesday evening, my father opened our home to teach from the Quran. Fifty or more men would come for the meetings. At that time, I had many opportunities to show my father, and Allah, I was a worthy servant. I worked alongside my mom and our maids to prepare the room each week. When the evening was completed, I would be the first to clean up. One Tuesday evening, I took it upon myself to start recording those teaching sessions. I eventually developed an audio library of those meetings. Later, those recordings became the basis for one of the nineteen books on Islam my father has published to date.

That desire to serve Allah extended to the mosque. There I handled jobs beyond my pay grade like rewiring light fixtures and re-installing them. True, I had no talent for such tasks, and it was a miracle I didn't set the mosque on fire, but I shied from no task that gave me a chance to show Allah the depth of my servitude.

While the adults looked on me as special and blessed, the other kids, my cousins especially, felt I was a bit of a freak. To be honest, they had a point. On one hand, I felt superior to the less devout around me. On the other hand, I felt inferior in just about every other way. My cousins were normal kids doing normal kid things. They went to the pool, watched movies and television programs, and listened to music. Meanwhile, I was living as a sixth-century Muslim. I was always the kid left behind.

Compared to my father, however, I was just treading water. I could never keep up with all he did in reverence to Allah. He fasted two days a week. He offered weekly animal sacrifices—he slaughtered the lamb, and I cut the meat into small packages and delivered them to the poor families in our community. He did this to atone for his sins, although I knew of no sin he was committing. The sacrifices continue to this day, I suspect, as a kind of insurance policy.

But that's not all. My dad built schools, bought books for school children, built mosques, and so much more. These types of benevolent acts were a significant part of his ministry, and most of this he did anonymously. All that mattered to him was that Allah saw. Meanwhile, he worked full-time and made a great deal of money to care for his family and to pour into Allah's kingdom.

I decided early on that being the weird kid was worth the effort if it meant I would reap the promises offered to the faithful. After all, if the blessings I saw in my dad's life were any indication, I would have been a fool to walk any other path. Earthly rewards were well and good, but the greatest riches awaited the faithful in heaven: peace and security; gardens filled with springs of ice-cold water; rivers of wine and milk; trees abundant with all manner of fruit; garments of silk and bracelets of gold, both forbidden in life on earth; and a throne upon which to repose while wives, young male slaves, and yes, seventy-two virgins tended to *every* need.

At least eighteen passages in the Quran told of the heaven that waited, a paradise offering everything a man could desire for all eternity. I was young but well on my way to claiming the greatest of Allah's promises, or so I hoped.

CHAPTER 6

MEETING A GOD I DID NOT KNOW

Do not take Christians and Jews as true friends. They are only true friends of one another and they are forever the enemies of Islam. If you become a true friend to them, then you will become one of them and god will punish you for that. If you stay steadfast and follow Allah, he will bring you conquest and will make you prevail over everyone.

—Quran 5:51–52

My father had it all, and I wanted nothing less. He could see the desire in my heart and knew I had the potential to reach my goals. I believed I was invincible and believed my faith was unshakable. It had not been that long since my dark room experience, but I impressed my father as being sufficiently grounded in my faith I could stand strong in a secular atmosphere.

This was a tremendous leap of faith on my father's part. He knew how hard it was to stay true to one's faith when surrounded by the enticements of a beguiling culture, but he hoped to spare

57

me a major stumbling block to his own success. Given the poverty of his youth, he had little exposure to the English language. Medical school classes, even in Egypt, were conducted in English, and my father struggled with the language all the way through. He had the resources to give me an opportunity he never had, even if it came with some risk.

In our community was a traditional British school renowned throughout the Middle East at the time. The student body was a mix of Christians, secularists, nominal Muslims, and perhaps a handful of devout Muslim kids. After much soul searching, my father concluded I should attend the school. His fear was the experience might challenge my devout walk with Allah, but my father believed I was up to the challenge and would master English.

MY FORMAL EDUCATION AT THE ENGLISH SCHOOL BEGINS

The English School, founded in the early 1900s as Victoria College, was a holdover from the days of British imperialism. The founders' goal was to free the region from the traditional Islamic educational model and provide a superior, secular education in a decidedly European style. The school adhered to that model for more than a half century under British administrations. In December 1956, Nasser purged the British educators when he seized power from the Egyptian monarchy, but the English educational model remained intact, language included.

The English School in Cairo emerged as the educational establishment of choice for most affluent citizens of the Middle East. Year after year, the school educated the children of prominent businessmen, of government leaders, and even of royalty. King Hussein of Jordan attended the school, as did actor Omar Sharif. Although my family was financially comfortable, we were considered "new money." Were it not for a very special connection, I might never have been accepted. As it happened, the wife of then-president Anwar Sadat arranged an interview for me with the principal of the school, Mrs. Enayat Saad El Din.

Mrs. El Din was born to teach, just as my dad. When my father and I went for my entrance interview, he and Mrs. El Din formed an immediate bond. I sat quietly and watched in awe how my dad spoke with her. He never had the chance to attend an elite school when he was a kid, and he had nothing in common with the well-born Mrs. El Din, but he was not at all intimidated. He has a remarkable ability to reach out to people across the religious, political, and socio-economic spectrum and form connections with them.

It is difficult to explain, but my father has a gift for entering a room as a regular guy and exiting as the man to know. Even as a boy, I could see he exuded Islam through his pores. His righteousness overwhelmed everyone in his presence, including Mrs. El Din. He left her in awe. He always seemed to do that.

Still, my father was not without his worries. Although he seemed in complete control, he approached that interview with a certain trepidation. He was afraid, and rightfully so, he was throwing his young son to the secular wolves. This was a calculated risk, but it was one he felt worth taking.

I was excited about starting school and getting to wear the official school uniform of a jacket and tie. To up my game, I found an old Samsonite briefcase my dad used to make house calls and turned it into my book bag. If I looked like "the man" ready to take on the world, in reality I was a scared little 5 year old kid who had no idea what I was walking into. As that first day approached, my father sat me down for a heart-to-heart talk.

"My son, the school will be very good for you, and you will learn a great deal that will help you later in life, much more than I ever learned," he told me, never failing to remind me my opportunities were greater than his. "But," he added emphatically, "there will be many influences and voices around you who are not living as Allah wills." I was listening. He made sure of it.

"Are you ready to reject anything that will separate you from Allah and take you from the right path?" he continued. "Are you going to always be on guard to protect your mind and heart from evil?"

"Yes! I am ready to fight the fight!" Deep inside, I was actually terrified. Who were these people and what were these awful voices he warned me about? I imagined all kinds of horrible monsters walking the halls, lurking behind the corners waiting to devour me as I walked past. My stomach was a tangled mass of knots. I had already learned the penalty for sin, and I never again wanted to go back to that place of fear and trembling. Just as powerful was my fear of being separated from the greatest teacher of all, my dad. As we walked into school that first day, I could feel my father's anxiety mounting. He and my mother said goodbye and left me alone with a teacher I didn't know and classmates I never met. It did not take long before the fear he placed in my heart overwhelmed my emotions, and I began to cry. Crying led to throwing up. Throwing up led to my father being called to come and pick me up. When he returned, however, he did not come to retrieve me. He came to encourage me to stay strong.

I stayed strong, but I did so by insulating myself from the other students. They were strangers, aliens even, who neither looked nor acted like me. I spent the first two years at the English School sitting alone in class, alone during recess, always alone. I refused to speak to anyone other than my teachers, and even then, only sparingly. Completely contrary to my nature, I played the introvert, and I was miserable. My days were a test of endurance, a struggle to hold together emotionally until I could get back to the safety of my home.

I was not overreacting. Rather, I was living the words of Allah and the Prophet. All Muslims were supposed to do what I was doing: distancing ourselves from outside influences that pulled us away from the faith. As Allah willed it, I was removing myself from temptations—*fitna*—and staying vigilant against a corrupted culture.

Of course, to properly insulate ourselves, we had to first recognize we were vulnerable to the temptations of the enemy. Only then could we put up the shield of Islam and immerse ourselves in Muslim homes, schools, and neighborhoods surrounded only by faithful Muslims. In the interim, if I had to be in a place of fitna, I wanted to reap the benefits of that exposure while rejecting the corruptions. This was not easy. To reinforce my submission to Allah, I engaged in extra rituals and doubled down on my faith. By the time I reached the third grade, I was secure enough in my faith to interact with my classmates. The student body was a good mix of Muslims, Egyptian Christians, and international students of all faiths and cultures. Given my background, this intermingling seemed very strange. About the only thing I had in common with most of the students was our shared need for food, water, and oxygen.

Unlike most schools in Egypt, the English School taught the art of critical thinking. We were encouraged to test, to question, and to challenge assumptions. This was not at all what I was used to doing. According to the Muslim way, the Quran and the words of the Prophet were not to be questioned, but to be acknowledged as truth.

The critical thinking skills I learned at the English School would one day change my life. My dad's worst fears would, in fact, be realized, but at the time, I was committed to becoming the best Muslim ever. I studied the passages from the Quran relentlessly and memorized the second chapter, the longest, before I was six years old. I remember its words to this day.

My exceptional abilities, however, did not curb my anxiety about one particular class: religious studies. Unlike the other classes, this one was segregated by faith. Each day, the Christian minority filed out of the classroom and went down the hall for their lessons. Although I wondered what they were taught, I had to focus on my religion class and make sure I learned everything I needed to pass my tests. There was much to learn.

When the Islamic schools—*madrasas*—were replaced by Westernized ones, Muslim countries mandated religious instruction in order to ensure a proper advancement of the faith. All Muslim students were obligated to learn the tenets of the faith as well as reading, writing, and science. By the time sixth grade was completed, every student had to memorize three to five chapters of the Quran and the foundation of Mohamed's story—the *Sira*. The latter included his sayings—the *Hadith* and his footsteps, *Sunnah*. Students also had to learn enough Islamic law—*sharia*—to handle day-to-day affairs on a personal and family level. They were also taught the fundamentals of jihad and the pride of Islamic conquests.

Even at the English School, I could not slack off in religious studies. Falling behind, even in third grade, would have been a serious failure, and I simply could not fail Allah. After all, he did not destroy me for my initial sin. In fact, he blessed me. I wasn't going to ruin that record now.

Once I came out of my shell and started interacting with other students, I found I made friends easily. One of my best friends was Emad, a green-eyed Egyptian Christian. I know my father would have been disappointed if he knew I befriended a Christian, but I never told him. I wasn't allowed to socialize outside of school with friends anyway, so I felt pretty safe with my secret. Besides, my desire was to overwhelm Emad over time with the legitimacy of Islam so he might forsake his false religion and convert. At school, we were the best of friends, always laughing together over something silly or playing games at recess.

GOD IS LOVE?

One day, while I was wringing my hands and racking my brain in preparation for my Islamic studies tests, I noticed Emad was as cool and casual as ever. "Why aren't you studying for your test?" I asked him. "Aren't you worried you won't do well?"

"No, I'm not scared of the test. It will be fun!" he laughed.

I knew Christians were not to be trusted, but I began to consider maybe my friend was just a little bit crazy. Didn't his performance on the tests carry the same weight as mine? If I didn't pass, I would be held back in school. I would destroy the confidence my father placed in my abilities. Worse still, I would fail Allah, giving him further reason to crush me.

I knew Emad was a super high achiever, just as I was. I could not understand his casual attitude. I was intrigued and just a little bit annoyed by his response. What were they doing in that other classroom down the hall?

One day, I decided to find out for myself and quietly slipped away during recess to have a look. I was full of curiosity and a great sense of fear. I certainly didn't want to be caught in a place I should not be. I crept down the hallway only to find the classroom door closed. My first thought was to turn around and run back to the playground where I was supposed to be, but the urge to know was too great. So I stood on my tiptoes and peered in through a small window.

Hmm. Nothing looked so very different. There were desks and books and everything appeared as it did in my classroom. But then my eyes landed on the blackboard at the front of the room. Written in chalk were three little words, "God is Love." *What?* I eased myself off my toes and stood there in disbelief. Could I have seen this right? "God is Love"? Just to be certain, I took another peek.

My brain felt like it was sloshing around in my head. *God is Love?* That was utter blasphemy! I knew Allah about as well as any kid anywhere, and he was certainly not love! Love is a feeling. Allah was not love. How could they downsize god into a feeling? My Allah was the judge. My god was judgmental. My god was going to strike me deaf and blind if I didn't follow him perfectly. How could that be love?

The Quran says Allah is an exacting judge who requires nothing short of perfect devotion. Nothing about that said love. I was expected to learn the ninety-nine names of Allah, and I knew them all. None of the names was "Love." The Quran says clearly in 22:19–21, *"But as for those who disbelieve, garments of fire will be cut out for them; boiling fluid will be poured down on their heads; Whereby that which is in their bellies, and their skins too, will be melted; And for them are hooked rods of iron."* Does that sound like love?

I trembled with fear everyone in the school would be struck dead for the blasphemy written on that chalkboard. I didn't want that to happen, and I didn't want Emad to be punished for the blasphemies he was being taught. Walking back to my own classroom, I felt my neck get hot. I was torn between anger and jealousy. I was jealous Emad was getting to enjoy studying his god, but I was angry my best friend would be condemned to hell for his blasphemy!

The warning of my father flashed before my eyes—the warning to protect my mind and heart from the lies of the enemy. I decided then and there I would no longer be jealous nor intrigued. Instead, I taught myself to feel sorry for Emad and all the other Christian students. My friend was destined for hellfire, and he was blissfully ignorant of that fact. Quran 5:50–52 made his fate clear: *"Look, how Christians invented a lie of forgiveness—that is an ultimate sin. Have you not seen those who were given a portion of the Scripture? Be aware of those who say that their scripture is better than yours. They are those whom Allah has cursed, and he whom Allah curses, you will not find for him (any) helper."*

MY COMMITMENT TO ALLAH GROWS

If the future was not bright for my friend, I knew I had the truth, and my devotion to Allah would save me. I proudly held my head high as I walked through the hall back to my classroom. I saw the lies and recognized the error. I resolved to embrace Allah and my faith with new fervor. My eternity in heaven or hell depended on it.

I walked out of school that day transformed. I knew blasphemy when I saw it, and I wanted like never before to reject it. If the Christians were going to spread their heresies in this secular school, I would make my life a statement of faith to counter those heresies.

It wasn't long before my commitment began to reveal its rewards. Every day, our religious studies instructor read passages to us from the Quran. We were expected to read along silently, commit the passages to memory, and come to school the next day prepared to recite them as best we could. One day, the teacher started reading a passage to the class, and my heart began to pound. I had already memorized that passage to perfection at home in my studies with my father. I knew the words coming out of my teacher's mouth before she said them. I mustered up my courage and raised my hand. "Yes, Mohamed?" said the teacher.

"May I recite the passage?" I asked.

"You know it?" she inquired.

"Yes, I do," I said confidently.

"Please, go ahead. Stand and share it with us."

With no book in my hand from which to follow the words, I rose from my desk. All eyes were upon me. I did not just recite the passage. I chanted it—*tarteel*—emphasizing the meaning of each word through my passionate delivery.

My voice filled the classroom as I chanted the words of Allah. In my heart, I did not seek glory for myself but for Allah alone. I garnered strength as I continued. The faces of my classmates revealed their astonishment and admiration. They no longer followed the text. Their mouths fell open in wonder, and the teacher stared in awe. When I finished, I quietly took my seat. Silence gave way to thunderous applause. When the teacher found her voice, she said, "Mohamed, that was perfect! From now on, you will read the text to the class."

From that moment, my classmates started treating me as an authority, which was astonishing. We were a school of high achievers, academic stars each and every one, and they recognized me for having a special gift. They thought of me as an imam, a teacher of Islam, and they continued to think of me as one until my final day of high school.

Some of my fellow students came to me not just with theological questions, but with personal questions as well. Many of them hoped to learn what the proper response under Islam should be to issues they were experiencing at home. Others mocked me and asked questions sarcastically. I held my ground through it all. Although I did not ask for this role, I believed it to be my reward for championing Islam, the victorious, in an environment where Islam was not championed before.

CHAPTER 7

AWAKENING

Allah has promised the faithful and righteous Muslims that he will make them rulers over the earth. He will bestow on the enforcer of Islam the inheritance of the world and establish the Islamic state and make them caliphs [kings].

—Quran 24:55

I have witnessed the power of Islam, and it is awe-inspiring. I saw it first in my father. When he entered a room, he only needed to speak a few words from the Quran to command the attention of everyone present. At a young age, I learned to do the same. Soon I was able to intimidate others with my faith and knowledge of Islam.

In reciting those nine verses from the Quran to my classmates that day I unleashed the power of Allah's wrath and silenced the room. The other students sensed my conviction. Speaking Allah's words with authority, I called them to righteousness and caused even the strong among them to own up to their weaknesses. Those words transformed me from a nobody to a somebody, Islam's greatest local champion. I tapped into a thirteen-hundred-year-old tradition calling out for revival.

There was never an occasion when I didn't have a question. Yes, I was that kind of kid. I was exceptionally enthusiastic and curious, and when I asked questions and didn't get an answer, I kept asking. While some would probably label me annoying, my determination and inquisitiveness served me well over the years. I just wanted to understand what people were thinking and why. Attending the English School and being introduced to the Western way of critical thinking at an early age encouraged my inquisitive nature.

When you're an inquisitive kid, there simply aren't enough hours in the day to absorb all the information available. I wore my dad out. Although he carved out as much time as possible for my relentless questioning, it was a difficult balancing act for him. He split his time between his work with the military, his work as a doctor, and his duties as a religious leader. Any one of those duties could have been a full-time job for the ordinary man. My father, however, was anything but ordinary.

Whenever I could, I went with him, no matter where the work took him. Regardless of where we were, our conversations revolved around Islam, politics, current events, and family matters. All conversations took us back to our original sources—the Quran and Mohamed. We viewed *everything* through the very narrow lens of Islam.

As a student at the English School, I needed more Islamic and Quranic studies to balance my schooling and to satisfy my extreme religious curiosity and hunger. My dad recruited an imam to meet with me daily at the nearby mosque. Every day after school, I went to the mosque to ask the imam questions and to read and recite the Quran with him. My cousins all thought of me as something of a nerd, and they were right. By the time I was nine, I was a walking Islamic encyclopedia. That was my goal.

I also spent many hours with my uncle, who taught me more about history and politics than I could possibly hope to learn from other sources. My idea of fun was to cross the corridor in our building and knock on his door to see if we could talk. I looked to Uncle Ahmed as a wise old man, a sage, and he was always happy to share his wisdom with me. We spent countless hours lost in conversations about most everything, and he was always patient with my questions.

Patience was a virtue he acquired behind bars. He once told me he made a conscious decision to use his imprisonment and torture to help strengthen his character. Rather than becoming angry and vengeful, he became observant and introspective. From my perspective, my father's life experiences made him a different kind of person. He became passionate and reactionary. When the three of us got together to discuss any topic, it was quite the stew. I always emerged from my time spent with them rich with wisdom.

None of my uncle's children were interested in spending time in deep discussion with their father. His routine was to withdraw to his study every evening to contemplate the events of the day. As for me, nerd that I was, I sought him out. It always gave Uncle Ahmed a chuckle when he answered the door and I strolled through, ready to tackle another evening of educational and philosophical pursuits. Just like my dad, he saw me as a man in a kid's body and was comfortable confiding in me his innermost observations. He was an instructor in need of someone to instruct, and I was just the person to fill the role of apprentice.

SADAT AWAKENS MUSLIMS TO WAGE JIHAD

One evening I boldly asked Uncle Ahmed about his release from prison, never really pausing to consider whether the topic would upset him. He got up from his chair, reached into his desk drawer, and produced a newspaper from 1970. On the front page was a picture of President Sadat, surrounded by his military leaders, breaking down the walls of the prison with a sledgehammer. The headline boldly proclaimed, "Sadat demolishes the imprisonment camps!"

President Sadat looked so strong in that black-and-white photo. I could see in my uncle's eyes Sadat's action was more than personal. It was a proclamation that everything was about to change, and did it ever! Sadat sent a powerful message to the world that Islam would no longer be suppressed. "We were vindicated,"

I said to my uncle. He replied, "And once we were free, we knew that Allah had a great work for us to do." As Uncle Ahmed explained, Nasser imprisoned them. He tried to silence us and silence Islam through the death of Sayyid Qutb. But Allah would be silenced no longer, and Nasser's Communist kingdom was falling apart. Within a very short time, Nasser was reduced to a shadow of the man he once was. After his humiliating defeat at the hands of Israel, he lost everything. When he died, his rejection of Islam died with him.

I thought about that for a moment and listened intently when my uncle began telling me about the amazing changes since Sadat took office. The Brotherhood was alive and well and had spread its message throughout the Middle East and into the rest of the world. Many answered the call to become more vocal and emboldened, hoping to educate a new generation in the curriculum of pure Islam. They took their message to Saudi Arabia, the United Emirates, Bahrain, Qatar, and throughout the Gulf region. Others went to Europe as doctors or in other professional roles. Still other members went to Canada and the United States. People I knew as close personal friends of my dad and my uncle, such as Dr. Maher Hathout, assumed key positions as influencers to high-level policy makers.

No matter where the duty assignment took them, Brotherhood members spread a common message. They learned from the lessons of the past. Never again would they allow a dictator to contain them. The seed was planted, and a greater victory was on the horizon—the victory of Islam over the world.

My uncle, a lawyer by trade, took a job at a large construction company as a legal consultant. I think some people viewed him as a broken, timid man who ran away from conflict. But that was not my uncle at all. I saw him as a brilliant hermit—a wise watcher who spoke few words, but when he did, watch out! They meant something. He kept a sharp eye on everything going on in the Islamic movement and kept my dad informed on important people and events. Since I was a part of these conversations I was always interrupting with questions.

"President Sadat was a very complicated man. He quite often thought he was outsmarting everybody and often did things according to his own devices," my uncle told me. "I do have lots of disagreements with him because this is not the way to do things according to Islam."

That much conceded, Uncle Ahmed added a useful caveat: "But yet Allah used Sadat to revive Islam in the Middle East after many decades of secular leadership. He resurrected the idea and the obligation of jihad, which had all but disappeared from the hearts of Muslims with the end of the caliphate in 1924."

When I asked how Sadat accomplished that, my uncle said it all began with the war of 1973. "Not long after our release, Sadat achieved a great victory for Islam. The victory was a manifesto of victory for Allah, alone, and martyrdom was re-established as the only absolute way to heaven. The martyrs are once again revered after many decades." I knew from hearing my dad's stories Egypt was humiliated after its defeat in the war of 1967. Israel, the arch-enemy of Egypt and Islam, came out on top and obliterated Egypt's military. What Egypt needed most after that devastating loss and the hopeless Communist policies of Nasser was a leader who could lift the country out of the quagmire and put it back on the world stage. Sadat was the man who wanted to make a statement for Egypt by defeating Israel and the Jews. The only sure way to accomplish that was to resurrect the true spirit of Islam and the duty of jihad and the rewards of martyrdom.

Redemption came in the form of a strategically brilliant trick— a surprise attack against Israel during the holiest day of the Jewish calendar, Yom Kippur. That date coincided with Ramadan, Islam's most holy time of year, and that was no accident. "Sadat was doing everything right," said my uncle. Sadat planned the offensive to take place during Ramadan. He appointed imams to guide the military in spiritual matters, urging members of the military to return to their faith. He encouraged them, for the first time in recent Egyptian history, to chant the call to prayers five times a day at military bases. He also built the first mosques in the military units and military hospitals in Egypt. He transformed a secular military operation into Allah's spearhead. Prayer would help them understand they would no longer be instruments of warfare for a nation. Instead, their calling was much higher. They were to wage jihad for Allah.

"Would you rather win a battle for Egypt or for Allah?" Uncle Ahmed asked me.

"Allah!" I said. "And jihad is a just battle against the enemy!"

"Yes," my uncle said. Requiring the military to focus on faith was a new idea to a secular military established by the British and then run by the Communists under Nasser. This was the first time our military was run by a leader with an allegiance to the faith.

"But how did Sadat do it?" I asked. "How did he trick the Jews and achieve a victory for Islam?"

"The Egyptian military was no match for Israel, especially after the defeat of 1967. The morale of the troops was at its lowest point. By resurrecting the victorious nature of Islam in the hearts and minds of the soldiers, Sadat assured them Allah would help them win against all odds. This was exactly what Islam teaches about Mohamed's victories. It was the only way to go."

"But Sadat was no fool," my uncle added. As he explained, Sadat knew a head-to-head military confrontation would have ended in disaster. His only true hope was to catch Israel off guard. Operation Badr, named for the first battle of Islam that also took place on Ramadan, turned the tide of history.

"And your dad was a crucial part of that great victory," added Uncle Ahmed generously.

Having lived through the persecution of the Brotherhood, he was able to see the military transform before his eyes. Under Sadat, he was able to serve Allah openly and boldly as a spiritual leader of the troops.

OPERATION BADR

As Uncle Ahmed described the events of Operation Badr, I listened, fascinated. He told me that to distract the enemy, Sadat called for his top military officers to make umrah, an abbreviated pilgrimage to

Mecca. This pilgrimage achieved a dual purpose: it convinced Israel they had nothing to fear since the military leaders were off praying in Mecca, and it convinced Egyptians embracing Islam was the only path to victory. My dad was right in the middle of Sadat's plan as a member of the military delegation that made umrah, and it made me so proud to know Allah used him to achieve his purposes.

Just before Sadat made his move, newspapers and other media outlets throughout the region announced the upcoming umrah, posting photos of smiling officers waving goodbye to their families as they set out to honor Allah. And when Israel least expected it, Egypt attacked. This war bore no resemblance to the one of 1967. This battle was waged for Allah, with Allah, and Allah rewarded Egypt with the victory.

For the first time since the Western occupation of Egypt and subsequent Communist rule, the military was united under one powerful banner—Islam. The Egyptian military massed along the shores of the Red Sea on October 6, 1973. At exactly 2 p.m. a chorus of "Allah Akbar" rang out. Every man was united in faith and vision as they swarmed across the Suez Canal. It must have been a powerful sight.

In affirming the supremacy of Allah, Egypt achieved both a military and spiritual victory, creating a tsunami of faith that swept through the Middle East and to the four corners of the earth. Israel's seeming defeat delivered a powerful message to the Muslim world—Allah was victorious, and Islam was supreme.

I had reason to admire President Sadat. Only Allah could have given him such a plan, and only Allah could have given us the victory. Uncle Ahmed and I talked for hours about Islam's victory. We also talked about how those devoted to the Brotherhood and the cause of Islam were becoming as numerous as the sands of the sea. That kind of power could not be ignored. Like a deluge of water thundering through the wadi after a desert rain, that power demanded the world pay attention. Just as Sadat put Israel on notice, Islam was putting the world on notice.

Muslims everywhere began to see the benefits of following Allah. Waging man's war for man's purposes achieved nothing.

But waging jihad, holy warfare for Allah, earned victory. In large numbers, Muslims started to rediscover their faith along with its duties and obligations, but not all Muslims.

Many nominal Muslims clung to the Western influences of the past, and some even held on to Communism. Angry conflicts broke out on the streets between the nominal and the devout. Standing on a foundation of the ancient texts, the devout condemned those unable or unwilling to defend the faith. As for the Communists, the undeniable failure of their system condemned them. There was no doubt—pure Islam was the true winner. Those who remained faithful were sure to be rewarded by Allah.

DAD DISCOVERS HIS PURPOSE

No matter who ruled over Egypt, my dad remained faithful. Nothing ever took him off course. He knew what the ancient texts said and what Allah required. He stepped up when Sadat needed a team to lead the umrah. Two years later, as a reward, he was commissioned to lead members of the military on the annual pilgrimage. It was then, and in that role, my father discovered his purpose, one that would become his mission for the rest of his life.

The fifth and final pillar is *hajj*—the pilgrimage to Mecca and a time of great renewal. The devout servant of Allah is expected to make at least one such pilgrimage in a lifetime. Ideally, he returns feeling as if he was born again. Making the pilgrimage is a vital part of the faith, but it was not always within reach of the average Muslim. Before the 1970s, not all Muslims even knew about the pilgrimage. This is how estranged they had become from Islam. Among those who knew about the pilgrimage and wanted to do it, only a few could afford the financial and physical hardships of either the hajj, the comprehensive pilgrimage, or umrah, the minor one.

In 1973, when Sadat resurrected the duty of jihad and holy war, he began sending his officers on the pilgrimage. This encouraged Egyptians to think they, too, could make this life-changing journey. Sadat helped make pilgrimages affordable by subsidizing anyone who wanted to go. My dad saw an opportunity and became one of the leaders of that effort.

Each time Dad led a pilgrimage to Saudi Arabia, I saw a new man walk through our front door on his return. The transformation stirred in me a longing to go and see Mecca for myself. I longed to visit Allah in his house, to touch the golden door, and to drink of the holy water. I longed for that feeling of unbreakable strength and renewed devotion I saw in my father on his return.

On one particular trip, my father became very ill. In fact, he thought he might receive Allah's reward of dying in that holy place. The Prophet said a death in Mecca should be every Muslim's hope.

I later told my dad I was afraid he would die in Mecca. Had he, I would have been an orphan, which is considered a punishment by Allah. "To die in hajj is like dying in jihad, assuring a straight path to heaven," my father corrected me. "You should not think of it as becoming an orphan. You should consider it an honor to be the child of a jihadi who is martyred." I believed his words, but they did not ease the conflict in my heart. I wanted to serve Allah *and* keep my father here with me. My overwhelming love for my father left me feeling guilty. I struggled to bring my heart into line with what Allah required.

MY FIRST HAJJ

In 1979, my father was offered the chance to Hajj, leading a group of prominent civilian doctors to Mecca. This was the first trip of its kind organized by a group outside the military, and it had the potential to change all our lives. Given my dad's experience as a military doctor and his expertise in leading the pilgrimage, he was invited to lead this one and bring his family to take part in what would prove to be a first-class experience. By sharing the experience of the pilgrimage with his own family, he knew it would inspire us all into being more faithful to Allah, especially my mother.

At the time, my mother was wearing the hijab and making a decent attempt at living a submissive Muslim life. She needed to make up for the many years before her marriage when she was inactive, however, and that inactivity was my father's greatest concern. Even now, Mom prayed but not five times a day. Educated in French schools, she could not easily read the Arabic text of the Quran, which is admittedly difficult, and never showed much desire to learn. Dad believed a pilgrimage would light a necessary fire within her.

As for me, the news totally energized me, and I was already on a spiritual high after my recitation of the Quran at school. It seemed at the time whenever I stood up for Allah, Allah rewarded me. I pictured the hajj in my mind many times, but now I would be able to describe the pilgrimage in vivid detail to all of my friends. I was certain a visit to meet my creator, whom I longed to know, would change me. How could it not?

The hajj would also give me bragging rights at my school where I already established myself as an authority on Islam. That appealed to my pride for sure, but I was more enamored with the idea I was going to be in the presence of something profound. I scarcely told a handful of friends when the principal leaked the news to everyone. The announcement sent shockwaves through the school. No one knew anyone who actually made the pilgrimage. My fellow students gathered around me and bombarded me with questions about my upcoming trip. I was dizzy with excitement.

The excitement was building at home too. My parents were busy preparing the mountain of paperwork needed to travel outside Egypt. Remnants of Communist policies restricted travel and required a full disclosure of travel plans be provided to government officials. Thankfully, dad's influence in the military and his close relationship with Sadat's daughter—he was her OB/Gyn—meant he obtained the signed yellow cards almost immediately.

Almost no one traveled outside Egypt when I was a kid. Many friends envied me for going *anywhere*. Others marveled at the incredible shopping awaiting us beyond Egypt's impoverished post-Soviet markets. Some riddled me with questions about what I might buy in Saudi Arabia.

The more devout asked us to pray for them when visiting Allah at his house. Some even shoved prayer requests into our hands.

These requests excited me the most. I welcomed the chance to offer up prayers close to my creator and to the Prophet. In this holiest of places, I also wanted to pray Allah would reward my future with wealth, health, and the ability to be a great doctor. I was going to ask for all the splendors of the earth Allah promised Mohamed and his followers.

My cousins, including Uncle Ahmed's kids, envied me. I couldn't help feeling a little smug about the upcoming trip. Up to this point they excluded me from their activities. It seemed only right that Allah would reward me with this trip. Let them have their movie theaters, TV, music, and other worldly entertainments. I was going to Allah's house!

My ever-thorough dad was going to make sure his family members were the best-prepared pilgrims ever. Just as he sat me down to talk about the English School, he sat our entire family down to talk about the pilgrimage. "We are blessed to be called to Allah's house," he said, and we knew it. "So, it's very important you understand the significance of each step we will take. If you are committed to understanding, the pilgrimage will change your lives. We must never mock Allah in his house by a lack of commitment and devotion."

Dad looked at Mom, and she lowered her head. "We are going to the most sacred place on earth. It is a holy place of refuge," he said. "You must not create any violence while there. That means you do not pull a hair from your head, clip a fingernail, kill an insect, or start an argument." I became terrified at the thought of stepping on a bug. I made a mental note to be fully aware of everything around me when I was in the house of Allah.

My dad, a perfectionist when it came to faith, was not going to take us on the pilgrimage if we weren't going to perform the rituals properly. He would be watching, but most importantly, he told us, Allah would be watching, too. "The pilgrimage represents dying to self and emerging renewed," he said.

This regeneration explained the required dress for male pilgrims. We were to wear sandals on our feet and two white towels draped across our bodies. The towels suggested the preparation of a body for burial. I have to laugh now when I remember how worried my mother was my brother and I might catch a chill and die. It was, after all, December, and the temperatures in Saudi Arabia could dip as low as the seventies! Just in case, in quiet defiance of my dad's Islamic teachings, she bought us each a white turtleneck to wear underneath.

"I want you to prepare your minds and your heart for pilgrimage. It is necessary that you have a pure and contrite spirit," Dad continued as I conjured up mental images of how everything would look. "Listen, learn, and become new," he said.

My father's instruction in our home during the weeks leading up to the pilgrimage was to become the signature of his ministry. It was not long after that trip when he produced his first book, a seminal work on the proper observance of the pilgrimage, *Hajj Mabrur*, which means the perfect hajj acceptable to Allah. His four-part training program was used, and still is today, to teach tens of thousands of Muslims throughout the Middle East. To this day, my dad continues to be the recognized expert in the Muslim world on the topic of hajj. His instruction heightened the experience for everyone who had the benefit of learning from it. As I would soon learn, other pilgrims looked at our group with envy and confusion. How did we know so much they did not? My dad was our mentor. That was how.

Allah's invitation brought our family together in unexpected ways. My mother, still struggling to become the kind

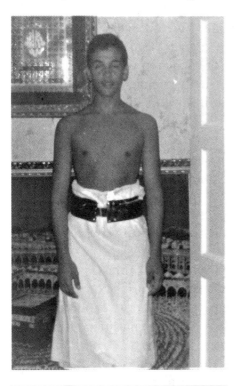

Mark getting ready for hajj.

of Muslim woman Allah said she should be, hoped to earn a measure of forgiveness. She also wanted to learn more about her path going forward. Dad was seeking continued confirmation of his purpose. And I, the kid who had emerged from a dark room beaten and bruised, was going to claim the reward of meeting my creator.

When the day arrived for us to depart, twenty to thirty of our family members accompanied us to the airport and waved us off, further evidence to me this trip was a really big deal. They wanted to be part of the experience, if even from the sidelines. Would they ever be able to make this trip? Who knew?

To keep my mother happy, I wore the turtleneck she gave me to the airport, but I took it off as soon as we boarded the plane. A turtleneck was not part of the perfect pilgrimage, and I aspired to be as much an Islamic perfectionist as my father. I was not going to let a little warmth stand between me and Allah's approval. Sitting in first class as the Saudi Arabian Airlines 747 took off, I felt as if I was walking on air. "This is how it feels to be rewarded by Allah," I said to myself.

As we lifted off into the sky, I was suddenly transported from the physical realm to some place uniquely spiritual. At this point, my dad began to lead the men in a chant, their voices strong and united. I joined in, confident of the words and the spirit behind them. They signaled the complete submission of a slave rushing to answer the call of a master.

"Here I am, Allah. I am all yours. Here I am, Allah, who alone is god, with no rival. Yours alone is all praise and all bounty. Yours alone is the sovereignty. You have no partners." Over and over we chanted, increasing our focus on Allah and entering a state of rapturous devotion. Our only goal was to worship and serve our master.

The plane from Cairo touched down in Jeddah, Saudi Arabia. The flight took two hours, but the time passed in what seemed like minutes, so lost was I in the experience. Jeddah was the jumping-off place for international pilgrims. There was no airport in Mecca. There never will be. Planes are expressly forbidden from flying over the house of Allah, the nexus between heaven and earth. Allah does not allow anything to fly over his home, not even birds or butterflies.

I was amazed at the grandeur of the airport in Jeddah. The wealth of Saudi Arabia was on full display. It seemed such a contrast to the rundown airport in Cairo. To me, Saudi Arabia was a land set apart, overflowing with milk and honey. I had to believe the Saudis prospered because they never bowed to any other faith or any other nation.

I found myself wishing Egypt looked more like this, but my country paid the price for allowing Islam to be suppressed. As I walked through the Jeddah airport, I saw Americans and other Westerners living and working in a strong Islamic country that had humbled them. Even Western women were properly covered in hijab, and everyone observed the dictates of sharia, whether it fit their belief systems or not. I hoped Egypt's great awakening would help us make up for lost time and gain Allah's blessing.

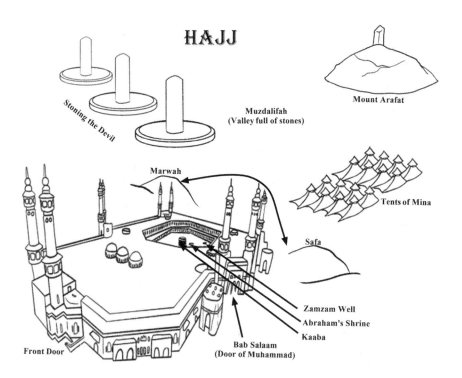

MECCA

We emerged from the airport and boarded a bus waiting to take us to Mecca. The anticipation only heightened my desire to take in every sight and sound. About fifty miles from Jeddah, we came to road signs detouring non-Muslims. The *kaffirs*, unclean and unworthy, were not allowed to come within twelve miles of Allah and his house. They had to circumnavigate Mecca by a wide margin. The road straight to Mecca was reserved for Muslims. If I hadn't already felt special to be Muslim, these signs would have done it for me.

All these years later, the memories and emotions of my first pilgrimage remain as vivid as they were then. The major milestones in my life have never faded or frayed around the edges. They retain a crispness transporting me mind, body, and spirit back to another time. Every sight, sound, and smell still resonates.

Mecca is in a valley. As we crested the last hill on our approach to our destination, the Masjid al-Haram, the Great Mosque, came into view. The air felt thick in my throat. Our chants, which we began again on the bus, were now reaching fever pitch. I could feel my dad's proud gaze on me but could not avert my eyes. At the center of the mosque was Allah's house, the *Kaaba*, and it was breathtaking! I could see its three-hundred-kilogram gold door gleaming in the distance, and I was swept away by the emotion of the moment. The chanting magnified the spectacle in front of me.

The bus pulled to a stop in front of our hotel, which was in front of the mosque. We disembarked and prepared to enter the mosque to begin the rituals of the umrah. Following a short break, my father briefed the group on our next steps. After his instruction, we readjusted our top towel to expose our right shoulder, just as Mohamed instructed us to do. I quickly took my position next to my dad who was leading the way.

Marching together to the mosque, we resumed our chanting. We entered through what is known as the Door of Peace, the archway through which Mohamed entered fourteen hundred years earlier when he conquered Mecca and cleansed it of the kaffirs, or non-Muslims. Indeed, the door of peace it is—that is, if you accept the Islamic meaning of "peace" as the after-effects of Muslim conquest and victory.

Prior to that cleansing, there were 360 statues of idols in the Kaaba. "How did Mohamed destroy them?" I thought to myself. "Did he walk the same steps I walk today?" I imagined the Prophet destroying the idols, removing all the false gods, and sparing only the house of Allah, and I smiled.

Fortuitously, that day happened to mark the beginning of the new Islamic century. Exactly fourteen hundred years since the Prophet's great work, I, Mohamed Abdullah, was walking through the same entrance. Millions of people crossed that very spot every year, but for me, it was personal. I stood taller as I contemplated the significance of the moment. My moment of reflection ended abruptly when armed guards stopped us. They proceeded to search each of us. I looked over at my dad, confused about why men with guns were present at the holiest place on earth, a place supposedly to be devoid of violence. I dared not ask any questions until the umrah was complete. I tried desperately to focus on the moment at hand.

After we got through the checkpoint, we gathered again and stepped inside the mosque. And then my eyes caught a glimpse of something red splattered on the pillars of the mosque. It was blood! Why was there blood everywhere? I saw a large number of people in uniform—police and other workers cleaning up the mess. They did not look like a normal cleaning squad. My mind began racing. My curiosity overtook my spirit.

My dad, however, refused to acknowledge the distraction. He focused our attention on the ritual we were about to perform. I turned my gaze to Abraham's Shrine and the expansive area around the Kaaba. Pilgrims circumnavigate the Kaaba, the house of Allah, during the rituals. Allah told us Abraham built the Kaaba on this very spot. Our group walked toward the shrine. I was sorely disappointed I was too short to see Abraham's footprints preserved in the rock. This mattered a great deal to me, and I made another mental note to tell my dad I wanted to look inside later.

We approached the eastern corner of the Kaaba. I gazed in wonder at a black stone entombed in a thick silver frame. An angel,

I learned, brought the stone here and gave it to Abraham. Abraham positioned it as the cornerstone when he and Ishmael—his son with his wife's Egyptian handmaiden, Hagar, built the house of Allah. For Muslims, the Kaaba is the most sacred place on earth. According to Muslim lore, angels originally built it as a house of worship. Adam and Eve used the house to worship Allah. The flood of Noah destroyed it, and finally Abraham rebuilt it.

Starting from that cornerstone, all of us pilgrims walked in circles around the Kaaba while reciting the ancient words of Mohamed. Seven times we went around, and each time I passed the stone, I reached out to touch it. I fully embraced the moment and could feel my spiritual eyes being opened in new ways. My curiosity was also awakened, and I couldn't help wondering whether Allah was sitting inside his house watching me as I walked by.

So few people were on site that day we were able to move freely around the Kaaba. For that, I was grateful. My later pilgrimages would find me lost in a sea of millions, and their presence distracted me. But this experience had my full attention. It would always stand apart from any subsequent visits.

When we completed the first part of the umrah, we were ready to go to the *Zamzam*. This was the sacred well which, according to the Quran, overflows with holy water. I tasted the water to see if I would be transformed. I was a little disappointed I didn't feel any different. Then I felt guilty and sinful for harboring those doubts. The Quran says the water is good for a number of purposes. If you need forgiveness, you will be forgiven. If you need healing, you will be healed. It is said to be good for passing tests, finding a good spouse, amassing wealth, and achieving good fortune, whatever one needs. For me, passing tests was my most urgent need, and I prayed I would continue to pass them once I returned to Egypt.

As we finished praying and reciting the Quran in the area where the holy water poured from faucets, we gathered again, and Dad pointed out the exact location of the well. It was behind barricades with many people hovering around. I was astonished. It looked strangely like a crime scene.

Now there were more questions I needed to ask my dad, but they had to wait. It was time for the last part of the umrah—the journey between the two hills, *Safa* and *Marwah*. The Quran teaches this is where Abraham, in obedience to Allah, brought his wife Hagar and his son Ishmael and left them in the desert with no food or water. I never really understood why he would just leave them there with nothing to eat or drink, but since he was obeying Allah, it was not for me to question. Allah required submission. If he led someone into the dessert with no food or water, that person was expected to be obedient.

Abraham left Hagar there with a prayer for Allah to take care of her and Ishmael. Hagar, as an obedient wife, didn't question Abraham. When Ishmael got hungry and started crying hysterically, Hagar did not know what to do. Being dehydrated, she was unable to nurse him. Suddenly, she caught sight of a water source on a hill in the distance and began running toward it. Halfway there, Satan tried to lure her to disobey her husband and Allah. She ran away from Satan and continued running to the hill called Marwah. When she arrived, however, there was no water. What she saw was a mirage.

When she looked back from where she came, she saw another hill with water, Safa. She ran halfway back, but Satan stopped her once more. Again she denied him and continued running. Reaching Safa, she saw the water was once more a mirage. Now water appeared once again at Marwah. Hagar ran back and forth seven times chasing mirages and was tempted seven times. When she reached Marwah the seventh time, the angel Gabriel came to her and said, "I will reward you for your obedience." Under Gabriel's feet, water sprung forth from the Zamzam well and continues running to this day.

The ritual representing this story requires the pilgrim travel a path of about seven hundred fifty feet, each way. The pilgrim walks the first two hundred twenty-five feet to the point where Satan tempted Hagar. There he will see a green light. This tells him to start running from Satan, and he runs about three hundred feet until he sees another green light, which alerts him to resume walking. He continues walking another two hundred twenty-five feet and returns to the starting point the same way. These steps are repeated a total of seven times, which is equal to about two miles total. The ritual is different for women. They are not allowed to run as the impact is jarring and may cause them to expose themselves by accident. If a husband accompanies his wife, he imitates running while remaining with his wife for protection.

In obedience, we each replicated the steps of Hagar and symbolically resisted the temptations of Satan. As soon as we reached our final destination at the hill of the Marwah, we experienced a great sense of satisfaction. A title of hajji was bestowed on each one of us, and it was as proud a moment as being knighted. We knew, however, a full pilgrimage would be required to earn total purification. Ultimately, that is what each of us was seeking—to be totally cleansed from our sins.

All the men gathered and thanked Allah for what he did. Allah invited us to his house and gave us the opportunity to be blessed by this experience. Once there, we asked him to accept our efforts. Then we made our way over to a reserved area to have our heads shaved. This final ritual represents the shedding of sins. Some sins, my dad later reminded us while reciting from the Quran and the teachings of Mohamed, were not forgiven by simply going on a pilgrimage. Those sins, like the failure to perform the five-times prayers and fasting, would require much more. All the rituals of the faith a person may have missed since puberty had to be compensated for. If not, that person would be punished in the grave. Allah does not forget his debt. Also, some other sins against Allah, *hudod*, have their own penalty. These cannot be forgiven without enduring the punishment set forth in the Quran.

Since women are forbidden from exposing their hair, my mom had just a little cut off the end. My little brother, also, had just a little cut. But when I jumped in line with the men, my mom looked at me chagrined. I had a beautiful head of hair, and she wasn't prepared to see it all shorn away by men wielding dirty razors. The more she protested, the more determined I was to have my head shaved. My father watched proudly as every last one of my hairs fell to the ground.

Some men just had a little cut off and then went to their own barber when they got home. Others had their entire head shaved. These days, many people take their own razors and shave each other. But devout Muslims want the full experience of having it done the way Mohamed did it—the way I did it.

When everything was complete, I felt clean and renewed as if all of my sins were cast far away. I didn't have many sins to atone for, so I felt as if I were washed completely clean. For my mother, though, it was only the beginning, a second chance to make amends for neglecting the rituals of prayer and fasting. As my dad hoped, the umrah shook something inside her. Now he was ready to explain the steps she would have to take were she to have any hope for forgiveness.

From the time she reached puberty until the umrah, my mother missed twenty years of prayers. To atone, she was facing twenty years' worth of makeup prayers, not an impossible task, but an overwhelming one. For missing the five-times daily prayers, she would have to perform the prayer ritual ten times each day for the next twenty years. She would have to specify to Allah those prayers said to make up for ones missed in the past. Thankfully, she had not missed as many fast days as she had missed daily prayers, but those too required additional fasts and monetary penalties.

After that first day, we all gathered and congratulated each other on our accomplishments, offering praise and thanks to Allah. Dad told the group they were free for the rest of the day and we would meet again tomorrow. My mom and little brother went back to the hotel to rest and reflect, but my dad, the devout Muslim he is, headed back to the Kaaba. Still excited from what I experienced, I asked him if I could join him. He consented and together we went back to the mosque, specifically to a site that became our favorite for years to come—Abraham's Shrine. We sat down together and performed some rituals from the Quran. Then I was free to ask my questions.

I still wanted to see inside. So dad took me over and boosted me up onto his shoulders. Abraham's footprints were right there. They were undeniable. But I was confused. How could Abraham have built the Kaaba standing on this stone three hundred feet away? How tall must he have been to make that work? How did he get to Saudi Arabia from Iraq, and why was he here? The questions came pouring out, and dad's answer was simply, "Allah knows. Allah is supreme."

I knew better than to press him, so we shifted our attention to the Kaaba. He explained how the original door was made of gold, but a few years prior a rich jeweler from Saudi Arabia had the gold on the door melted down so he could add more. Said my father in awe, "Now it is made of more than seven hundred pounds of pure gold!"

The most holy place to pray to Allah is in front of this golden door. The bottom edge is six feet above the ground. Anyone would need a ladder to go inside, but the only person allowed in is the king of Saudi Arabia. The elevation signifies the slave of Allah is not on the same level as Allah, who is superior. I was extremely curious about what the inside looked like. Questions darted through my mind as I imagined what was behind that massive door. Sometimes I wondered with my nine-year-old mind, *Did Allah live inside there? Did he ever come out? Was there furniture?* But I quickly suppressed those thoughts and asked Allah to forgive me.

TERRORISTS SEIZE THE KAABA

As I sat there looking at the Kaaba, I saw some of the panels covering the building were torn in spots. Like the well and the blood on the posts, the Kaaba looked like a crime scene. I saw further evidence in what appeared to be bullet holes. I asked Dad what was going on. "Why were there men with guns and blood on the posts?" I queried. "And why couldn't we see the Zamzam well from above ground?"

He took a deep, agonized breath and explained in a way I could understand how this holy site was seized by Muslims seeking the overthrow of the House of Saud, the royal family. At 5 a.m., when some five hundred worshipers were getting ready for Morning Prayer, men stormed the mosque with their weapons drawn. They chained all the doors and held the worshipers hostage. The leader of the group, Mohammad Abdullah al-Qahtani, proclaimed himself the *Mahdi*, the redeemer of Islam, and called for other Muslims to join him in standing against the Saudi royal family. He was outraged by their alliance with the United States and their failure to wage jihad throughout the Muslim world. Abdullah al-Qahtani's goal was to reestablish the caliphate system.

The bin Laden family, owners of the world's largest construction company, was appointed by the king to provide the care and maintenance of the mosque. Dad said, at the time of the siege a bin Laden employee was working in one of the minarets when he saw the siege begin. He was able to get word out that help was needed. I asked myself why this "Mohamed Abdullah," a devout Muslim, could claim to be the Mahdi. What made him different from me? I also was a Mohamed Abdullah, a devout Muslim. I could never claim such a title, nor would I if I could. I asked my father why this man claimed to be the redeemer.

My dad said al-Qahtani and his followers thought the Saudi family was applying Islamic law incorrectly. They believed the House of Saud had become soft and Westernized, just like the rest of the Middle East. Because of his name and because of his devoutness, al-Qahtani believed he would be the redeemer of Islam. He and his followers chose November 20, 1979, for the attack because it was the first day of the year 1400 according to the Islamic calendar. This tied in with the tradition of the *mujaddid*.

According to the Hadith, the mujaddid is a person who appears at the turn of every century to revive Islam, cleansing it of impure elements and restoring it to its original state. Al-Qahtani wanted to expel all non-Muslims from the country, to outlaw television and other entertainment, and to require strict adherence to sharia law. My dad said the Saudis were more observant Muslims than the Egyptians, but they were still not what Mohamed would have wanted them to be. My father believed the Muslim attackers had a point but their methods were wrong.

As my father explained what happened, I sat in rapt attention, trying to understand how such violence could have taken place here. He said the bin Ladens, after reporting the siege, contacted the oldest brother, Salem bin Laden, the son of the founder and patriarch of the family. He was American-educated, married to an American woman, and had very strong ties to the United States. He contacted the Saudi king to see what should be done next. Without any better options, the king accepted bin Laden's suggestion of seeking American help.

Salem bin Laden established a cover operation to break the siege with the help of American Special Forces. This, of course, was not common knowledge at the time, but my father had sources within the House of Saud who confirmed the assistance of America. Publicly, it was accomplished with a team of three French commandoes who were already working with the Saudi Forces and who were willing to go through a short ceremony to become Muslim. Then the Americans took over and spearheaded the operation. In the process of retaking the mosque, one of Salem's brothers was killed. This created a fracture within the bin Laden family, the ramifications of which reached far into the future. This was the kind of inside information my dad frequently shared with me.

The commandoes tried pumping gas into the underground chambers, but the gas failed and the resistance continued. With casualties climbing, these special forces finally drilled holes into the courtyard and dropped grenades into the rooms below, killing many hostages but driving the remaining rebels into open areas where sharpshooters picked them off. More than two weeks after the assault began, the surviving rebels finally surrendered. Sixty-eight of them were later beheaded.

Word spread about how the mosque was retaken with help from the West. Because non-Muslims are not allowed in this holy land of Mecca and because Muslim people called on Christians to kill fellow Muslims, the Muslim populaces were enraged. This fueled angry anti-American demonstrations throughout the Muslim world. In Pakistan and in Libya, mobs overran U.S. embassies and burned them to the ground.

I asked Dad what happened to the leader. He told me that during the cleanup, crews discovered al-Qahtani's body, beheaded, at the bottom of the Zamzam well. For that reason, authorities boarded up the original above-ground access to the well, forcing pilgrims to go to a below-ground level to see the well. The cleanup was still going on. The appearance of the Zamzam well was changed forever. The above-ground access was forever blocked and was replaced with a sign on the ground and a window glass showing the original well.

SAUDI ARABIA'S REACTION

The siege happened only a few weeks before our arrival. My dad was confident, however, Saudi Arabia was going to be more devout than ever. Within two weeks of the siege, King Fahd issued a royal decree formally creating the Committee for the Promotion of Virtue and the Prevention of Vice. He charged the committee with ensuring Saudis and foreign residents respected traditional Islamic morality as defined by sharia. This meant there would be no more movie theaters, music, or any other forms of entertainment. Photographs of women in newspapers were banned. Women could no longer appear on television. Gender segregation was extended to all public places, and women were no longer allowed to drive. In addition, school curricula were changed to provide many more hours of religious studies and to eliminate classes on subjects like non-Islamic history. The decree also made sure there would be police on the streets enforcing sharia law in every aspect.

My dad's words were prophetic. As Saudi Arabia tightened the reins on the social and political lives of its people, enforcing proper sharia, the nation prospered. Allah never fails to reward the faithful. My father and I agreed Saudi Arabia's response was in complete compliance with Mohamed's teachings and his deathbed wishes. The response showed me that even though devout Muslims can be good, Allah requires they always work on getting better. Saudi Arabia got a wake-up call. Al-Qahtani may have led the siege, but Allah sent the message to return to strict observance of sharia. Saudi Arabia immediately took notice and made the required change. Muslims, I was certain, needed to make the same reforms in Egypt and throughout the world.

AMERICA'S INVOLVEMENT IN THE MIDDLE EAST

When dad mentioned the involvement of America, it got me thinking about what Uncle Ahmed told me. He said President Sadat was once good, but now he was doing bad things because of his association with America and our hated enemies, the Jews. This prompted me to ask my dad what he thought about the United States and their involvement in the Middle East. He told me how President Jimmy Carter, at about the same time as the siege of the mosque, interfered in the politics of Iran and caused a revolution leading to the rise of Ayatollah Khomeini and the Shia caliphate.

This was a problem. Sunnis consider Shias apostates and not true Muslims because Shiites blasphemously elevate the prophet Mohamed's family and kinsmen to the level of prophethood. The fact Shiites were getting more powerful could not be good for the Sunnis, who are the only true Muslims.

I was overwhelmed with information but came to the conclusion Allah's laws were clear and his word was indisputable. Although Islam might have been special, I could see individual Muslim leaders needed a dark room experience of their own to return to pure faith. I had mine at age five. My dad had his in the desert after a brutal defeat by Israel. Egypt had it when they allowed the British and the Communists to subjugate Islam. And Saudi Arabia and the royal family had their experience through the siege of the holy mosque. Allah's condemnation preceded the awakening—always.

.

CHAPTER 8

THE ISLAMIC STATE
IS BORN

Indeed! Allah himself, together with His angels, gathers together and worships the Prophet Mohamed. So, all you Muslims must follow accord and do the same to Mohamed and praise him favorably with enthusiasm.

—Quran 33:56

The bond between my dad and me was—and is—indissoluble. At nine years of age, I felt as if we were two parts of the same whole. I could read his thoughts, and he could read mine. There was an unspoken understanding between us I realized even then was rare. Immersed in a shared spiritual experience, we bonded. It was as if the tendrils of a vine wrapped our hearts and minds together. Even today with the chasm separating us, the connection remains, and is perhaps the source of his and my greatest sorrow.

The time I spent with my dad in Mecca at the Grand Mosque stoked the fire within me to learn more, do more, and be a better Muslim. My dad anticipated that effect. I wanted to see more places in Mecca—to walk in the footsteps of Mohamed and experience everything possible. My curiosity was unlimited, and my dad was proud of my youthful enthusiasm. "I'll have a surprise for you tomorrow," he said.

A SPECIAL SURPRISE

Never could I have dreamed of the surprise he had in store. That next day, the deputy for the Ministry of Hajj and Umrah, a role filled by a prince from the royal family, pulled up to our hotel in his shiny black Cadillac. He had come to take us on a very special journey Dad arranged through his longstanding friendship with the prince. As a kid, I was amazed at the power and connections of my father, a friend to presidents and royals. I was proud to be his son and embraced the blessings associated with being a devout, faithful Muslim.

Having participated in the umrah, my mother just wanted to relax and enjoy a little vacation. She chose to remain at the hotel with my little brother, which was just as well. As a woman, my mother would have burdened us and limited our experience. We would have to submit her to all sharia law and the Islamic rules and regulations of what a woman could and could not do. Her presence would have just complicated the excursion. As for me, I was happy not to have any distractions as I set out to learn more about the roots of my faith.

HIRA CAVE

We were about to visit the key places of Mohamed's journey to Mecca, the birthplace of Islam. This experience would give me a glimpse of what I could expect when I reached puberty and returned for the full hajj. Our first stop was the Hira Cave—the place where it all began. The cave was Mohamed's chosen spot for meditation and where he, at age forty, received the first revelations that would become the foundation of Islam.

When we reached our destination, I was a little surprised by how small and unassuming the cave was. Grand events happened here in this tiny place. It is where the Angel Gabriel appeared to Mohamed and commissioned him to be a messenger to the world.

The message Gabriel gave him that day was simple but profound: Allah is one, and all other faiths are false.

I was in the presence of something amazing. I couldn't help but wonder, though, why Mohamed's first wife Khadija and his early followers failed to record this incredible event. Nor did the Prophet have his scribes document this angelic encounter. It was not until twenty-three years after Mohamed's death when Aisha, his third wife, first mentioned the cave. This was the story of the genesis of Islam. Had I seen an angel, I was sure I would have been telling everyone!

I was drawn into the conversation when my dad remarked how Mohamed journeyed every day several miles over rugged terrain to meditate in the little cave. Tradition says he ran back and forth between his home and the cave, a round trip that would have taken several hours, and I was astonished. "How did he do it?" I asked aloud, knowing Mohamed was also responsible for the day-to-day management of his wife's business. Dad answered it was a religious obligation, so he just did it. This increased my admiration for the Prophet even more. Allah must have given him superior strength to carry out his religious duties, and I wished for the same strength.

Hira Cave was only the beginning. I wanted to see all the sites important to the Prophet's story, but I was also eager to learn as much as possible about Abraham's time in Saudi Arabia. Abraham too was a central figure in Islam. Earlier, we worshiped and prayed for hours at his shrine inside the mosque.

THE FOOTPRINTS OF ABRAHAM

"Can we visit the places Abraham went?" I asked. Our escort, the prince, smiled and complimented my curiosity, which in turn made my father beam with pride. And so, we continued our journey on the Hajj Road, and I pressed my face against the window of the sedan to take in all the scenery.

I knew from my studies about Abraham making three visits to Mecca. The first time he brought Hagar and Ishmael and left them in the desert. The second time he returned to sacrifice his son, and the third time he rebuilt the Kaaba with his son by his side. I saw his footprints from that visit. All three visits were made with the help of the speediest of creatures—a flying horse with a human face named "Buraq." This supernatural beast transported Abraham at the speed of light. Later, Mohamed rode Buraq for another important journey, and I wished more than anything I could ride him too, but I knew this was an experience reserved only for the prophets.

After a brief stop at the royal family's cabin at Mina, we paused to discuss the significance of the area. The area around Mina is where Satan stopped Abraham on his way to sacrifice his son, Ishmael, and tried to tempt him to disobey Allah. Three different times Satan called to Abraham, but Abraham was not to be deterred. He threw rocks at Satan, and Satan fled. In remembrance of that event, pilgrims camp out at Mina and emerge from their tents each morning to throw stones at Satan.

They get those stones from *Muzdalifah*, which was our next destination. It is important for every good Muslim to be prepared to reject Satan's temptation to disobey Allah. I admired Abraham, who was strong and faithful to Allah in the face of the temptations, and I aspired to be just as strong and faithful. I renewed my commitment to be diligent and thoughtful in service to Allah, vowing to remember the stones that could keep Satan at bay.

MT. ARAFAT

The day had already been filled with learning milestones strengthening my connection to the patriarchs. But we weren't finished. We were going to the mountain—Mt. Arafat. It was on the rocky heights of Mt. Arafat where Allah saved Abraham from having to sacrifice his son, Ishmael. And it was upon this spot Mohamed delivered his final speech, the last words to his followers before he died.

"Well, what do you think?" my father asked. "How does it feel to be here and walk in this special place?" He knew my answer without my having to say a word. I understood why he returned from pilgrimage the way he did. Transformed. Forever changed. Resolute in commitment, I dug my feet more firmly into the soil, hoping it would allow me to become one with the history that unfolded here.

We remained on Mt. Arafat, waiting for the call to prayer. We went into the mosque to answer the call of prayers, thus fulfilling our religious duty, and then thank Allah for his many blessings, chief among them this unforgettable trip. I bowed in prayer and touched my forehead to the ground over and over again, enthusiastically submitting myself to Allah as his slave for the rest of my life.

I looked forward to returning for the full hajj and participating as a man. Alongside my father, I observed the rituals of the umrah and walked four hours to Mt. Arafat to sit by the hillside and meditate. In the evening, we walked together to Mina. We stopped at Muzdalifah to pick up forty-nine small stones to throw at Satan. And together with other pilgrims we celebrated our faith.

I sat quietly in the car as we made our way back to the hotel that evening. I was lost in my thoughts about what it must have been like for Mohamed to walk this land and establish Allah's kingdom on earth. I wanted to honor him and emulate him in every way. At my urging, my father took me to purchase a *galabeya*, the traditional clothing of the region. The clothing may have seemed insignificant to some, but to me it perfectly expressed what was in my heart.

BREAKFAST WITH A PRINCE

On the last day before we departed Mecca for the next significant stop on our faith exploration, Medina, we went on one more adventure with the prince. This time one of his sons joined us. Only a year older than I, we formed an immediate bond. We met at the mosque and participated together in the 3 a.m. prayers and then went back to his palace to share a meal. I got to see up close and personal what it meant to receive the "royal treatment."

Walking into the prince's home, I had great difficulty keeping my jaw from hitting the floor. The airport in Jeddah impressed me, but there were no words for the wealth surrounding me in that palace. Ornate chandeliers shone down onto the granite floors where we reclined. There we were served a traditional Egyptian breakfast with Arabian coffee. I felt more like a man than a boy as the four of us sat together eating and laughing. I knew if this was how Allah rewarded faithfulness, I wanted these rewards for myself. I saw no women in the palace, but they were there somewhere. In observance of sharia, strictly adhered to in Saudi Arabia, women were not to be seen by strangers in any home, even a palace.

As the sun came up over the horizon, we headed for another cave integral to the faith. Upon arriving, we parked the car at the base of a mountain and began our ascent. The first half of the hike was quite easy, but the terrain became more challenging as we continued. We had to make numerous rest stops so my dad could nurse a knee injured in 1967 when he jumped off a burning tank. We climbed over boulders, and I thought of the Prophet making this same trek, fleeing the people of Mecca who were chasing him and bent on killing him. Our destination, like his, was a hiding place at the top of the mountain.

GHAR THOWR

Hot and tired, we eventually arrived at *Ghar Thowr*, Mohamed's cave of refuge. Once there I replayed in my mind the events carrying him to this place. Mohamed delivered the message given to him by the Angel Gabriel, but that message angered many people, especially those who worshiped idols. The idea that Allah was superior to all other gods was not popular. If I were in the shoes of these idolaters, I suppose I could understand. Who was this man telling them their faith and their gods were invalid?

There were some who embraced his message, but a good many of them were slaves attracted to Mohamed's idea that man should be a slave only to Allah. Mohamed went so far as to try to buy the slaves' freedom. When he failed to raise enough money to free all the slaves who followed him, he urged them to flee to Ethiopia. This quickly drew the ire of the slave owners. Slavery was a profitable business at that time in Arabia, and Mohamed's message threatened the wealth of the locals as well as their gods. Then as now, the strongest relationships can fall apart when faith and finances are challenged.

All that saved Mohamed from the angry citizens of Mecca was the prominence of his uncle Talib and Mohamed's first wife, Khadija. A prominent business owner, Khadija used her wealth and influence to protect her husband.

For a brief period, Mohamed continued to preach his message without reproach, but in AD 619 Khadija died, and so did Mohamed's uncle. Their deaths cost him his home, his means of support, and their protection. I have often wondered what happened to Khadija's assets when she died, but I've not found a historical account. I do know this so-called "Year of the Sorrow" marked a turning point in Mohamed's life and in the development of Islam.

Many considered Mohamed a nobody—a crazy man with a crazy message. With his protection gone, some decided the time was right to eliminate him. Just when things looked their bleakest, however, Mohamed's fortunes changed on one particular night. We celebrate this night every year in remembrance, *Lailat al Miraj*.

THE NIGHT JOURNEY

I was taught to believe this was the time when Allah intervened to save his messenger and to designate him a prophet. As our ascent to the cave continued, I mentally replayed the events of that amazing journey in AD 622. That night Mohamed was awakened by a knock at the door and found himself face-to-face with the Angel Gabriel once again. By Gabriel's side was Buraq, the beautiful white man-beast that transported Abraham in the past.

Gabriel instructed Mohamed to mount Buraq for a special journey, but Buraq, bucking and resisting, had a mind of his own. That part of the story always made me laugh. Didn't Buraq know he was about to be mounted by the best man ever? He soon found out. Gabriel promptly informed Buraq that Mohamed was greater than Moses, Abraham, or any prophet who ever lived. Buraq changed his mind and moved in close so Mohamed could climb onto his back.

Buraq, whose name means "travels at the speed of light," flew into the night skies. He headed to Jerusalem and to the Temple Mount, where the Aqsa Mosque stands. I've often wondered why Allah sent them to Jerusalem instead of to the Kaaba in Mecca. According to the Quran, the hadiths, and the Islamic teachings, Kaaba is the direct connection between earth and Allah. But who was I, after all, to question Allah?

When he arrived in Jerusalem, Mohamed tied Buraq to one of the mosque doors, and Gabriel offered him something to drink. Faced with the choice between milk and wine, Mohamed chose milk, for which Gabriel praised him. Islam still permitted moderate use of alcohol at that time. Later, after it contributed to a military defeat, Mohamed completely forbade it. Rivers of alcohol, however, are said to await faithful Muslims in heaven.

All the prophets—Abraham, Jesus, Moses—greeted Mohamed at the mosque. They welcomed him with great joy and ushered him to the front to lead them in prayer. He was understandably shy about leading these great prophets, but Gabriel told him it was a direct order from Allah, so he obeyed.

I paused long enough to marvel at the idea that Mohamed was sleeping in his bed one moment, and a moment later the prophets of old were according him the greatest honor by asking to lead them in prayers. In so doing, they acknowledged his superiority!

Once the prayers were concluded, the prophets were jubilant. Gabriel then led Mohamed to the rock of Mount Moriah next to the mosque. It was from this spot Mohamed began an even more exciting journey than the ride on Baraq. He and Gabriel stood on the rock, and together they ascended into the heavens. Mohamed was going to meet Allah.

Much like ascending seven flights in a building, Mohamed and Gabriel ascended through the seven levels of heaven. I imagined myself climbing into the heavens as I continued my climb up the mountainside. But whereas I struggled, Mohamed soared supernaturally into the presence of Allah. At each level, Gabriel knocked at the door and announced, "I am with the chosen man and the seal of the Prophet." The phrase, "the chosen one," translates to the name "Mohamed." At each level, the response was, "Oh, the time has come for him. Hallelujah, let him in!" This was the first time the Prophet was called "Mohamed," the chosen one. His given name was bin Abdullah, meaning "son of the slave of Abdullah."

Adam, the first man, greeted Mohamed on the first level of heaven with the affirmation that Mohamed was indeed the chosen one. Jesus and John the Baptist greeted him at the second level and acknowledged him as "the promise," the one for whom they had been waiting. On the third level, Mohamed and Gabriel met Joseph. He met Idris on the fourth level and Aaron on the fifth. Moses was waiting for Mohamed at the sixth level, and Abraham was waiting at the seventh. Finally, Mohamed was ready to come into the place of worship for all of the angels, Gabriel's final stop. Gabriel advised Mohamed, "You must ascend from here alone. Anyone else will be burned."

In the first few years after my dark room experience, I believed with all my heart in Mohamed, as well as in all of the prophets who preceded him. In studying the events of the night journey, I began to understand my Prophet's elevated status among the others. I also understood the meaning of his name and the power it embodied. There was blessing and power in being a true, obedient slave to Allah and a follower of Mohamed. I was proud to share his name.

Alone, Mohamed stood in the presence of Allah. Here, he was shown wonders and proclaimed a prophet unlike any other who came before. Mohamed was the promise of Abraham and the prophecy of Jesus, the highest prophet and the final messenger. I wondered what it must have been like to stand in the presence of Allah and have him commission you to build his kingdom on earth. I wondered whether Mohamed was afraid, surprised, or humbled.

The experience had to be overwhelming. Allah elevated Mohamed to a station attained by no other prophet in the history of the world. He became the final Prophet, second only to Allah. Given his status, Allah revealed to him when the Day of Judgment would come. That would be the day when the flag of Islam rose in every corner of the planet, and Allah's name was worshiped above all others.

While in the heavens, Mohamed went to the mosque where the angels pray, Al Bait al Mamour. This mosque sits directly above the Kaaba. I had to ask myself why he didn't ascend from the Kaaba in Mecca instead of traveling all the way to Jerusalem. Since these thoughts were not honoring Allah, I immediately stopped myself and asked for Allah's forgiveness. Mohamed saw the many rewards of heaven with its jewels, its gold, its flowing milk and honey. Allah showed him the dark side as well. He took Mohamed to hell so he could warn his people about what awaited those who rejected the faith. The Prophet's account of the punishments beyond the grave was the stuff of nightmares. His detailed descriptions of the afterlife terrified me as a child and haunted my dreams even as I grew into an adult.

While still in the presence of Allah, Mohamed was told he must require his people to pray fifty times a day. There had previously been no required prayers for Muslims. The new religion was given the name "Islam," and the faith was going to demand much more in the way of observance from its followers.

Thankfully, the story did not end there. On his descent from heaven, Moses stopped Mohamed and asked what Allah advised. When the Prophet told him about the fifty prayer times, Moses told him it couldn't be done. Forewarned, Mohamed went back to Allah repeatedly to plead the case of his people. When the negotiations were finished, Allah settled on five times a day.

And just like that, the journey was over. Mohamed remarked later it took place in an instant. His bed was still warm when he returned to it. The next morning he excitedly told the cousin with whom he was living, about his encounter with Allah. "Don't tell anyone!" she warned. "No one will believe you, and they will certainly kill you."

MOHAMED ANNOUNCES HIS MISSION

Mohamed didn't listen. He wanted to share Allah's words with all the people of Mecca. He gathered anyone who would listen and told of the revelations he received. From that moment forward, he demanded his listeners pledge allegiance to both Allah and

Mohamed. He also demanded they accompany him to the Kaaba five times a day and pray toward Jerusalem.

Six years later Mohamed intensified the prayer ritual. It became a rule that if a man neglected his five-times prayers three days in a row without a legitimate excuse, Mohamed would have his acolytes burn down the man's home. Mohamed soon amended this, saying burning was Allah's punishment in the afterlife. Instead, according to the Quran—surahs 8:12 and 47:4—he made beheading the required penalty for apostates.

THERE WERE MANY SKEPTICS

Many laughed at what Mohamed was saying about his encounter with Allah and his night journey. Others were skeptical and thought him crazy. Still others just walked away. Undaunted, Mohamed provided evidence of the trip. He described a caravan on its way to Mecca and due to arrive within hours. He claimed he saw the caravan from the back of Buraq. Much to the surprise of many, the caravan arrived just as he predicted.

Mohamed also described the mosque in Jerusalem down to the last detail. Those who claimed to have visited the mosque affirmed his story. When people went to Abu Bakr and told him this unbeliev-able story, Abu Bakr stepped forward and said, "If Mohamed said it, then I believe him." The people were astonished by Abu Bakr's response, but because of his wealth and influence, they remained silent. Abu Bakr's affirmation of Mohamed's story stood as the most important evidence that Mohamed was not making it up.

I struggled to understand every detail of the story and the many questions it brought to mind. I wondered whether the mosque in Jerusalem was the same one that existed now. I wondered too who built it when there was no Islamic religion at the time. Nor were there any Muslims to build it. According to the historic record, the mosque wasn't built until fifty years after Mohamed's death. If this were true, I wondered how other people could affirm his description of it? When, I wondered, was it really built?

I also couldn't help but wonder why the cousin with whom he was living at the time, Fakhitah Bint Abi Talib, did not believe him.

Nor did she affirm his story. She should have at least heard the commotion at the door when Gabriel was picking up Mohamed. Why, in response to her disbelief, did Mohamed ask this cousin to divorce her husband and marry him? Why did she not become a Muslim until years later when Mohamed conquered Mecca and her husband had to flee the city? Once again, though, I suspended this line of thought and asked Allah for his forgiveness.

MOHAMED MEETS RESISTANCE AND ESCAPES MECCA

Whether the people of Mecca believed or not, Mohamed knew Allah commissioned him to build the Islamic state. He promptly began to make that happen. He met with delegates from Yathrib, a city three hundred miles north of Mecca, and selected twelve from his clan to lay the groundwork. Rumors started spreading through Mecca as people went missing and later showed up in Yathrib. There they were working to establish the kingdom of Islam, further angering many residents of Mecca.

Mohamed was becoming a problem for people of Mecca. Hoping to prevent others from following this "madman" to another city, they thought of killing Mohamed. They feared, however, his death would start a tribal war. So they devised a clever plan. They planned to gather a few men from every tribe in the city to break into Mohamed's house. Together, they would beat him to death. All the tribes would have blood on their hands, and none would be vulnerable to revenge.

Allah did not allow this plot to succeed. He warned Mohamed and urged him to have his cousin Ali sleep in his bed as a decoy. Later that night, Allah put all the would-be assassins to sleep and told Mohamed to flee. Mohamed walked outside into the middle of these men, picked up sand from the ground, and threw it in their faces. He was mocking them and leaving proof behind of Allah's victory. Their dozing off gave him enough time to escape with his friend and confidant, Abu Bakr. Together they started their journey to Yathrib, stopping five miles beyond Mecca to hide in a cave.

When the assassins woke up and discovered Ali in the bed instead of Mohamed, they began a frantic search for Mohamed in the direction of Yathrib. Although Ali thought he was going to be a martyr, Allah preserved him as promised. Mohamed advised Ali that, once spared, he should stay behind for a few days to return the possessions previously entrusted to the Prophet by the non-believers.

MOHAMED HIDES IN GHAR THOWR

I visited the cave, *Ghar Thowr*, in which Mohamed hid. Standing in this spot sent chills up my spine as I remembered how Allah miraculously protected him. His pursuers suspected the cave to be a hideout and followed his footsteps to the cave, but Allah had already employed a spider and a dove to protect Mohamed. Every Muslim child knows the story of how the spider spun his intricate web across the entrance of the cave and how the dove flew just outside the cave's entrance to prepare a nest for its eggs. As the angry hordes approached, they saw the web and nest and reasoned that no one could be inside.

Allah provided the necessary distraction, and Mohamed's life was spared. That cave also provided the first opportunity to reveal how Allah favored Mohamed above all others. In securing the cave as their hideaway, Abu Bakr sat down in front of a small hole to protect Mohamed from creatures that might slip through. While Mohamed slept safely with his head in his friend's lap, a scorpion bit Abu Bakr on his buttocks. He suppressed the pain so as not to awaken his friend, but he could not block the tears. They fell onto Mohamed's face and woke him from his deep sleep. When Abu Bakr told Mohamed about the bite, Mohamed spat into his hands and rubbed the site of the bite. This action drew the venom out of the wound and gave Abu Bakr much welcome relief.

I was embarrassed as my own tears began to flow. My heart was overcome with sorrow that Mohamed had to run for his life and take refuge in a cave in order to escape those who rejected his message. I also wept for joy that, ultimately, he received his revenge on his pursuers and emerged victorious. None of them could have imagined that in less than a decade Mohamed would build a mighty army, return, and take over the city.

My time in Mecca left me in awe. The solemnity. The holiness. The history. I went to the house of Allah in my quest for unity with my creator. I touched the places where Islam was born, and I was overcome with a sense of my inadequacy as Allah's slave. I was as close to my creator as I could come in Mecca, yet the void was not yet filled, and my longing was not fully satisfied. One thing I knew, however, was I was forever changed.

YATHRIB (MEDINA)

Having seen Mecca, it was time to go to Yathrib. This was the city that became the first seat of the Islamic State and the home from which Mohamed began to exercise his Allah-given authority. We said goodbye to our royal tour guides and rejoined the group of doctors with whom we began our pilgrimage. Together, we flew to the city formerly known as Yathrib, today known as Medina, the City of Mohamed.

From above I watched the landscape change from the dry rugged mountains around Mecca to the lush, green oasis of Medina. This transition seemed almost a metaphor for the journey. I loved Mecca with its rigid rules. I soon learned to love Medina, for being the city that welcomed a fleeing Prophet as a victorious king. The story of what happened to Mohamed in Medina—the fulfillment of Allah's promise to establish his kingdom was nothing short of miraculous.

Medina was originally settled by Jewish tribes. Dispersed by the Romans, they turned this strip of desert into an oasis. Their success attracted two Arab tribes from other parts of the Arabian Peninsula challenging the Jews for the land. What they all needed was a mediator. This they found in Mohamed. The *hijra*, Mohamed's migration from Mecca to Medina, marks the start of the Islamic age and the Islamic calendar. On July 15, 622, everything changed, including the name of the city. Yathrib came to be called, in Arabic, "Medina, the city of Mohamed." Later, the name was shortened to just "Medina," which means "The City."

We arrived in Medina and checked in at my first five-star hotel. My dad and I relaxed in our suite and discussed the many adventures we would have. Meanwhile Mom busily made lists of items she wanted to purchase from the mall for her mom and sisters. None of these women had ever been to Saudi Arabia, and my mother hoped she could bring a piece of it back for them. Medina gave us the opportunity to do the shopping about which so many of our friends and relatives inquired before we left Cairo.

As we waited for the call to prayer, I peppered my dad with questions about what I should expect at the Prophet's Mosque, the first stop on every pilgrim's journey to Medina. "You will see many great things there," my dad said. "The Prophet's Mosque was a home, a place of worship, and the seat of a great government that spread across the globe from this very location."

Dad explained that Mohamed's house stood at the site of the mosque. From there, he governed. He was buried there as well. According to Islamic teaching, his body is still there and has never decayed. All other bodies turned to dust, but the body of the Prophet remained intact. Worms were forbidden to eat him. My father advised me that his spirit was also there so we had to show complete respect when visiting his burial site. It made me nervous to know he would be listening to everything I said. I did not want to mess this up. It was, after all, going to be my first formal introduction to the Prophet.

In preparation for our visit to Mohamed, according to his directives, we cleansed and perfumed ourselves, dressed in our best clothes, and when the call to prayer was issued, we rushed to the mosque to perform the ritual. We then went to visit the Prophet. The spectacular green dome of the mosque caught my eye. It loomed above Mohamed's last home on earth, the home he shared with Aisha, his third wife and daughter of Abu Bakr.

We approached the mosque respectfully and found a place in the courtyard to sit and pray. Afterward, our group walked toward the Prophet's living quarters. Dad gave his final instructions to be on my best behavior as we entered this special section of heaven. "Allah is watching us closely," he said.

We spoke only in hushed tones as we approached the tomb directly beneath the dome. I gazed in wonder, lost in thought about the man who lay on the other side of the golden door, the man whom Allah forbade the earth to consume. My dad leaned over to me and whispered, "All the respect Mohamed received when he was alive must be given to him today. You are stepping into an area that is holy, and he is listening to everything we say."

Two giant doors loomed directly in front of me. The door on the left had a large circle cut into the right side about halfway up. This was where Mohamed was entombed. The second door had two circles. The circle on the left marked the site where Abu Bakr was placed. The one on the right marked Umar's gravesite.

At my father's prompting, I greeted Mohamed aloud with the highest praise a nine-year-old boy could muster. My adoration poured out like a flood as I told him how much Allah and the angels loved him; how I too was overwhelmed with feelings of love for him, the greatest man of all, one worthy of all praise and glory. I loved him so much I could actually feel his presence. I believed he was showering me with love as well.

I stepped to the right to the burial site of Abu Bakr and began to utter words of praise and affirmation for all he did to stand by Mohamed during his lifetime. He was his defender—a rock on which the Prophet could always depend. I told him how grateful I was for how he stood up to the infidels after Mohamed died, and I thanked him for killing the apostates and those who doubted Islam.

Finally, I stepped over to Umar's grave and greeted him. He was the first martyred caliph. I thanked him for his bravery and for being the great conqueror. I thanked him for cleansing my home country from Christianity and bringing Islam into Egypt. I praised him for his boldness, his strength, and for raising Allah above many nations by conquering the Persians, Romans, and Christians. He was a great hero to me and every Muslim kid. We all wanted to be like him.

Then I looked back to the first door. One day, I learned, a second circle would be added to the door where Mohamed was buried to mark the burial site of Jesus. The Quran teaches that Jesus never died but was raised up to heaven and will return in the last days to proclaim Islam victorious. Overwhelmed to the point of tears, I longed for the day when Jesus would return and raise the sword of Islam throughout the world. When this mission was complete, only then would Jesus die and assume his place beside my Prophet.

Like the prince's home, the Prophet's Mosque was a woman-free zone. Women could only visit Mohamed's grave during specially designated hours. Mohamed taught us women could be overtaken by emotion and act inappropriately. Men would have to watch over them, a needless distraction. Women were also considered a major source of temptation. Men had to guard them to protect other men from sinning, another distraction. I was happy to be there among men alone, free from such distractions.

Mohamed was buried in the room he shared with his third wife, Aisha. The most beloved of his wives, she had the privilege of living with him since she was nine years old and having him die in her arms. His thirteen other wives and concubines lived outside the walls of the mosque. Their homes have been destroyed over the centuries.

Some in our group decided to walk around the mosque again to find a place to pray. Dad and I continued walking, trying to find a corner of heaven, *rawda*, where we could read the Quran, perform some rituals, and talk quietly. We looked for a good spot and finally squeezed into a corner. I was happiest when I could sit with my father in these holy places and pray.

After a while, duty called. I had to leave my dad and go with my mom to the mall. She was not allowed to go on her own according to sharia. I was frustrated I had to come down off of my spiritual high to go shopping, but it was the first time for me to see a mall, and I have to admit it was exciting. When the call to prayer was issued, however, no one was allowed to buy or sell. Everything stopped as men, women, and children performed their religious duties. Once the prayer concluded, life picked right back up where it left off. Coming from a semi-communist country, I was amazed there seemed to be no fear of people stealing, especially during the call to prayer.

In the mall, I saw products I never saw before. I could only attribute this bounty of goods to the fact Allah blessed the Saudis for following him. I believed Egyptians could be this blessed if they did the same. Victory, wealth, success, good health, political superiority, and longevity were all signs of Allah's approval. The only way one could achieve all of that was by being a good Muslim.

The morning after the mall visit, I stirred myself awake to prepare for the 3 a.m. call to prayer. I couldn't wait to get back to the mosque with my father. Holding his hand as we left the hotel, I still remember how fresh the morning air felt as we walked across the street to the giant doors of the mosque. We were the first to enter that day. We visited Mohamed again and then found a nice spot next to him in the corner of heaven to do our morning prayer. The sun was rising as we concluded, and we walked outside to talk. Dad pointed out the area where Mohamed's other wives lived. In the courtyard, he remarked on the new flooring. "There was a shrine over here for the Prophet's dad, but it has been completely demolished and removed. If you were here with me two years ago, you would have seen it."

With that, a question bubbled to the surface: "How did Mohamed's dad end up being buried in Medina three hundred miles away from Mecca? I thought he had no connections to this city before the migration."

"No, that's not true my son," Dad began. He explained that Mohamed came to Medina when he was seven years old to visit his dad's gravesite. "But just in the last two years," my dad continued, "the Saudi government demolished the shrine and removed any signs of it. They paved over it."

"Why would they do that?" I asked. "Because shrines are a form of idolatry," he told me. "The man's only reason to be on this earth was to father Mohamed. He died before the Prophet was born. Mohamed himself said his father was in hell. He wasn't a believer. He wasn't Muslim."

Dad knew I had more questions and this was only my opening salvo. I looked around, taking in the significance of this amazing place and the world-changing events that happened there. "Why did Mohamed build his home here and why did the people accept him as their king? And how was he able to rename the city," I asked, all my thoughts gushing out at once.

YATHRIB – A CITY WITH A HISTORY

My dad laughed and directed my attention throughout the expansive area. "Let's start with the first question," he said. "Why did Mohamed build his home here? The story says that this is where Allah directed Mohamed's camel to sit down after he entered the city. So, this is where he felt he was supposed to establish his home." My father told me about the hadith describing how Mohamed designated himself the elder and king of the city in which his family owned land, then wrote the rules that would govern the city.

My father continued, "He was welcomed and greeted as their new leader upon the death of one of his uncles who was the former chief of the Banu Khazraj tribe, part of the Najjar clan." He began to tell me the story revealed in the hadiths of this transfer of power. As my father explained, at the time of hijra, the city of Medina was under the control of two large tribes, Banu Khazraj and Banu Aus. Mohamed's clan was in charge of the Banu Khazraj tribe, and one of his uncles was the king. Since the former king, Asad, left no sons, the leaders of Najjar asked Mohamed to appoint a new leader. Mohamed replied, "You are my clan, and we belong together, so I will be your leader." The Najjar clan was pleased to have Mohamed as its new chief. Mohamed later ordered the assassination of Kab ibn Al-Ashraf, the head of Banu Aus tribe. This murder gave him complete control of Medina.

I was standing in the presence of history—the history of my faith, the history of the law, and the foundation of all I knew to be true. All the lessons of Islamic history I learned in school originated here. From this place Mohamed welcomed delegations from Arab tribes and earned their allegiance, thereby uniting the Arabian Peninsula. From this place, Abu Bakr waged a two-year war against the apostates and then Umar spread Islam throughout Northern Africa and Asia Minor.

As I looked around the expanse of the mosque, which at that time held seven hundred thousand worshipers and can accommodate two million today, I was awed. My gratitude and pride left me speechless. I could not imagine any other place on earth with this kind of historical and spiritual significance. There could be no rival. Within its boundaries were placards marking the location of the homes of Abu Bakr and Umar, whose daughters Mohamed married. From within these walls, a great faith was born and a great government was established. And it all happened within eight short years.

My Prophet was a victorious warrior and brave leader. I was so proud of everything he accomplished for Allah. He was fearless, and Allah always assured his victory. If his armies were not adequate for the fight, angels joined the battle. I took note of every holy spot, and my heart swelled.

Dad and I walked into the al-Baqi' graveyard next to the mosque. I knew the men lucky enough to be buried there had an easy road to heaven. Not many nine-year-olds thought about death, but I knew dying in Medina was a blessing. According to the hadith, "The Messenger of Allah (blessings and peace of Allah be upon him) said: 'Whoever can manage to die in Medina, let him die there, for I will intercede for whoever dies there.'"

That's why Dad said he would count himself blessed if he could die either at the house of Allah in Mecca or at the house of the Prophet in Medina. Any Muslim should be so blessed as to die in either place. The next day we went to the oldest mosque in Islam built by the Prophet's own hands, the Quba mosque. The Quba mosque, also known as Ali's mosque, was the rendezvous site for the leaders of the faith—Mohamed, Abu Bakr, Umar, and Ali.

Inside the mosque, Dad directed my attention to three corners marked by arrows pointing to the cornerstones. The first stone was placed by Mohamed, the second by Abu Bakr, and the third by Umar. Cornerstones have great meaning. The way the stones were placed indicated the order of their authority within the faith. The placement of the stones reminded the people of the city that all three men were leaders in this new movement.

I also noticed the stone placed by Mohamed faced Jerusalem. A few years after he laid the cornerstone, the Prophet changed the *qibla* (prayer direction) from Jerusalem to Mecca where it remains. This first mosque held a special place in Mohamed's heart, and he went there twice every Saturday to offer his prayers. A hadith promised anyone who offered two prayers would be rewarded with the equivalent of performing the umrah.

SLAUGHTER OF THE BANU QURAYZA TRIBE

One of our final stops in Medina was a shopping district. Although not a holy site, amazing events took place in this ancient market, events that forever changed history. We were going into the *souk*, the ancient market at which Islam achieved its first victory over the Jewish people.

My dad had a mantra when I was growing up that went something like this: "The Jews have always been bad. We should never trust the Jews." And I believed him. He showed me the battlefield in Sinai. I saw the bunkers and heard the stories of Egypt's ongoing warfare with the state of Israel. In 1979, Israel was still Egypt's and Islam's greatest enemy. As I walked through the souk, I rejoiced that this city, which was built by the Jews, had been claimed for Islam.

Mohamed, as ruler of the city, encountered frequent challenges to his kingship, and he was forced to fight several defensive battles against encroaching pagan Arab tribes. He didn't expect to have trouble with the resident Jews, but he received word from an angel that they were about to betray him. Trusting the words of the angel, Mohamed put the Banu Qurayza tribe under siege and rounded up all the Jewish men and boys who had reached puberty, somewhere between seven hundred and nine hundred males in all. He had them bound and brought into the souk. He then ordered the beheading of each one. He also killed one woman who challenged his authority. The remaining Jewish women and their daughters were the spoils of war. They were offered as reward to the Muslim men who assisted in eliminating the betrayers.

Mohamed took one of those women, Rayhana, the daughter of the head of the clan, as a concubine, and later he married her (Quran 33:9–10, 26–27).

I left the souk that day happy and fulfilled. Our pilgrimage was ending, but the memories would never fade. I would come many times in the following years , but nothing would ever compare to this first visit. As the plane soared into the Saudi Arabian skies, I replayed the events of the last two weeks in my head. Through it all, I gained an unexpected appreciation for the Saudi people. Unlike the people of my country and other nations of the Middle East, I saw in the Saudis an uncommon devotion to Islam. They adhered to sharia and tried to perfect it every day. It seemed to me Allah was repaying them with overflowing wealth. Their example revealed to me in that historic land and on that holy ground the secret to the successful Muslim life—as a slave of Allah, the more you please your master, the more riches he will bestow upon you.

MY TAKE-AWAY

I knew what I had to do. I had to live my life as a good Muslim, vigilant in prayer and good works before Allah so my reward in heaven would be great. I never wanted to be like the elderly pilgrims I saw in Mecca, desperately washing their shrouds in the holy water in hopes this act would spare them the harshest penalties of the grave.

One day as we were departing the Kaaba heading to our hotel for a short, deserved rest from the relentless worship and rituals, I saw these pilgrims. Men and women of all ages were working in groups doing what looked like laundry. Intrigued by the sight, I asked my father what those people were doing. Were they allowed to wash their clothes in the sacred mosque? Why did all their clothes appear to be very long sheets of fabric? "These are not their clothes," said my father. "These are their shrouds, the shrouds in which they are planning to be buried. They want them blessed." "Why?" I asked. "And why are they spreading them as if they were trying to dry them?"

"It is very sad really," he answered. "These people are hoping for a miracle of forgiveness. They think if they bring their shrouds to the Holy Land, immerse them into Zamzam water, and dry them seven times, the angels will see them in the grave wrapped in their blessed shrouds and be more forgiving. They hope Allah will also have mercy on them on the Day of Judgment." My father had no pity on them. "They are imbeciles," he added. "I guess when we are desperate and fearful of an imminent fate, we resort to irrational measures. But that will never work with Allah. He is the all-knowing and a ferocious, untamed judge." He cited a verse from the Quran to make his case: *"Verily! The hearing, and the sight, and the heart; about each of those, you will be questioned by Allah"* (Quran 17:36). He followed that with another: *"Then, on the day of judgment, you shall be asked about the delight you indulged in, in this world"* (Quran 102:8).

I judged these pilgrims then and every day of my life as a Muslim, but I also understood. The images of hell and the terrors of the grave the Prophet explained were the stuff of the harshest nightmares. The knowledge of what awaited beyond the grave could drive any one to do crazy things. This knowledge would soon drive my own mother to the brink of madness.

CHAPTER 9

AN EYE TOWARD THE GRAVE

When the soul leaps up to the throat and you are helplessly watching that he is on the verge of death, if he is one of the true submissive Muslim believers of Allah, then happiness and delight and gardens of bliss are his. He is welcomed by the words, "Peace be to you." But if he is one of those who went astray, then he will be served boiling water, scorched by the hell fires. That indeed is the absolute truth.

—Quran 56:83–95

Back home in Egypt, life was different because I was different. I knew nothing would ever be the same again. It couldn't be. I saw and experienced far too much to come back unaffected. When we returned from our life-changing trip, I embraced my destiny—to live a devout, rewarded life, and become a leader, just like my dad. I was going to be someone who made a difference in the Muslim world. I knew it to my core.

My mom, though, was a mystery to me. Although she went through the dark room experience with me and endured many other attempts by my dad to get her to be a submissive Muslim believer, she had not fully committed to Islam. I could see her faith was edified by participating in the umrah. That was evident. But the trip did not have the same effect on her as it did on me. Was it because she was a woman, I wondered? Was it because she wasn't fully invested? I didn't know. Eventually, though, she would get the wake-up call she never knew she needed.

Dad and I came back with a stronger bond than we had when we left Egypt. Helping others grow in their faith through the hajj became our shared passion. In time, that passion became a burden. We wanted everyone to make the pilgrimage before they died. My dad felt a special urgency to get his own father and mother to Saudi Arabia for their first pilgrimage. They were in their seventies. Time was short and growing shorter with each passing day.

When Dad suggested leading them on the hajj, they were delighted. Being devout, they knew they desperately needed to take this step so Allah would reward their obedience when they drew their last breaths. I was deliriously excited when my dad told me he was planning a trip for my grandparents, and I immediately asked to go along again. "Another time, Mohamed," he laughed. "You will make the full pilgrimage soon, but we need to let your hormones catch up to your enthusiasm!"

It seems silly, but after my phenomenal journey through the roots of my faith, I almost forgot I was still just a kid. A few more years needed to pass before I reached puberty and could participate in the full hajj. I had to console myself with the idea I could help prepare my grandparents for the journey just as Dad prepared me. At least I could relive those wonderful days vicariously through them.

Eighteen months passed before all the arrangements were in order. In September 1980, my grandparents were ready to make the trip. And the answer was no—I had still not reached puberty. Dad and I left our house in Cairo early one morning to pick them up. Every time we pulled up in front of their small, rundown house in the country, I said a prayer of thanks to Allah for the blessing of my nice home, my excellent school, and our indoor plumbing.

On the drive over, my dad and I talked about how vital it was for his parents to take this journey before they died—how important it was for every Muslim to do so before they came face-to-face with the Angel of Death. I know it sounds morbid, but good Muslims always have death on their minds. The Quran and hadiths leave nothing to the imagination about what happens after we die. The urgency of the matter is clear. Everyone should live a properly observant life, or else. What I prayed for most was no one I loved would have to experience the "or else."

When we got back to our house with my grandparents, Dad launched into his teaching on the perfect hajj. This made his parents proud. They had the benefit of being led by the best teacher there was. The fact he was their son was an added blessing in their eternal account. My dad also received a blessing because of my devotion and knowledge, which I happily and earnestly shared. I illuminated the points my father was making and added personal details. I had an insider's perspective, and my heart overflowed with gratitude for Allah's blessing in having allowed me to go to his house.

As excited I was for my grandparents, I was surprised by my own tears when they departed. What prompted the tears was not jealousy but fear. My soul was conflicted between faith and love. My faith told me it would be better if my grandparents died in the house of Allah. If they did, they would avoid the torments of the grave and be immediately swept up to heaven.

But I was still a kid, and I selfishly wished for their safe return so they could continue to be part of my life. The struggle between human nature and religious obligation is a constant in the life of any devout Muslim. Submission to Allah must always come first, but it doesn't always come easily. I prayed and counted down the days until the three of them returned. Not until they all walked through our front door did I breathe easily. I couldn't wait to hear my grandparents' stories about the hajj and what it meant to them. Those were some of the best days I ever spent with my grandfather.

Sitting together hour after hour, I listened intently as this wise, elderly man recounted his pilgrimage, the pinnacle of his life. Little did I suspect these were some of the last days we would ever spend together.

After a few weeks at our home, we took my grandparents back to their little village. Our grand adventure together was over, and I was sad to see them go. Less than a week later, we received a phone call that my grandfather was hit by a van. He complained only of a sore arm and shoulder, and the village medical personnel told him he had no broken bones. So he went home to recuperate. Days later he suffered a stroke and was rushed to El Mahdi Medical Center.

DEATH BECOMES PERSONAL

For ten days, he lingered in the intensive care unit, and Dad and I were constantly at his side. It was clear to us the end was near. As his way of coping, my father chose those days at the hospital to explain to me Islam's theology regarding death. He wanted me to understand what was about to happen to his father so, together, we could pray for Allah to spare my grandfather the agonies of the grave.

Many people ignore the fact we all die. They either deliberately remain ignorant about the afterlife or entertain the fantasy the afterlife will be all good. Most consider death a seamless passage into the afterlife. Not all. True Muslim believers are the most wary. The Quran is very clear that death is our greatest *fitna*, or test. Some picture the sinful souls in hell being poked, prodded, and pierced while raging fires lick at their flesh. Yet even these images fail to capture the enormity of what the Quran teaches about punishment after death. In fact, the concept of death may be the most powerful motivator of behavior on this earth.

As my grandfather neared the end, the words I read came to life and plunged deep into my heart. From that moment forward, death and its consequences would never leave my thoughts. I prayed my grandfather's recent pilgrimage meant Allah would show some mercy toward him. But even if Allah did, I knew not all grandfather's sins were erased. There were some for which he would have to stand accountable.

"If he is going to die, I wish he had done it in Mecca," I cried out to my dad as the days dragged on with no improvement in grandfather's condition. "At least he would have died a martyr." My dad couldn't argue with me. Death was a terror, a terror with which even the Prophet struggled as he lay upon his deathbed. "Soon your grandfather will draw his last breath, and the two angels, Munkar and Nakir, will come to show him his place for eternity—heaven or hell," my father said. We prayed the angels would show him a place in heaven.

"Following close behind is Azraiel, the Angel of Death. He will come and remove his spirit. There can be great pain. It all depends on how he conducted his life." Mohamed described this extraction of the spirit as a needle being pulled through wool, shredding the flesh as the spirit departs. I prayed my grandfather's spirit would slip easily from his body. He was faithful to Allah and deserved a better fate than the unfaithful.

Grandfather did so many things right. He was devout all his life. He read the Quran daily and never missed a day of fasting. But even that was not enough to avoid spending time in hell. Every Muslim, aside from the martyr who dies for the cause of Islam, is promised some time in that storied place of fire and torment. It is an unavoidable reality, and I prayed my grandfather's time of suffering would be short and would ultimately lead him heavenward.

Some talk of death and hellfire is common in Muslim households. Parents try to instill the fear of Allah in the hearts of their children as a way of encouraging them to stay faithful. But our discussions were candid well beyond the norm. Dad knew however, I could take it, and together we went over verse after verse dealing with the darkest of all topics. *"And the stupor of death will come in truth; that is what you were trying to escape"* (Quran 102:8). This verse told me nothing was hidden from Allah. Other verses reinforced this theme.

The day will come when the unbelievers and unfaithful will both face the agonies of death. That day Allah's angels will mock those sinners and tell them *"Go ahead and save yourselves if you can. Today you will receive the punishment and humiliation that you deserve"* (Quran 6:93). The day of judgment is the day every soul will be presented with all the good they did and all the bad they did. *"Some will wish their bad is hidden but Allah is warning you about his just nature and he will punish the sinners"* (Quran 3:30).

There was more, of course, so much more, including Mohamed's firsthand accounts of the agonies of hell. Then as now, Muslims heard all the verses filled with admonitions to live a righteous life. Most, however, got so lost in their day-to-day existence they failed to pay attention unless they were forced, as I was, to confront their faith through a dark room experience.

I thought of the pilgrims I saw in Mecca desperately washing their shrouds in holy water. I asked my father if that would help them, even a little. "No, a clean shroud offers no hope for the dying," said my father. "A clean, devout life is the only hope." Hearing this, I felt sad for the people at the well.

During those ten days at the hospital, I spent much time in thoughtful consideration of death and what it would mean to me. I knew I was uncommonly lucky to have come to a faithful life as a kid. My record was almost spotless. But if I fell short, even a little, the penalties would be high. My mom and most of the people around me weren't so fortunate. They had a lifetime of sins for which they would ultimately have to pay.

As expected, my grandfather died. Although I did not see them, the angels came and did what they had to do with his dear soul. I prayed that the process be painless. For days after I prayed he had already left hell and found his way to a place in heaven. I prayed, yes, but there was no way for me to know. I had to live with uncertainty from that moment forward.

My poor mother chose to close her eyes. When reality forced them open, she became consumed with a creeping fear that spread like a cancer. Her father died when I was still just a baby. She grieved the loss of her father, but at the time she understood little about death and the grave. In her mind, her dad was a good man who should have been blessed in the afterlife. That opinion, however, came from a place of ignorance. The Quran teaches there are no good men. Everyone will have a price to pay and Allah will be the judge. The only true standard of goodness was whether or not a person lived as an obedient slave. In that measure, my mom's father fell egregiously short.

MOM'S FAMILY FALLS APART

Mom also foolishly believed that because her father was a "good" man he would go to a "good" place in the afterlife. But her idea of the afterlife was a product of her Western ideals, nothing more. Had she been an observant Muslim, she would have had a clearer idea of her father's fate, and it would have torn her apart.

In a patriarchal society, even among nominally observant religious families, the death of a father upends the family structure. That was certainly true in my mother's case. Her family imploded with her father's death. Her brothers started fighting over money, the inheritance, and the disposition of their father's construction company. Things got messy quickly. Assets were frozen, lawsuits followed, and my maternal grandmother, Fatima, was left to handle the problem. Leaving their ailing mother with no income and with the family's considerable assets frozen, the sons scattered and vowed to deal with family matters later. There in her big house, surrounded by her memories and expensive Italianate furniture, Fatima was forgotten. It broke my mother's heart.

Whenever the conversation turned to my mom's family, my father and uncle would quickly remind us that all their struggles were due to one thing: not properly following Allah. I couldn't argue with what they were saying, but I felt pity for my grandmother and my mother. Fatima was a good and loving woman. She was the peacemaker of the family, always stepping in when there was conflict to try to make things better. She loved me and took care of me, and I loved her dearly. But none of those virtues could spare her.

I was twelve when her health started to deteriorate. I vividly remember standing just outside her room trying to see how she was doing. Through the crack in the door, I saw Mom and a few of her sisters fussing over Fatima as she clung to the edge of the chair gasping for breath. They urged her to go to the hospital, but she stubbornly refused.

Knowing my grandmother never properly observed Islamic rituals and her sins came at a high price, I slipped into her room when no one else was around to pray for her. As I held her hand in mine, I asked Allah to save her, suspecting all the while I would never see her again. Although Fatima was a good woman, she never consistently observed Muslim rituals. She tried in the last few years of her life to be more observant, but it wasn't enough to pay all her dues to Allah. I begged Allah to forgive her nonetheless.

If there were another standard by which to measure her, Fatima would have excelled. She was a giver, always doing good things for her family and friends, and she cared for a sister during her time of need. But I never saw her read the Quran, and she didn't pray five times a day. Even though my mother and her sisters raised enough money to send Fatima on the pilgrimage before she died, her spiritual debt was enormous. I had no idea how much time she would spend in hell for it.

I shared my grief with my dad. He wanted to comfort me, but his bold nature and his faith gave him little room to maneuver. He told me matter-of-factly that Fatima brought her fate upon herself. If I wanted to do something to help her, he advised me to pay some of her debt to Allah by dedicating prayers or doing other rituals on her behalf.

This was yet another of those teaching moments for him, and I was amazed at how he could lock his feelings away so deftly. He mastered the art of shutting out his human nature and embracing his role as a slave to Allah and a soldier in his army. Over the years I occasionally saw him slip, and a bit of his humanity surfaced, but he would quickly catch himself. Even on my best days as a good Muslim, I sometimes struggled to hold my human emotions in check.

Fatima died at the age of fifty-eight, and Mom's family came completely unglued. It started with Mom's oldest brother Sabah. One morning he proclaimed the best way for the family to reclaim some of its wealth was to sell their childhood residence. My mom, as a female, was not asked her opinion, but the idea of losing her family home crushed her emotionally. The home was so much more than a dwelling. It was her only remembrance of a carefree youth. Losing it would mean losing another piece of herself. She dared to speak her feelings aloud. "There are other things we can sell," she told her brother. "We don't have to sell the home where we shared holidays and happy times as a family!" Sabah, though, would not hear it. "You are a spoiled brat," he shouted at her. He reminded her she was married to a doctor and living very comfortably. "You have no need for the money," he raged. "The rest of us do! Two of our sisters are widows. How do you expect them to survive?"

Sabah vented the anger and bitterness he felt about my dad and dismissed her longings out of hand. It was a losing battle, and my father was no help. He reminded my mother her family deserved their ill fortune. "And whoever turns away from my remembrance and won't worship me and won't stay adherent and faithful to my way will have a miserable, depressed, and failing life," he quoted from the Quran. Over and over he used that verse in describing Mom's family. Sadly, the depth of their failure was to become glaringly real to my mother.

Shortly after the family meeting in which he humiliated my mother, Sabah went to the hospital to take a stress test for his chest pains. That afternoon, he invited some of his sisters, again excluding my mother, to his house for dinner and entertainment. After dinner he excused himself and said he wasn't feeling well. When his sisters went to check on him, they found him dead.

Mom's angry words to her brother were still hot in her heart when she learned Sabah suffered a massive heart attack. He likely had the same heart condition as their father, but my mother felt responsible for his death. She knew too her siblings secretly blamed her.

For three days, my mom tried to reach out to her sisters, and each time they shut her out. I found her in her bedroom huddled in the corner, weeping. Mom's guilt was consuming her. Rather than comforting her, my father decided it was the proper time to educate her on what Sabah could expect in the afterlife. He had me actively participate in the conversation. "Can I tell him I'm sorry?" Mom asked in desperation. "What can I do to make this right?" We answered her questions in turn, each of us lifting the veil from her eyes so she could see clearly what Allah promises when we die. From that moment forward, Mom could no longer claim ignorance. Although she did not attend the burial when her parents died, she chose to attend her brother's. She watched as the attendants lowered his shrouded body into the grave, placed it on his side facing Mecca, and tossed sand over his face. As her brother's tormented afterlife began, my mom had to acknowledge she was in similar jeopardy. That was when she really started to grieve.

MOM SPIRALS DOWNHILL

The mother I knew died at that gravesite. The grief was no longer about her brother or what her sisters thought of her. It became personal. Over the years, I have seen many lives transformed at the grave of a loved one when the reality of death manifests itself, but I've never witnessed a transformation like that of my mother.

In the months following her close encounter with death, my mother developed dark circles under her lower eyelids, and her skin became ashen. Her nights were long and restless as she was forced to confront the fact she too fell short of Allah's demands and would have to face his judgments. She frantically enlisted my help in her daily struggle with reading and memorizing the Quran, and it hurt me to see her suffer.

Mom got a notebook and drew up a spreadsheet to calculate how many days of prayers and fasting she missed in her life. If she could buy her way out of Allah's wrath by giving to approved charities, she planned to do so. But when all was calculated, Mom realized her debt was far too large for an easy penance.

I had to give her credit. She tried. She attempted to read the Quran, but the Arabic was too difficult for her. She simply couldn't understand what the words meant. To help her understand, we bought her a Quran on tape along with a small tape player and headphones. She spent hours every day with those headphones on, the Quran in her lap, trying to follow along, her box of Kleenex always nearby. And every day, her failures and frustrations spilled from her eyes and onto her notebook.

I was always by her side. To help calm her, I held her hand and offered words of assurance. She understood perhaps 10 percent of what she read and heard, but her attempts to read the Arabic earned her some points toward redemption. That hope inspired her to continue. She kept the tapes in a red box next to her chair and kept the notebook with spreadsheets under her pillow. When I saw how desperately she struggled, I had to wonder how Muslims in non-Arabic countries dealt with this same issue. Credit for redemption is earned only if the text is read in Arabic.

My dad has always had the philosophy that it's best to strike while the iron is hot, and that was certainly true with regard to my mother. She experienced an "awakening" at her brother's grave. Hoping to keep her on track, Dad took her back to Mecca for another umrah. He and I spent hours explaining how her inevitable death must govern what she does with the rest of her life. All of her hours of hard work were vital to her afterlife experience.

ALLAH DEMANDS PUNISHMENT

It never ceased to amaze me how many Muslims were surprised at what the Quran said about death, my mother included. They lived in ignorance either by active choice or by their shallow grasp of the Quran and the teachings of Mohamed. But for those devout souls committed to honoring the faith, this preoccupation has always been central. In Islam, death is not the end. The grave is a holding area until Allah pronounces his final judgment.

This new "life" in the grave is called *al-barzakh* and begins the same for everyone—with the arrival of the two angels who ask the three crucial questions: "Who is your Lord? What is your religion? Who is your Prophet?" The answers for the righteous will come without hesitation. "Allah, Islam, Mohamed!"

Dad and I believed we would answer swiftly, and our reward would be a glimpse of our heavenly future. We hoped our graves would be filled with light thanks to our endless reading and memorization of the Quran. But we knew too even the most virtu-ous among us would spend time in hell. The Prophet said no one was sinless, and everyone would receive some measure of torment, but I hoped and prayed daily my time would be short. The thought of hell scared me enough to keep me from sinning. As the perfect embodiment of Islam, Mohamed too had an overwhelming fear of death and the agonies of the afterlife. Islamic texts made that clear.

Aisha his wife said, "When death approached prophet Mohamed and while his head was on my thigh, he became uncon-scious and then recovered consciousness. He then looked at the ceiling of the house and said, *'There is no god but Allah; death indeed is painful and has its agonies. O Allah, forgive me and bestow me your Mercy on me, please accept me with the highest companions on Your Side.'"*[7]

If my beloved Prophet feared what was to come, who was I to fear any less? Although he did not die a martyr, Mohamed was diligent and faithful in all things. But what about those who were not diligent, those who missed prayers or the fast? What about people like my mom? To hesitate answering the angels, even for a second, would reveal the condition of her heart. For those poor souls, severe punishment was in store. The angels would beat them mercilessly with heavy iron rods, crushing their bones. The ground around their bodies would close in, disintegrating their ribs and sending their anguished cries heavenward. The Prophet said all the creatures of the earth but man would hear their screams of sorrow. And for the unfaithful the grave was just the beginning. Darkness, pain, and agony would continue unabated until the Day of Judg-ment. As you can imagine, the more we educated my mother, the more we terrified her.

My mother had reason to be afraid, but non-Muslims had even more reason. They were immediately sent to hell for all eternity. They had no hope of ever achieving a place in heaven. Mohamed's own father and mother were said to be in hell. It didn't matter who you were or whom you knew. It was all about submitting yourself to Allah and living your life accordingly.

If a man failed to properly clean himself before just one prayer, he could expect to be whipped and have his grave filled with fire. The foot cleansing required males to wash up to the Achilles tendon. I remember regularly looking around the mosque at the grown men who failed to wash properly. Their feet were wet, but their Achilles tendons were dry. *They are going to be whipped in hell*, I thought to myself.

That was only one sin. If a person were too lazy to get up and pray at the directed times, his head would be crushed by a rock. Those who withheld their wealth and failed to help the poor would have to eat rotten food. Those who caused dissension would have their lips cut off with iron scissors. Some sinners would be force-fed rocks they would later have to excrete. Others would be hung by their breasts. Others still would be forced to eat flesh cut from their sides. Fire would consume many of the damned. Serpents would strike at the necks and ankles of others.

I never stopped to question why Allah would punish everyone, even the faithful, in the grave and beyond. Allah was just, and if he were angry, disobedience must have provoked it, mine included. Ultimately, I knew, we would all receive penalties according to our level of offense. Given we could sin through the heart, the eye, the ear, the mouth, the tongue, the stomach, the private parts, the hand, the foot, everything, I couldn't imagine anyone ever walking the earth sinless.

THE ONLY ESCAPE

No trial in life was as difficult as the grave. Jihad, the spilling of one's own blood in the cause of Allah, was the only real escape. But a woman could not be a martyr; the Prophet forbade it. Only under the most extreme circumstances, where there was no man to perform the act of jihad, was a woman allowed martyrdom, and even then, Allah was to be the judge of its necessity.

Had martyrdom been an option for my mom, I have no doubt she would have seized it. The desperation, the agony, the pain, the fear, and the sleepless nights made her a prime candidate for jihad.

Through the years, I have seen countless men equally desperate to pay their debt to Allah. Many rushed to the field of jihad to secure their place in heaven and avoid the punishment they felt they deserved.

Only martyrs bypassed the questioning, the crushing of the earth, the time in hell. They received their immediate reward without having to wait anxiously until the Day of Judgment. Any man who knew the penalty for the sins he committed in his lifetime would readily accept the opportunity to advance heavenward with a clean slate.

The grave was the great unifying factor for all Muslims—man, woman, rich, poor, Middle Eastern or Western European. It was every man's dark room, a never-ending one in which the glaring light of a lifetime of sins pierced the soul and brought him to his knees. For an imam, each funeral offered a new opportunity to instill the fear of Allah and to call Muslims to repentance. Dad and I embraced this opportunity throughout the years. We preached about the afterlife and did so in graphic detail, reminding funeral attendees that they, too, would be left alone in a dark grave with the worms devouring their decaying flesh. This practice might sound harsh, but we knew we were giving them the gift of knowledge and time to do something about it. Although late to an understanding, my mother poured herself into earning her redemption. She will never stop until the day she draws her last breath.

CHAPTER 10

SADAT MAKES CONCESSIONS WITH THE WEST

All of you Muslims take note that the Christians and the Jews are unclean so never let them approach the holy mosque in Mecca even if it causes you despair and loss of money and fight hard those who do not believe in Allah and are not Muslims until they become Muslim or pay the poll tax and are willingly humiliated.

—Quran 9:28–29

Julius Caesar once said, "Experience is the teacher of all things." That sentiment was never more true than in my case. The fact Caesar, one of my personal heroes, said as much reinforced the point's legitimacy. Even though Western or Christian characters like Caesar should not have been part of my thinking as a true Muslim, my exposure to that and more at school was inevitable. The knowledge I acquired about history, politics, the Middle East, and Islam came more from my own experience and that of others close to me than through book learning. My young adult years were spent in the company of presidents, kings, princes, Muslim Brotherhood leaders, and all manner of influential men.

I was convinced all of these influencers entered my life by divine appointment. I was, after all, an average teen, not born of royal blood or from a political dynasty. My father, however, always managed to be in a position of influence, and I was always with him. Although uninterested in public office, he was the keenest observer of all. In every situation, my watchful dad formed judgments about everyone he met and their actions. "Are they behaving as properly devout Muslims? Are their actions sanctioned by Allah?" And on and on. I too learned to be an observer and a judge, just like Dad.

Dad's military service gave him access to many truly important people. Our country had long been controlled by the military, and *anything* that took place in Egypt went through military intelligence channels first. It's ironic my father's military career began as a way of evading arrest for his Muslim Brotherhood ties and later became the source of some of his greatest blessings.

Sadat's Yom Kippur War gambit led to my father's lifelong career as spiritual leader for the hajj. This position put him in close contact with the most wealthy and powerful men in the Middle East. To this day, Egypt's military intelligence orchestrates the hajj for civilians as well as for military personnel and their families. Retired veterans of the intelligence service have parlayed their experience into profitable businesses arranging pilgrimages for the public. They also orchestrate high-end operations catering to the elite and the influential. Ministers, government office holders, and wealthy civilians alike have sought out these intelligence veterans both for their knowledge and for the added security they provide.

A proven spiritual leader with high-level security clearance, my dad emerged as *the* foremost spiritual leader for hajj at that time. This status enabled him to make frequent umrahs and the annual hajj. He stayed in the finest hotels and received the royal treatment. In time he became the trusted spiritual advisor of the most important men in Egypt and Saudi Arabia. In that role he had unprecedented access to the private world these men inhabited. As his constant companion, I did too.

I never really stopped to think about it then, but as my dad's sidekick I was reaping the benefits of his blessings. He was gaining material wealth and influence. I was gaining knowledge a book could never teach. Eventually, I was able to step right into his shoes. But first, I had some growing up to do.

For as long as I can remember, I have been a seeker. I have always been reluctant to accept only one historical account, only one person's word, or even the word of a noted authority. By watching my father, I learned to analyze everything. Everyone, I sensed, had an agenda, and every written word had a subtext. My father helped me see only by adhering to the ancient texts could I be my own authentic self. I had to answer to no one but Allah.

From age twelve to twenty, years of emotional upheaval for any adolescent, I was pressed to put my father's lessons into practice on a daily basis. The changes in the environment reflected the changes within me. The Middle East was becoming more Islamic. Leaders were reclaiming some of the ground lost when the last caliphate fell. It was an exhilarating time to be a Muslim youth, especially one whose personal faith was ascendant as well.

Islam is and must be both a system of governance and faith. From the beginning, it was intended to provide the direction every individual needed for every area of life. In pure Islam, I understood, the individual was a Muslim above all else. Ideally, the law and social codes would be Islamic as well, and good Muslims knew this. To desire some other governance is and was always a sin. I saw every reason to desire what Allah prescribed and to resist every temptation keeping me from being a slave to Allah.

I had no doubt outside influences destroyed the Middle East. The only hope we in Egypt had to rise from the ashes was to do as Saudi Arabia did, at least as a start—return to the governance of pure, unvarnished Islam. President Sadat understood. Had he not, he would never have released Brotherhood members from the prisons and enlisted their help.

For reasons unclear to me, however, Sadat lost his way. While he was busy making peace with the Jews, he butted heads with

Umar al-Tilmisani, the spiritual leader of the Muslim Brotherhood at the time. As a result of this conflict, Sadat rounded up fifteen hundred Brotherhood leaders and tossed them back into prison. Other leaders were arrested as well, including the Coptic Pope who built an alliance with the Muslim Brotherhood over its stance on Israel. Largely as a result of the 1979 peace treaty with Israel, the president's popularity hit an all-time low. He was such a smart man. I was confused about why he thought he could betray us with impunity.

The day after the mass arrests, I sat with my uncle and watched the president give a nationally televised address. Afterward, my uncle turned to me and said matter-of-factly, "Sadat is dead meat." I was stunned. I knew mistakes were made, but I never imagined Sadat could fall so far from Allah's favor as to deserve death. My uncle did not have inside knowledge, but he did have a keen understanding of how the Brotherhood worked. He knew some of its members would take decisive action against the president, the man who they felt betrayed them.

AN ESCAPE PLAN

Immediately after that address, my uncle and my dad began planning. They did not want to be in the country when the inevitable happened. My uncle had no desire to get thrown back into prison because of his Brotherhood ties, nor did my dad. The safest course of action was to head back over to Saudi Arabia for a pilgrimage until the deed was done. Afterward, they could safely return if the conditions were right. Plans were made. It was impossible for normal people to make pilgrimage plans so quickly, but with my dad's connections he was able to get the paperwork taken care of. Within days my parents and my uncle boarded the plane for Saudi Arabia while my brother and I stayed behind with Uncle Ahmed's wife and children.

As usual, I had difficulty separating my emotions from the realities of Islam. I was afraid for Sadat and for my own family. Remembering happier times saddened me. Dad, as Sadat's daughter's physician, had access to the president on a personal level. I remember visiting Sadat at his farm and having breakfast with him at a big table. It was a thrill to sit with such an important man. Such wonderful memories were clouded by the very real prospect that someone was about to kill a man I grew to care for deeply.

In October of 1981, my uncle's prophecy came to pass. The occasion was an event celebrating Egypt's crossing of the Suez Canal eight years earlier in their defeat of the Jews. Standing in salute to the military convoy as it passed, the president was caught off guard. Four men, allegedly members of the Egyptian Army, jumped from a vehicle and began shooting. Lieutenant Khalid Istanbouli led the assault in response to a *fatwa* issued by cleric Omar Abdel-Rahman. Abdel-Rahman, the so-called "Blind Sheik," was later convicted in the U.S. for the 1993 World Trade Center bombing. Abdel-Rahman declared Sadat an apostate who forsook the faith by his actions and by his association with Islam's mortal enemies, the Christians and the Jews. Worse, Omar Abdel-Rahman called for Egyptian jihadists, likely from the Brotherhood, to assassinate the president. At the end of the two-minute barrage of gunfire, Sadat and ten others were dead or dying.

Glued to my uncle's TV, I watched the entire spectacle from the site of the shooting to the El Mahdi hospital where Sadat died. The funeral was also televised. As I watched, I tried to figure out why everything happened as it did. I was not sure whether Sadat was a martyr who died in the cause of Allah or a traitor gone astray. I longed to discuss my questions with my mentors, my uncle, and my dad. It wasn't until three weeks later, after the government made all its arrests, my father and uncle were finally able to return home.

On one hand, Sadat was a faithful Muslim who resurrected the ritual of jihad and transformed the Egyptian military. On the other hand, he developed a strong relationship with the Jews and Christian Americans. I did not know whether he befriended the West to deceive the enemy or whether he was deceived. One answer led Sadat to heaven, the other to hell. The difference was that stark. I was as conflicted as I was when my grandmother died. I loved Sadat but had no choice but to put a lock on my heart until I could assess his faithfulness to Islam. I knew I had to cut anyone and anything out of my life not faithful to Allah.

MUBARAK CHANGES DIRECTION IN EGYPT— THE MUSLIM BROTHERHOOD FLOURISHES

Sadat's death led to more changes in Egypt. The new president, Hosni Mubarak, started working to remove anyone he deemed "extreme" in the military. His eye was clearly on the Brotherhood, but he was no fool. Playing it smarter than Nasser, Mubarak tried to work with the Brotherhood. He gave the members willing to work with him enough room to bring about positive change while keeping them on a short leash. If anyone posed a significant threat, that person went to prison.

In fact, two of the key men who started al Qaida—Ayman al-Zawahiri and Palestinian scholar Abdullah Yusuf Azzam—served prison terms but were released after short sentences. Had Mubarak instead crushed the Brotherhood's extremist elements, al Qaida would never have gotten off the ground. It was through the Brotherhood's military branch, *Gama Islamia*, al Qaida was born. Mubarak, learning his lessons from Nasser, chose not to crush the Brotherhood, not even its secret militant wing. Many of those militants were and still are the power behind the Islamic jihadi movement. The al Qaida organization and the al Gamaat Islamiael movement were a result of Mubarak's decision.

An unexpected outcome of the new president's policies was the mainstream Muslim Brotherhood flourished. Members ran for parliament. They exercised influence over unions. They continued to maintain roles in universities, commerce, military, and even the government. Civilization jihad, taking control by infiltrating every key organization and operation, was alive and well. And rather than being reined in, the Brotherhood was getting more powerful than ever before. Its influence reached into Europe and beyond.

Mubarak's policy changes affected my father. As a known spiritual figure, he was subject to suspicion as an extremist. He had to make a choice: either retire from the military or remain in service but minimize the "extra" preaching he was doing. That "extra" included the Tuesday evening lessons in our home. He also had to stop gathering people for preaching Islamic lessons after the midday obligatory prayers at the military base hospital mosque. Going forward, he had only fifteen minutes to lead his prayers, not the usual two hours. Mubarak was shutting down the Islamic window Sadat opened in 1971. My dad was heartbroken, but he had to find another way to express his zeal. After much internal debate, he agreed to dial back his teaching, at least publicly.

DAD GETS HIS CERTIFICATION

There was also the problem of his being an imam. Mubarak directed that if a man wanted to preach in Egypt, he was required to have a certificate from government-controlled Al-Azhar University. Otherwise, he had to cease teaching immediately. Al-Azhar has represented Sunni Islam to the entire world for more than eleven hundred years. My dad did not have a degree from Al-Azhar, nor did he want one. He taught himself by studying the works of the ancients. We both believed the Quran and these ancient texts had much more legitimacy than an institution serving as the religious arm of the government since the British colonization sixty years prior. Up until Mubarak's directive, my father was the first man to teach in the mosques without a license, and he was never before challenged.

My unflappable father, a man who built a solid reputation as a champion of the faith, was not deterred. He built two religious schools at the cost of about one million Egyptian pounds. As a known leader and authority on Islam, he had already altered the culture. So he did exactly what his friends knew he would do. He took it right to the top. He sought out the grand imam of the university, Gad al-haq Ali Gad al-Haq, and—*voila!*—he got all the certification he needed.

My father smashed every obstacle put in his way, and I was a front-row witness. I could see Allah was on his side. I wanted more than ever to be just like this amazing man. Sure, he followed the rules, but he was always faithful to Allah in doing so. His faithfulness was soon rewarded. Dad emerged stronger. He preached to thousands, wrote books, and taught on television. He started making videos and writing more books about how to make a pilgrimage. He even made a business deal with military intelligence and Egypt Air, the official airline for the pilgrimage. The gist of the deal was all those going to hajj got a copy of his book as they boarded their flights. His books expanded his income and his influence. He was a mega-preacher before Egypt knew what a mega-preacher was.

Dad also had great success in his medical practice and was able to reap many rewards by building his own clinics and hospital. He was an excellent doctor and was credited to be the first physician in Egypt to use ultrasound and the laparoscope. I often went to work with him at the clinic on base, where tanks were my playground and the troops my soccer mates. Dad even allowed me into the operating rooms as he delivered babies or performed surgery. This kind of access wasn't normal, but it was my normal.

When we weren't on base or at the mosque, my father and I attended Muslim Brotherhood meetings and kitchen-table strategy sessions. I was studying ancient empires and political dynamics at school, but nothing in a textbook could ever compare to the education I received by my father's side. Daily discussions with two of the smartest men I knew, my dad and uncle, inspired me to study ancient maps and analyze historical accounts. And as a good Muslim, I had no distractions. Allah did not allow them. I knew of no other kid who spent as much time with his father and other powerful men as I did. I decided this was a far more satisfying way to spend time than, say, sneaking out to see movies.

CHOOSING MY OWN PATH

My father used to say, "You can decide what you want to be. The choice is yours." Sure, I could choose to be an engineer like my mother's relatives and risk my father's scorn, or I could choose to be a doctor. For me, the choice was obvious. I always knew I would be a doctor, just like my dad. There are photos of me as a small child reading the Quran with a stethoscope draped around my neck. Those early images portrayed everything I aspired to be as an adult—a good Muslim and a physician.

Allah was central to my life plan, and I wanted to teach others. And just like Dad, I rejected the idea of going to Al-Azhar. As a government-controlled school, the leaders there taught a politically influenced form of Islam, and the correctness was determined by those in power. I preferred uncorrected Islam—Allah's pure, unfiltered word.

Another possibility was to join the Brotherhood and see where that path took me. I rejected that option. Like my dad, I did not want to be defined by the company I kept. I also didn't want to owe anyone anything. I was going to reach my goals the old school way. I would learn from devout imams and original sources and free myself from the labels attached to a group or a school. Besides, I already had access to the benefits the Brotherhood could offer. If the political climate turned chilly, membership could get me thrown into prison. I had no good reason to consider that option.

I made my decision in concert with my dad and uncle. I would pursue a mainstream education to become a doctor, and enrich my education with Islamic instruction from some of the best Islamic teachers available. A couple of imams helped me memorize the Quran. Later, a group of faithful Muslims opened a nearby qur'anic school, *Talaa al Kamal,* which means "Perfect Budding Youth." I attended on weekends during the school year and on every summer day. And I couldn't get enough! Other kids thought I was crazy for craving more and more education, and perhaps I was, but I was driven to emulate my father's success.

No, I was not normal at all. I preferred to call myself "unique," and I was very comfortable in my Muslim skin. At school I was known as the smart religious kid. Outside of school my dad made me his second in command and gave me adult responsibilities. I was a curiosity to be sure, but thankfully my outgoing personality helped me make friends and kept me from being the school freak.

Friends posed a dilemma, though, and I learned to walk a very fine line. My dad never allowed me to have friends over to the house, and honestly, that was for the best. My home life would have shocked them. Dad never permitted me to spend time at my friends' homes either. There was zero chance their families would be as devout as ours. All my social interaction had to take place at school where the lures to stray were enormous.

More than once I longed to be just like everyone else and embrace pop culture. The temptations were huge, and I lost a battle or two along the way. Other kids were into Michael Jackson, Madonna, and George Michael. I was into the hajj and teaching grown men the meaning of the Quran. I did sneak a listen to Michael Jackson's "Billie Jean" once. I liked to hear a good joke. I wanted to have a good time, but I was my own prison guard, inevitably shielding myself from anything that would anger Allah.

My diligence came with an emotional price tag. Everything in Islam did. Unseen forces were always at work: watching, waiting, and recording every thought and deed, all to surface on Judgment Day. Every Muslim who has reached puberty knows about the angels who reside on our shoulders recording our every deed until death. If I looked at a girl with lust in my heart, the angel recorded it. If I missed a prayer, even one, the angel made record. Even if I managed to hide my sin from my father or my teachers, I could never hide it from the angels.

Life was a struggle. I had to resist the charms of a beautiful girl in one of my classes named Doaa. I used to watch her perform on our gymnastics team, and I often looked for occasions to run into her. One day a friend told me Doaa liked me, and now I had a real problem. I *knew* I liked her too. She was bolder than I was and obviously less observant in her faith. One memorable day she approached me and asked me to call her. I wanted to so badly. You cannot imagine how badly! I actually made several attempts, but as soon as I heard her voice, I silently hung up the phone. I felt so stupid. But I was terrified of my attraction to her, an attraction expressly forbidden in Islam.

With my raging hormones imploring me to give in to her flirtation, I remained unyielding. I began to think Allah was testing me to see if I could resist. Doaa persisted for two years and finally gave up. If I were to see her on the streets today, I would be hard pressed to recognize her. The culture changed. So did she.

The fact we didn't have a television until my father began a televised teaching show made me even more socially awkward. I had to be content with watching Dad's show or the news while my peers were watching entertainment and sports. When something other than his show or the news was on, my dad covered the TV with a large, opaque plastic bag. I had to agree with my father that watching television was a waste of time. Nevertheless, I enjoyed an occasional televised soccer match with my uncle in his house, always a special treat. Even my uncle did not live up to my dad's righteousness.

Once, though, I remember watching *Top Gun* on TV while my father was at work. Tom Cruise, fighter jets, and action sequences filled the screen, and wow, it looked amazing. To make sure I didn't get caught, I had the sound turned off. I also took two chickens from our freezer and placed them on the television tube in the back. I figured the cold chicken would absorb the heat from the TV, and I was right.

My plan worked perfectly. When the movie ended, I quickly replaced the plastic cover to hide my sin. My father was never the wiser, but I'm sure my shoulder angels took note, and I was wracked with guilt for what I did. I prayed to Allah five hundred times on a rosary and hoped it would suffice.

Looking back, I realize how awful my teen years were. I had to tamp down my natural desires while watching others enjoy the most carefree time of their lives. "Carefree," however, was not a word in my father's vocabulary, and so it was not in mine either. Everyone else was dating. Not me. In fact, I never even talked to a female unless I had to for a class project.

Sincerely terrified of the punishment for sin, I tried to do no wrong. Besides, as a teacher's assistant instructing other students in the Quran, I lived under a microscope. I couldn't allow myself to stray. Some of the boys teased and bullied me. Although I liked to think I didn't care, deep inside, I did. That said, my commitment to a higher calling always won out. I liked to think I gained some respect from others by setting that standard for myself.

I won't lie. It wasn't easy. As hard as I tried to be a carbon copy of my dad, we were two very different people. I was extremely social, and I loved being with people. My father loathed social occasions. He was a straight arrow, still is. We both were compared to the "greats" of Islam, but in very different ways. My dad was like Umar, the third caliph, focused and serious. I was compared to Abu Bakr, a people person. I enjoyed interaction.

Regardless our differences, my dad was my hero. It did not matter that he placed a heavy yoke around my neck at age five and held me to impossible standards. I held him up as everything I wanted to become. And for that reason, I was his hope. I was to be everything Allah required of the perfect slave. I was to earn him a measure of redemption and be a better Muslim than he ever dreamed possible.

GROWING AS A RELIGIOUS LEADER

I readily assumed that responsibility. At age twelve, I took it upon myself to go to the mosque and issue the call to prayer. It was my first real taste of leadership. The desire to be a man kept me moving ahead on the right path. True, I didn't sound much like a man then as my aunts often reminded me. They chuckled aloud about my squeaky voice coming over the microphone. But issuing the call was empowering. Whenever Dad was out of town, I stepped up to lead the prayer. Later I even dared to lead prayers when he was there.

My knowledge of the Quran and sharia law and theology was tested at numerous competitions organized by the Talaa el Kamal Islamic school I was attending. Between the outside lessons, instruction from my father, and private lessons with some of the top Islamic imams, I was better prepared than any of my contemporaries to begin preaching. By the time I was thirteen, I was recognized for my knowledge and received my certification as an imam.

At the time we lived in an upscale neighborhood, and there were several mosques close by. By our standards, however, these government-controlled mosques were politically controlled. Looking for an alternative, I found an unused basement in a nearby building and asked the building owner if we could turn the space into a new independent mosque. He consented as long as we agreed to finish out the space. I was fourteen at the time and very excited.

My dad liked the idea, and together we went down to take a look. In no time at all, Dad hired workers to add a bathroom, carpeting, and a sound system. Once the space was ready, I started leading prayers in "my" mosque. In my heart, I was on my way to becoming the greatest imam of all.

Around this same time, my school was adapting to the Islamic awakening. It astonished me a school built by the British and championing Western education was now investing in a mosque on the school grounds. I praised Allah for his victories! When the administrators were ready to build the mosque, they turned to my dad. They were a bit star-struck. Dad was, after all, renowned for his television show, for his work as a great spiritual leader on the hajj, and for the hospital he co-established near the school.

A mosque on the grounds of my British school was a sure sign the times were changing. It wasn't staffed full-time by a regular imam, but was left open for the students to enter and pray anytime they wished. I made the call to prayer over the loudspeaker for the third prayer, *Asar*, at 3:20 p.m. every day. It broke my heart that this big, beautiful mosque was left empty the rest of the day and during weekends. At first there were only a few students who came, but eventually more staff and students joined.

BUILDING CASTLES IN HEAVEN

By the mid-1980s, Egypt's economy was beginning to boom, and Dad was getting wealthier by the minute thanks to his careful investments. His work leading pilgrimages was flourishing, and his medical clinic and hospital were growing. He was reaping from all he had sown. At home, though, we didn't see much change. Dad believed strongly in the principle that wealth was to be invested in the afterlife. "Don't be upset if I give all of my money to Allah," he told me one day. "It is important to invest in heaven. I am doing well, but Allah expects me to turn that blessing back into his kingdom on earth."

That he did. He built a new hospital catering to the poorest residents of the city. He also decided to use the money he made from his investments to build a mosque and school in his home village. It wasn't going to be easy to bring modern infrastructure to an area with no sewer system, no electricity, and limited water sources, but he was determined. Construction would be a several-month process.

The village was more than sixty miles from Cairo. I spent weekends there observing the construction and serving as my dad's eyes and ears. I walked the same roads my father walked as a child, and I stayed in his childhood home. Dad's mother had long since moved to a nice apartment in the city. Other than the occasional construction worker, I had the place to myself. Often, I stayed there alone, terrified of my frequent visitors—rats!

Dad's uncles and other kin still lived in the village, and I had the chance to get to know them better. They had nowhere near my father's level of education, wealth, or ambition. One was a heavy smoker, a practice forbidden in Islam. Dad's judgment on him became mine as well, and I considered him a black sheep. Still, I liked them all and enjoyed their company even while secretly condemning them as Islam demanded.

Through Dad's numerous connections, he was able to get power extended to the village for free. The first lights in the village shone from my grandfather's house. Dad also got a special permit for a modern sewer system. With an expected three hundred kids in our school, sewerage was vital.

Just two days before the grand opening, my father told me the story of how he walked home, a broken man after the 1967 war. Together we marveled at the fact that just twenty years later, he was walking those same roads as a man of wealth and influence. He changed his way with Allah, and his life changed accordingly. The evidence was undeniable.

In the days leading up to the grand opening, it was not unusual to see a line of people snaking around the building hoping to get employment or to enroll their children. On my dad's birthday, May 25, 1987, the school and mosque opened. This gift to the community offered hope that other children would be blessed as he was blessed. The educational component was important since his father was a teacher. More importantly, he wanted to provide an Islamic foundation for all Muslims. He was building himself a castle in heaven. The Quran gave him reason to hope: "Whoever builds a mosque for Allah, Allah will build for him a castle in Paradise."[8]

Dad eventually opened a total of nine schools and three mosques. Keeping a mental record of Dad's accomplishments was important to me because Allah promised wealth and success if I obeyed him. I learned that when an individual submitted himself totally to Allah, he would provide, and my dad was a great example. I believed the way my dad and I honored Allah was the proper way. At the time, no one could shake that conviction.

THE WAR IN AFGHANISTAN AWAKENS A GIANT

For nearly sixty years, many Muslims were religious in name only and allowed the faith to be buried under mounds of Western and Communist ideas. In 1973, however, Sadat's Yom Kippur War put the concept of jihad back into the minds of Muslims, and six years later the war between Afghanistan and Russia gave many of us, me included, the opportunity to exercise our obligations as a Muslim in service to the Islamic state. If Sadat gave Islam a nudge, Afghanistan awakened the giant!

Jihad is not an intrinsic act of aggression or violence. It is a ritualistic act calling upon Muslim men to fulfill Mohamed's prophesies and Allah's mission. Since the day jihad was first ordered by Mohamed, it has always been guided by strict rules and regulations. One major rule was no Muslim could go off and wage jihad without Mohamed's approval. That authority passed to his successor after his death and to successive caliphs after that.

In AD 711 Tariq ibn Ziyad waged war on his own without waiting for the approval of the caliph. He conquered parts of Europe all the way to the borders of France. Upon his return to the caliph, proud of the great lands he conquered, ibn Ziyad was expecting to be celebrated. Instead, the caliph threw him in jail.

When Sadat made the call of jihad in 1973, he was not adhering to Islamic protocol. His rationale was there was no longer an

Islamic caliph after the last one was abolished in 1924. He also justified his calling for jihad because he was the president of a Muslim nation about to fight the mortal enemies of Islam. The goal was to recapture a land originally conquered by Islam years before. Another argument he advanced was all Muslim countries and territories would be involved in the war. The Saudis, the Pakistanis, Libyans, Syrians, and many more sent troops to fight at his side.

After the war, however, when Sadat entered peace talks with the Jews without the approval of the rest of the Muslim world, he was deemed a traitor. In the mind of many Muslims, he betrayed Islam and committed apostasy. All Muslim nations turned their backs on Sadat, and later he was killed for his actions. By issuing the call of jihad in 1973, however, Sadat set a precedent in Islamic jurisprudence. Henceforward, a Muslim king or president could issue a legitimate call for jihad.

Ten years later a new era dawned. A war in Afghanistan broke out between the Muslims and the Soviets. At first, Muslim men were reluctant to join in the fight because it did not meet all the necessary requirements to be considered a legitimate jihad or holy war. For one, no caliph or designated leader issued the call. For another, no official Islamic military forces were participating, only militias and sporadic fighting groups.

Afghan Muslims were not sure their martyrdom would be rewarded by Allah. But when the Islamic Jurors of Egypt and the Grand Jurist of Saudi Arabia issued fatwas, the jihad in Afghanistan became legitimate. Those decrees changed everything, not only for that war, but for years to come. These fatwas opened the door for jihad by Muslim men all over the world without waiting for a declaration from a caliph or even a political leader.

I could see the change. People who practiced all types of debauchery suddenly became devout and left to go to jihad. Many Muslims who went to fight came back and told the people about the war. Eyes were opened at the sight of victory, and those victories inspired more and more people to jihad. A fire was starting in the hearts of Muslims with a momentum that seemed to have no limits.

CIVILIZATION JIHAD AT HOME

Disinclined to fight, I still wanted to answer the call to jihad. I decided to exercise civilization jihad by collecting money to support the war effort. Everyone was called to support the fighters, the *mujahideen*, and I was happy to answer the call. On nearly every street corner, people were collecting money and items to sell for cash, and trucks canvassed the neighborhoods to gather donated goods.

My mom and her sisters managed to hold onto a number of personal items following the deaths of their parents. I believed the clothes, jewelry, silver, and furniture gathering dust could serve a better purpose as a funding source for Allah. These objects had a sentimental value for them, but shortening their time in hell would mean a whole lot more.

I carefully determined how to broach the subject with Mom first and then with the rest of her sisters. I then went in to plead my case. "Grandmother died and I loved her so much," I said. "But her clothes and things are collecting dust and nobody is ever going to use them." Not sure this was persuasive enough, I added, "Do you want her to spend more time in hell paying for her sins? Selling her things will earn her rewards. By giving this stuff to the cause of jihad, it will lessen her time in hell and make that time less painful. Allah will reward her and forgive her sins even now."

The reminder about the grave and hell did the trick. My mother and her sisters let go of all of those meaningful items in the hope of redeeming their parents. I started seeing real signs of an Islamic awakening in her sisters and her family. As for me, I satisfied my goal of contributing something of substance to the battle for the Islamic State.

THE MUKHABARAT CONNECTION (EGYPT'S MILITARY INTELLIGENCE)

There is no better place to understand what is really going on in Egypt, in the Muslim world, and globally for that matter than to have full access to privileged intelligence from a well-organized, highly trained organization such as the Egyptian Intelligence Directorate, the *Mukhabarat*. In the beginning, the Mukhabarat mimicked the organization of Hitler's intelligence arm. Later, the KGB trained and officially organized the Mukhabarat for more than twenty years. When the Soviets were driven out, the Mukhabarat turned completely to the CIA for methods, tools, and support. Egypt was a friend of all, and enemy of all.

The Mukhabarat participated in the pilgrimage to Saudi Arabia since the ruse of 1973. My dad was part of that ruse. Starting in 1975 he became the Mukhabarat's spiritual leader. He handled the pilgrimage branch of the Mukhabarat for years to come with full access to the information flowing through the agency. My father filtered that information through a critical eye and then passed it down to me for discussion on a daily basis. I was his Mini-Me, his closest confidant. He and I routinely stopped by the central command of the Egyptian military to discuss life, Islam, politics, and many other things. Even when I did not go with him, he shared that day's information with me, and we analyzed every bit of it.

A CLOSE ENCOUNTER WITH AL QAIDA

About that same time, I had an encounter with a man named Ayman al-Zawahiri. Released from jail by the direct orders of Hosni Mubarak, he was imprisoned for his involvement in the assassination of Anwar Sadat a few years earlier. His release order dictated he leave Egypt and find a new home. His plan was to secure a job as a physician at one of the hospitals in Saudi Arabia. Or so he said. He was about to leave for that job the day we met. His public stance was he was not going to answer the call for jihad in Afghanistan. Rather he would pursue his career in medicine and continue preaching the pure word of Allah outside the battlefield. That never happened. After his arrival in Saudi Arabia, he met with Osama bin Laden at the Grand Mosque in Mecca and was joined there by Abdullah Yusuf Azzam.

Osama bin Laden was a very wealthy young man from a very famous family and an heir to the bin Laden construction company.

The deeply dissatisfied bin Laden held a grudge against his older brothers and the Saudi royal family at large. He spoke to al-Zawahiri and Azzam about the Sadat assassination and Sadat's work with America and Israel. The three also discussed the 1975 assassination of King Faisal of Saudi Arabia. His assassin was an American-educated nephew who had just returned from the United States. Many believed the assassination was orchestrated by the CIA because of King Faisal's very effective oil embargo against the West and America in 1973. His opposition to American-led peace talks between Islamic countries and Israel further estranged him from United States.

Bin Laden was in despair. He perceived the assassination as a betrayal of Islam. On a personal level, Osama was angry at his family. Many of his older half-brothers looked down on him because his own mother, Syrian by background, was not from a Saudi royal family. Nor was she a devout Muslim. Osama also resented the ongoing affiliation of his brothers with the United States, a relationship culminating in their mutual involvement in ending the 1979 mosque siege in Mecca. The fact Osama lost a brother and a cousin during that siege further alienated him.

Smart and soft-spoken, al-Zawahiri was able to seize the moment. Together with Azzam and bin Laden, he pledged to leave everything behind and answer the call of jihad in Afghanistan. These three formed the "base"—in Arabic, *al Qaida*—from which they and their fellow jihadis would defeat the Soviets and create a pure and new Islamic state. In the process, they would rid the Muslim world of its traitorous leaders. Al Qaida would then annihilate Israel and eventually defeat the West and the United States. Just as Mohamed built his base in Medina and from there conquered the world, they would do the same.

About that time, I attended a large wedding of an affluent and influential family, and many members of the al-Zawahiri family were there. My dad knew his father, Dr. Muhammed Rabie al-Zawahiri. He was one of Dad's mentors in medical school. In the middle of this particular wedding celebration, the afternoon call to prayer was issued. Many celebrants opted to catch up during the next call to prayer, but the more faithful Muslims pulled away to pray right then. My dad and I, along with a handful of others, left the room in search of a place to wash and pray.

Al-Zawahiri was among those who left with us. We removed our suit jackets, shoes, socks, and jewelry, washed, and entered a carpeted room to pray. It was then al-Zawahiri spoke up and suggested he lead the prayer. Others naturally chose my father. Why al-Zawahiri thought he deserved that honor was beyond me.

When the prayers were concluded, each of us greeted our brothers with a handshake and an expression of hope that Allah would receive our prayers as customary. As al-Zawahiri took my hand, he asked, "Where do you go to school?" When I answered, "The English School," he tightened his grip and began to challenge me. This was odd as he too seemed to have received a Western-inspired education given he spoke perfect English.

"Is this how you shake the hands of the girls at your English School?" he asked me.

"No," I said, shocked by his accusation. "I do not shake the hands of the girls at school."

"Do you lust after the girls with their short skirts and tight shirts?" he continued. Again, I denied his accusations. He continued, "Getting close to the sin is the same as committing the sin itself."

Al-Zawahiri could have been angry at being denied the opportunity to lead the prayers. Or he might have been appalled by my fancy suit. Whatever the reason, he was determined to get under my skin. He had a lot of nerve to instruct me in what Allah required. I had the best teachers in the Middle East, and he knew it. He was simply looking for a gap in my soul.

To encourage obedience to Allah and fidelity to Islam, Muslims routinely shame one another to show how naked we are in the light of full obedience and enslavement to Allah. This was a particularly effective strategy in recruiting foot soldiers. Men like al-Zawahiri were always on the lookout for broken souls willing to die as martyrs to assuage their guilt. For many, martyrdom was the *only* path to absolution. Had I been less well-schooled, in Islam, my encounter with al-Zawahiri would have fit this pattern perfectly. Once a man like al-Zawahiri reduced an unschooled young Muslim to a state of complete despair, he would show the recruit how violent jihad provided a path to make peace with Allah.

In the video footage shown of the 9-11 hijackers one detail stands out. None of these men who were about to perform jihad and die as martyrs looked angry. Rather, they seemed focused and relieved they were about to be forgiven for all their sins, receive their rewards of heaven, and make eternal peace with Allah.

For all his efforts, al-Zawahiri had no effect on me. I was conscious of the temptations I faced, but I was willing to do the hard work, the heavy lifting, to resist them. I was secure in doing everything in my power to be a good Muslim, just like my father, and I had plans to be a jihadi of a different sort: I would equip myself to convince the masses of the Prophet Mohamed's legitimacy and Islam's exclusive path to Allah and heaven.

Deep inside I knew I wasn't blessed with the innate aggression and fighting skills of a warrior. But I also knew jihad in the battlefield was the only form of jihad worthy of the rewards of martyrdom. So I knew if I were obligated to fight for the kingdom of Allah, I would answer the call. Otherwise I would be condemned just like those men who refused to answer Mohamed's call. Quran 9:39 tells us if you do not answer the call to jihad and you do not mobilize with the troops, Allah will punish you with an extremely painful punishment. He will replace you with someone else. Your lack of action will not harm Allah but will harm you because he is all powerful.

If Al-Zawahiri did not succeed in piercing my soul, he did cause me to take inventory of the influences around me at school and to continue to guard my heart. This was to be a full-time job.

CHAPTER 11

OF SUMMITS, TRAINS, AND SWORDS

But when the forbidden months are past, then fight and slay the Pagans wherever ye find them, and seize them, beleaguer them, and lie in wait for them in every stratagem but if they repent, and establish regular prayers and practice regular charity, then open the way for them: for Allah is Oft-forgiving, Most Merciful.

—Quran 9:5

Looking back at my childhood and youth, my upbringing and life experience was not normal. So when I was a fifteen-year-old boy, and was offered this opportunity to go to Mecca one more time, for pilgrimage, not only as a worshiper but as a guide, and a leader, I was following in line with my past experiences.

I did not allow myself the mindless teenage activities others enjoyed. I had a clear goal in mind, becoming a doctor and an Islamic spiritual leader. So I strived to make excellent grades in the English School and finished middle school with a solid A.

Simultaneously, I continued attending my Islamic school during the weekends and the summer, working hard to excel in my Quranic studies. I continued on my path to memorize the Quran, one chapter at a time, and I was studying Islamic theology and religious law with remarkable teachers and imams.

I remember one incident when my Islamic school sponsored a national competition, and I made the school team. The competition was a really big deal. Proud parents beamed as I and other students underwent vigorous questioning on Quranic memorization, recitation, Islamic jurisprudence, and sharia law. The contest was intimidating, but I managed to win first place in two categories and earn third place in the overall competition. I will never forget the look on my father's face when I received my award. He was so proud of the man I was becoming.

My hunger for information and studying Islamic teachings was stoked and I was no longer satisfied with the sporadic chances I was afforded to learn about my faith. I needed more. I suggested to my father to clear one room in our house and make it into an Islamic library. I told him it will be a great place for him to sit in reclusion, surrounded by all his resources and books. I told him it would be a perfect place for him to prepare for his Islamic lessons as well as his weekly preaching. I encouraged him to start and organize his own library we could continuously add to, and of course I would be using it regularly.

After the library was assembled and furnished nicely, another idea was sparked. A professional video, a documentary of sorts, would be created illustrating the steps, the rules, and the regulations of the pilgrimage. It would complement the books my father already wrote on the subject and would add a visual dimension, taking advantage of the latest technology, the VCR.

When it was time to recruit the talent to be featured in the documentary and reenact the steps of the pilgrims, I was the best candidate with my vast knowledge and, of course, as my mother said, the best looking one as well. It was clear to us both my dreams of being an Islamic authority and a physician were within reach. As long as I remained focused, I was sure I would have a good life ahead of me.

Throughout the years, I traveled to Mecca numerous times with my dad to perform the hajj and the umrah. I was delighted to go whenever the opportunity presented itself. The experience never got stale. Every time I went, I hoped to get closer to Allah, to learn new things, and to reach new heights.

STEPPING UP TO A LEADERSHIP ROLE

The summer of 1986 will stay with me as the most memorable experience of them all. It gave me an extraordinary opportunity. Since l reached puberty a few years earlier, I was fully accountable for all my deeds to Allah. The Islamic rituals were obligatory and would be fully rewarded. When it came to pilgrimage, if I paid for it with my own money I would be truly fulfilled in the eyes of Allah.

As a reward for all of my hard work, my father offered me another opportunity to go on pilgrimage with him. He told me I would pay for it with my own money. "But I do not have that kind of money to pay my own way. I do not have a job yet," I said. He said, "You will be working as a spiritual guide to the group, and for your time and efforts you will be paid to cover all the expenses, and you will get some extra after you get back."

He appointed me his right-hand man for the fifteen-day pilgrimage. During the past few years, my father led military groups to Mecca. It became his passion and the spearhead of his Islamic leadership. Private tourist companies jumped on the new lucrative spiritual business, still under the direction of the military intelligence agency, to benefit from its influence and long reach. They were now offering pilgrimage opportunities to a wider range of people. Among these people were some of the more affluent members of Egyptian society.

Travel between countries in the Middle East was strictly choreographed. Politics was at the center of everything. If Saudi Arabia was at odds with another Muslim nation, which happened often with the rollercoaster of ever-changing geopolitical spectrum in the Muslim world, the Saudis would simply deny those citizens travel permits. Securing permits required proper procedures and a little finesse. For that reason, Egyptian military intelligence was well equipped to negotiate the process.

It was no surprise intelligence veterans started private companies offering civilian travel or were recruited by the already existing travel companies wanting to embark on the pilgrimage business. My father was moving into a new role consulting and leading the spiritual aspect of these travel groups. Dad was a prize in their crown, and they immediately snagged him as one of their prime leaders for hajj. He soon became the most sought-after teacher for rich and famous travelers and was able to dictate his terms.

Dad was, after all, the most knowledgeable and authoritative teacher in Egypt at the time. He was particularly famous for leading deeply passionate prayers on Mt. Arafat, the epicenter of the pilgrimage component. Mt. Arafat was the site of the Prophet's final message, a place of great Islamic significance and the highlight of the pilgrimage experience. From this extraordinary site, Mohamed called for unity of all Muslims despite racial differences, established our superiority over all races and backgrounds for being Muslims, bade us to act mercifully to one another and to show no mercy to those who rejected the faith.

From this rocky hillside, millions of pilgrims have called out to Allah to forgive their sins. For the pilgrim it is the quintessential moment. All other rituals pale in comparison. Such a moment can only be entrusted to the most revered, most sincere, most experienced of all spiritual leaders. And no one was more revered or experienced than my father.

I was shocked to my core when he suggested a new plan for this particular trip. "This year, I would like to try something different, and I believe you are ready for this responsibility," my dad explained. "I would like to lead the group from Golden Tours. The group is having some very high-profile individuals, and they asked me to pay more attention to their group, and to do that I will put you in my place with the military contingent."

"How is that possible?" I asked nervously. "I am not in the military and I'm still just a kid! Will they even respect me?" I had just turned fifteen. I was not at all sure I could pull it off.

"I will work out the details," my father assured me. "You are theologically equipped for this. You are ready, and I will be there for you if you need anything." His plan was unprecedented. My heart dropped into my stomach. I could barely comprehend what he was telling me. Although lacking confidence, I knew by heart everything required of me, having assisted my father so many times in the past. I knew every word of my father's pilgrimage preparation classes. I could easily

Mark in Mecca.

impart the information to my group without hesitation. I knew when, where, and how to pass out the packets of materials the pilgrims needed. I agreed to step into the role he believed I was ready to assume.

My father and I, though still a team, flew over with our respective groups—my father with the Golden Tours group in first-class a day or two earlier than me. I followed with the military group. His lodging was in a five-star hotel just outside the mosque. Mine was a little farther out, and we slept four men to a room. The room was modified with mattresses on the floor to accommodate the extra occupancies.

I was a little shy and hesitant in the beginning but quickly assumed my role and started leading. In the end, I was doing pilgrimage as usual. I was not one to cut corners or perform rituals half-heartedly. I had a particularly strong aversion to the practice of paying to slaughter a lamb. Many pilgrims, at least those who could afford it, would slaughter a lamb as a sacrifice in order to be relieved of some required rituals and steps. I didn't want to spend the extra money to slaughter the lamb, but more importantly, I did not want to skip anything. It was important for me to do everything as Mohamed required. That was my personal conviction, and it made an impression on the other worshipers in my group.

My hair was unkempt, but since losing a single hair was forbidden, I dared not trouble myself with it. My wraps became more and more soiled—a drop of orange juice here, dirt and grime there. It was of no consequence to me. My focus was on Allah, alone, and I embraced the perfect pilgrimage by doing everything to the letter. I arrived for prayers early and stayed late. I meditated outside the Kaaba. I rarely took time to eat. I made myself available to answer questions and provide spiritual direction.

That pilgrimage was of great significance to me. The day for the pilgrimage to camp on Mt. Arafat was August 15, 1986, "a Friday," just as it was for Mohamed when he performed the ritual of pilgrimage and gave his last and famous farewell sermon. Mohamed performed the pilgrimage ritual only once and that was it. That first year the day fell on a Friday, which meant something special for every pilgrim in attendance. This one day was the equivalent of performing seventy pilgrimages, as the prophet Mohamed instructed.

As the days passed, I began to feel confident in my abilities. That said, I knew I would not have to carry the responsibility of leadership alone. My dad and I worked out a plan for him to lead his own group most of the time, but he would occasionally join our group to take some of the pressure off my shoulders, show his presence, and legitimize my leadership position.

As we camped on Mt. Arafat, the time came to pay homage to Allah; it was the hour before sunset. We all got up and joined in a plea for Allah to bestow his mercy on us all. I believed, as Mohamed instructed us, Allah would speak at the pilgrimage as he watched his faithful slaves pour their hearts and souls out, begging for his mercy. I was filled with great anticipation but also with fear. I was trying to prove myself as a budding leader and prove to Allah I was a slave most worthy of his mercy and forgiveness. This was a dream only true martyrs could achieve.

I led my group up the hillside and took a position on a large rock. With two thousand men and women behind me, I looked up to heaven and called out to Allah, pleading the case for me and all my fellow Muslims. My mind was fixed on my mother, and the words coming from my mouth flowed right from my heart. I pleaded with Allah to have mercy on us on the Day of Judgment for the heavy weight and consequences of our sins, to give us the strength and means to repent, to help us make up for all our missing prayers, and the failures at fasting on the required days, and to give us the strength to repay all our debts to him. Our sins are limitless because our obligations and rituals are many. The best slave to Allah knows he will always fall short of what is expected from him by Allah.

A chorus of "Amens" rose from the worshipers behind me. As my tears began to flow, so did those of every man and woman within earshot. I spoke to Allah about the grave and the fact we would all go there someday. I cried out for his mercy. I asked that he grant us a reprieve from hell's fury. I recited a special prayer Mohamed used regularly as a reminder of the crushing horrors of the grave, pleading with Allah to have mercy on us while we are under the heaps of dirt and sand, being devoured by flies, and ground worms, alone in despair. That prayer puts the wrath of Allah to a different level and reminds us of our fate of death and facing him on the Day of Judgment. The strongest men burst into tears when they hear or pray that prayer which sparks a sincere urgency for repentance. I asked Allah to unite us as Muslims and make us supreme over all mankind. "Amen" rang out over and over as I touched on the sins of humanity. I earnestly beseeched Allah to forgive us of all our sins.

My father arrived at some point during that hour, but I scarcely took notice. I had transcended the earthly plane and was lost in a spiritual moment. Dad touched my shoulder, led the prayers for roughly ten minutes, and then stepped away to allow me to conclude. When the hour was completed, I had emptied my soul on the side of Mt. Arafat. The pilgrims in my group did the same.

Fighting for eternity as we were, for the hope of being forgiven, we gave it everything we had. We could do no less. And then we were finished. Nothing more could be said. Nothing more could be done. It was only one hour after all, and, as Quran 14:42 reminds us, master Allah is forever the ultimate judge, and his wrath has no limits.

I wish I could say the pilgrims walked away knowing they achieved Allah's forgiveness. There is a huge difference between the assurance of forgiveness, and the hope to be forgiven. Waiting for the verdict literally takes a lifetime because it will only be at the Day of Judgment when our fate is declared. Living a life of anticipation and working hard, begging hard, fighting hard is all we can do.

It was agonizing to see many of my fellow Muslims boarding the plane to Mecca, investing a great deal of wealth and effort in the hope of being forgiven for their past sins, hanging on the broad brush of statements about the forgiveness that pilgrimage will offer, only to see their souls crushed after they become aware of the fine print. In truth, they leave knowing only they begged for forgiveness. Afterward, they would just have to continue keeping the faith. There was no assurance. It was like going to say goodbye to a beloved family member at the graveside, saddened by their departure but pained to think about the huge burden they had to pay to get straight with Allah. In Islam, there was always more work to be done. According to Quran 6:162–164, *"Indeed, our prayer, our rites of sacrifice, our life and our death are all for Allah. And when we die and return to Allah, he will only then inform us if our work was acceptable or not and our eternal fate."*

Leading the prayer on Mount Arafat, I knew, was an important role. I met the challenge boldly. Even in the midst of my tears I began to claim the status to which I felt entitled. I was strong, emboldened, and deserving of this honor. My father always talked to me as if I were a man, even though he and I both knew I was anything but. On this day, though, I became a man, equal on every level with the man whose approval I always sought.

At the conclusion of the Mt. Arafat rituals, I was simultaneously exhilarated and drained. Our fellow pilgrims immediately started heading toward the buses that would take them to the next rite location and accommodations, but Dad and I opted to remain behind and walk instead. The Prophet Mohamed walked so we would do the same, adamant not to take advantage of any modern technology or luxury.

Sitting on an air-conditioned bus after a long day in August in Saudi Arabia sounds like heaven, but it is a short-lived heaven. We only aspire to an eternal heaven, and nothing will get us there except trying our best to follow in the footsteps of prophet Mohamed. With nearly three million men and women sitting on hundreds of buses, it would be some time before the area around Mt. Arafat was totally cleared. At that rate, we knew we could rest awhile, walk the distance, and still beat many of them back to our destination.

Dad was tired and told me so. I realized I should give him a chance to rest, but I was excited beyond description. Within minutes of sitting down, Dad was asleep. I was thankful for the opportunity to sit for just a couple hours and reflect on everything that took place thus far in the pilgrimage. I watched as throngs of people descended the mountain, their tear-stained faces reflecting weariness and a hope that, somehow, Allah heard their pleas.

I thought about the woman in my group who came to me for hope. "I promised Allah that if he will heal my son, I would give him two thousand dollars. But I don't have it. Will Allah forgive me for that?" she asked me.

"You must pay that money," I advised. "You must always honor your promises before Allah. By making that promise to Allah you made it an obligation on yourself and Allah will severely punish you if you don't fulfill your promise to him."

I also considered the woman who asked me how to deal with her husband taking another wife. "You must get all jealousy out of your heart and support your husband and his other wife. You must not question what Allah has ordained and made lawful."

I sounded so much like my father. In many ways, though, I believed I surpassed him. My tears were a genuine expression of my devotion to Allah. My pleas were impassioned, desperate, and breathless. Dad, on the other hand, seemed distracted by fulfilling his duties and promises to different groups, and trying to be in many places at the same time. I was concerned for him not being fully invested and submissive to Allah and that he had to work at producing his tears. He was going through the motions rather than storming heaven with the urgency of a person desperate to avoid hell.

Contemplating whether to raise my concerns with him or not, I figured obedience to Allah is the highest aspiration, I recalled also his words to me in the dark room when he was beating me into the obedience of Allah, instructing me in how I should have corrected my mother and not follow her to the movie theatre. I made my choice, I told him so when he awoke. "Dad," I said, "it seems like you have too much going on to get focused." For the first time in my life I was judging him. The competitive juices stirred within me. The fact he didn't correct me sent a clear signal he knew I was a man. "You did a good job, son," he said. "You prayed, and I hope the angels heard your prayer and reported it to Allah. Many people see the potential you have to be a great leader. You're also building relationships that will be important for your future."

Had Allah not ordained that I should lead the prayers, I never would have. But he did, in this most holy hour, in the most holy place. I never thought, though, that leading pilgrimages would be my special ministry. That was my dad's. And even though I succeeded, my spiritual goals went well beyond this task. I had very specific gifts, and they were different from my father's. Wherever Allah ultimately directed me, I wanted to be his best slave. I just needed for him to designate my field of battle.

ALLAH'S REWARD

My return from that trip was unlike any other. Within days I was receiving invitations from important people. First, my father received word the head of the military forces in the south, a man who shared my accommodations in Mecca, wanted to host us for a tour of his area. He flew us into Luxor, provided housing in one of Sadat's former presidential retreats, and showed us the sites. We were treated to amazing dinners and traveled everywhere in an impressive motorcade. It occurred to me this was the beginning of something awesome in my own life. I saw it in my dad's role, but now it was my turn.

Another high-ranking officer wanted to show his appreciation for my service by inviting us to dine at a country club under his command on the Nile. Dad was right—I was getting noticed. I made military brass weep on Mt. Arafat, and the doors of mercy were opening. Allah was pouring out his blessings.

This, I was convinced, was just a glimpse into Allah's plan for my life. My mission field was about to come into full view.

Not long after the pilgrimage, Dad started talking to me about his plans for the future. He was weary of his service at the military hospital. He felt constrained by the strict boundaries on his preaching imposed on him by President Mubarak and other seculars within the military. He wanted to be free from worry that his preaching could damage his medical career. His passion to preach Islam and to bring more nominal Muslims into true devotion burned brighter than ever, and he wanted to continue leading the pilgrimage.

At the same time, he hoped to expand his medical practice. He had very real concerns, however, about how separation from Al Maadi Military Hospital would affect the scope of his patient care. We discussed his options for hours on end, bouncing ideas off one another. Once he was assured his role as spiritual leader of the hajj was secure for life, he was ready to announce his retirement from military service.

The second step in his plan involved expanding his medical clinic and offering services never before available in Egypt. With his own money, he purchased an ultrasound machine to set up in his private clinic. Even more, though, he wanted to offer his patients laparoscopic surgery, otherwise unavailable at that time in Egypt.

Never one to run from a challenge, my dad partnered with a local businessman and together they opened a hospital and outfitted it with state-of-the-art equipment. It was a great business plan firmly establishing my dad as a pioneer in the country. He offered up-to-date medical care in line with what Europe was practicing at the time in the field of female medicine, while at the same time serving as a Muslim leader and preacher to the core.

THE MEETING ON THE TRAIN CHANGED EVERYTHING!

Late in 1986, my father made a trip to Amsterdam to receive specialized training to operate the new medical equipment he purchased. Visiting Europe and the West was not a regular event. He was going outside the borders of the Muslim world and crossing into Christendom. Even though the Islamic empire was dissolved by the fall of the caliphate system in 1924, in the hearts and minds of all Muslims the empire is still alive and well. There will always be the Muslim world and the "other." Muslims live everyday with the hope our Islamic empire and world will once again leave our imagination and find its place on the world map—united, vibrant, and victorious, better than ever.

I also was very clear with my dad that he had to buy me authentic, top-of-the-line Adidas soccer cleats, as well as some sports outfits and the jerseys for my favorite European soccer teams. When he returned from the trip, as was customary after major events, he and I and my uncle met to contemplate and reflect. He discussed all he saw and experienced. I listened wide-eyed as he detailed the amazing medical advances in Europe. He also talked about the orderliness, the work ethic, the respect for human dignity, the conspicuous wealth, the tidy, clean, and organized streets as well as the carefree culture and lack of morality.

"But there are less than ten mosques in the whole country," he said of the Netherlands. "They barely know anything about Islam. They are totally and completely morally bankrupt." He told us about neighborhoods in Amsterdam where women were literally framed in windows and prostituted. He described drunkenness and other immoral behavior in the streets. "They are a godless people," he concluded.

That statement alone snapped me to attention. They needed to know Allah and his Prophet. Someone needed to take Islam to the West. As I considered that thought, Dad started telling us about an excursion he took to Brussels. Before I could inquire why he went there, he told me about an encounter he had on the train.

Dad said when it was time to pray, he stood, quietly made the call to prayer, and prayed right there in the aisle. No one stopped him. Knowing my dad, I doubt he would have stopped in any case. I am sure he saw his prayers as a way to spread the word about Allah.

As soon as he took his seat, a European man approached him. "He said he was intrigued by the Middle East and asked where I was from," Dad said. "When I told him Egypt, he replied, 'That is a beautiful country with lots of history. Ancient Egyptians were pioneers in sciences, religion, and astronomy. There is lots of Christian history and unique historical churches and architecture.' "He then boldly asked me, 'Why are you a Muslim?'" My uncle chimed in immediately. "Obviously that man knows a lot about Egypt and the Muslim world. He must have been an Orientalist!" "What is that?" I asked eagerly. I could not imagine any Westerner questioning my father about Islam in such a manner.

"An Orientalist," my uncle began, "is a Western spy, a traitor. Orientalists originated in the sixteenth century when Europe and Christendom were engulfed in the dark ages. They represented a failed system; empty vessels with no spirituality, no emotional barometer, no economic prowess, and no original scientific thought! They were living in a world of black magic and human sacrifice. The Muslim world was ahead of the rest of the world— leading in science, architecture, technology, medicine, and all other areas. Because of their jealousy, the European leaders sent the Orientals to spy and steal our ideas and technology. They kept doing this until Napoleon decided to invade and take over the Middle East. This later paved the way to colonization."

I had never heard this and was fascinated by my uncle's passionate description. "Their Renaissance was due to one thing and one thing only. They stole from Islam. The Prophet was the mercy to humanity and the seal of the prophets. Muslims brought to the world the best religion and the most perfect political system that humanity has ever known."

My uncle was a master of historical thought. His narrative of these historic events was like nothing I had ever heard at the

English School. "The Islamic State flourished, and we enjoyed a golden age for centuries," he told me. "And then a very bad thing happened. We started losing our grasp on the teachings of our Prophet. The West took advantage of us in every way and tried to erase our impact."

My uncle had much more to say. "Once Westerners did that," he continued, "it was a natural progression to crush the Muslim lands. The Europeans' jealousy was their guide. They were thieves who should have paid us or embraced our values. Instead, Muslims fell victim to their snares, helping them steal from our treasures without requiring them to honor our ideals. Allah stopped bestowing on Islamic lands the splendors of the earth."

I had always believed Europeans were living in a bubble of lies, propagated by their own devious leaders. They were blocking the amazing truths of Islam, and that is the only reason, in my mind, most Europeans knew very little about the beauty and the legitimacy of Islam or its history.

"What did the man say to you next?" I inquired.

"He had the audacity to say to me that he thinks Islam is a fake religion, that it is only spread by the sword, and exists today only because of its stern punishment for apostasy," my father answered, practically spitting the words out of his mouth.

I was stunned when my father recounted those words. I had never heard anything like that before and was shocked by the man's boldness. How dare anyone, especially someone outside the faith, say something like that? "What was your answer to him?" I asked. It was my firmly held belief that anyone who heard about Islam would immediately embrace it as the only legitimate faith.

"He was a worthless buffoon, a mule who didn't deserve an answer. The Quran 74:50 mentioned people like him and how to answer them. Rest assured, son, Allah will take care of them in this life and hereafter, but just for the sake of his argument I told him, "The sword liberates people and exposes them to the truth of Islam, which they willingly embrace when given the opportunity."

That was it? That was my father's answer to this man who was clearly trying to disparage the Prophet Mohamed, and to convert my father to the polytheistic religion of Christianity or get him to turn away from the one true faith? I was so disappointed in my father, a great champion of the faith. When given the opportunity, he failed to answer with authority. I did better than this when talking to my fellow students at my English school.

I went to bed that night with our conversation still ringing in my ears. Perhaps my father wasn't equipped to answer him. Perhaps he wasn't used to being around Europeans and didn't know how to respond to someone outside the Middle East. Maybe his command of the language wasn't strong enough. I didn't know. Or maybe taking Islam to Europe was not his calling. Maybe it would be mine.

MY LIFE GOAL BECOMES CLEAR

I was angry. Mine was a righteous, burning anger that kept me awake all night. I worked through how I would have handled the conversation if I were the one sitting across from this man on the train. If given the opportunity, I would meet this challenge head-on. My dad did not envision mosques in Europe. I did. I would build them. Europeans did not know who the true legitimate, seal of the prophet, Mohamed is. I would introduce them.

I would become a doctor and take my practice to Europe. From that home base, I would bring Islam to the Europeans and to the whole of Christendom. I had a newly ignited fire in my soul to spread Islam far and wide. I would have an answer for that European "Orientalist" and any other I met. I would have these answers ready so I could destroy such fools with my superior religious knowledge, historical facts, debates, and arguments.

Often, I saw my dad leave people quaking in their shoes because of his superior knowledge of Islam. I would leave Westerners quaking by proving the legitimacy of Islam scientifically, historically, and theologically. I dreamed of the day I could practice medicine in Europe and bring the continent into submission to the one true faith. The urge to get on with this task overwhelmed me. I needed to step up to this challenge and answer the call. I would be Allah's soldier to the West. First, of course, I had to finish high school.

High school in Egypt is a three-year program, but I couldn't wait to pursue my life goals. So I enrolled into a faster program and worked furiously to make sure I graduated in two years instead, routinely spending sixteen hours a day in study. My upcoming tests would determine everything. It was imperative I ace all of them for one reason: only with a high score would I be allowed to study medicine. Egypt's educational system is set up like a draft. Students who score the highest get first choice on professional schools and can choose to be doctors. Students with slightly lower scores can choose other medical fields such as pharmacy or dentistry. Students below that can choose engineering or law or, if no other option exists, teaching.

I was going to be a doctor. I had no doubt about it. I knew it since I was a little boy playing pretend. Then later, I was there in the operating room with my father during hysterectomies and many other surgeries. I never doubted my abilities. But when I received my test scores, I stared at the posting dumbstruck. I read it again. Maybe I was looking at the wrong score. No, I wasn't. I missed it. I scored a fraction below what I needed to go into medicine.

I was shocked. Perhaps I did it to myself. Maybe I shouldn't have pushed so hard to finish early. I felt so high standing on the rocky hillside of Mt. Arafat, and so low absorbing my failure. I was crushed. If I couldn't be a medical doctor, I couldn't practice in Europe. And if I couldn't practice in Europe, I couldn't take Islam to the Europeans. That fractional difference stole my purpose. I was distraught. I was so obsessed with my dream I had to get it "all or nothing." I didn't even think about what opportunities there would be in dentistry.

THE DEATH OF MY DREAM

My father was disappointed, but he assured me dentistry was a noble profession and I should be proud. Mom was exuberant and couldn't wait to brag about her son who finished high school in only two years and scored among the top students. She called up all of her family and threw a big party with lots of food and celebration. Everyone was happy. Except me. I was a failure. I just wanted to slink over into the corner and hide. It took every bit of resolve I could muster to smile and make pleasantries with the well-wishers.

I spent the next few weeks grieving the death of a dream. Everything I hoped to do for Allah slipped away. My future that looked so bright now looked bleak. No matter. I had to be a doctor. It was in that frame of mind I showed up for my first day of dental school.

The dental school occupied one building among a complex of other medical buildings at Cairo University. I pulled up to the school and almost immediately ran into a person whose existence I tried to ignore, Ramy, the son of my father's second wife.

When I was in the fifth grade, Ramy came into my life. According to Islamic law, it was perfectly acceptable for my dad to take a second wife. At the time, I had no idea what was going on. This woman seemed nice enough and had a couple of kids for me to play with. It never occurred to me dad was in the process of signing marriage documents.

This part of my father's life was kept entirely separate from our own. I often provided cover when he was away from home for extended periods. I believed my mom and her family were not devout Muslims and I was looking down on her. Judging her. So when my dad wanted to take a second wife I was happy for him and I lied to my mother on his behalf. Mohamed told us it is lawful for a man to lie to his wife in the same hadith he says it is lawful to lie to non-Muslims, and my mom fit both categories since she was on many occasions not a fully devout Muslim.

My dad kept his second marriage a secret and only I knew about it. Not that he felt any shame about his second marriage. On the contrary, it was his escape, a welcome respite from my mother and her fragile emotional state. If he even hinted he planned to take another wife, she devolved into fits of hysteria. So Dad adopted a "what she doesn't know won't hurt her" mentality, and

I did nothing to upset the balance of his plan. My presence with him when he visited his second wife was a good ruse so she wouldn't be jealous or suspicious since I was with him.

I only saw Ramy when I occasionally played with him while Dad was visiting his second wife, but we were never friends. His second wife was a widow with two kids from a deceased husband. Ramy was one of them. When I walked into dental school the first day he was there greeting me as if he was my older brother. It was the first time for us to be together in public. He too was a dental student. A few years older, he immediately took his "little brother" under his wing, but I was *not* his little brother. Adding insult to injury, he was using my father's name, among his close friends, laying claim to an identity as my father's oldest son. I hardened my heart to the reality my dad was sharing himself with another family. By passing himself off as the son of my father, Ramy ripped the bandage from that wound. He was stealing my identity, and he wanted my tacit approval for his theft.

I found it increasingly difficult to elude Ramy and his friends. He was fake, and I didn't want to support the lie he was selling. Any time he found me on campus, he hovered around, trying to pull me into his group of friends as if we were buddies, as if we were brothers. Although I never made a scene, he disgusted me. My situation disgusted me. And I was heartsick that my life seemed to be falling apart. Humiliating too was the sight of some of my former English School classmates who made it to the medical school at Cairo University across campus. Their presence was a constant reminder of their success and my failure.

A NEW PLAN

To escape Ramy's suffocating overtures, I occasionally ventured over to the medical school to talk with them. They were kind, cognizant of my misery, and quick to offer advice. They told me if I hadn't spent so much time and effort trying to finish high school early, I could have enrolled in a pre-med program in England. "You could be on your way to being a doctor," they said.

I had no idea there was such an option. For several weeks I plied them with questions about how the process worked. I continued to go to my classes at dental school but began an immediate investigation into finding a way to get into medical school. When I was fully armed with the information, I went to my father.

"If I enroll in a pre-med program in London, the Egyptian Ministry of Education will accept my work there in combination with my high school scores and admit me to the medical program," I told him. He had no idea about this back channel and was intrigued with the idea. That said, he was not sure I was up for the task. He may have been more disappointed about my test scores than he let on.

"You cannot do it. You'll never get into medical school," he said. His words stung. I was not sure whether he was challenging me with a bit of reverse psychology or showing a genuine lack of faith in my abilities. I would never know, but I was determined to prove him wrong.

In retrospect, I believe my dad had a scar on his heart because of his own denied dreams. After his graduation from medical school he took a job as an assistant professor at Cairo University medical school. It is a medical school founded by the British and as was customary he would get extra training in England if he continued in his job, but his plans fell to the wayside in 1966 when fate forced him into the military. England, however, seemed to me a natural progression from my twelve years at the English School. I intended to pick up my dad's dream and see it through to completion by practicing medicine in Europe and taking Islam to the skeptics of the West.

"I have no faith you can do it," Dad told me bluntly. "If you want to enroll in the English pre-med program, I will give you the money, but you must sign a paper saying you will pay it back if you don't succeed." I signed his papers vowing to pay back every dime if I failed because I knew there was no chance I would fail. Then my dad put another obstacle in my way. He said, "I will still not assist you financially until you prove yourself and get all A's in the upcoming mid-semester at the dental school," which I did.

The pre-med program in London was a one-year deal. I decided right away I would knock it out in a semester. Unheard of, yes, impossible, no.

I jumped over all the obstacles Dad put in my way. Now, convinced I was serious, we went to pick up the required study guides for the pre-med program. The program required I begin my studies in Alexandria. My father rented me an apartment while studying and attending classes there. I stayed there for 5 weeks and then I moved to England to go to mandatory classes in London during the last two weeks of the program. I studied like a crazy man. This time I would not let my future slip away. I had no interest in playing the part of Ramy's little brother.

Once I arrived in London, I took up residence with an uncle. He kept an eye on me and made sure I lacked for nothing. Aside from attending classes, I had little chance to check out life in England. I was certainly curious, though, and even my short trip to class revealed a great deal. I found the advances of humankind fascinating. The streets were organized. Traffic was orderly, and the quiet calm of the crowds stood in stark contrast to the manic chaos of downtown Cairo.

Professors spoke to me and treated me with dignity as they did with all their students. These interactions fascinated me because they were nothing like what I was accustomed to in Egypt. Still, although everything looked perfect on the surface, I knew these people were totally lost. Islam made their advancement possible, but they had not embraced its truth. They needed Allah and his law, and someday I would return and share the real source of their success.

I completed the program in January 1989. It took me just one semester, and my scores would ultimately earn my admission to medical school. I was anxious to get back to Cairo and set my life plan in motion, but I felt a sense of melancholy on my departure. As the plane soared into the skies over Heathrow Airport, I looked down onto the city below. "I will be back. I will be back to give you the truth," I said, my resolve strong.

ACCEPTANCE TO MEDICAL SCHOOL

Once I was accepted to medical school, beginning in October 1990, I stopped attending dental school altogether. There was no need to waste any more time there dodging Ramy and his friends. In that he already considered me a fellow doctor, my dad and I grew even closer during the time between schools. Everything changed, and pride overtook my misery. Life was good again.

I got a new car, and I relished the freedom it gave me. I also had an amazing opportunity to move into my own apartment. In Egypt, it was unheard of for a student to have a home of his own in the late 1980s. The country had a dismal infrastructure, over-populated cities, and chronic economic problems. I also found ways to support myself. I played semi-professional soccer from which I earned a stipend.

In a post-Communist market simple goods are not readily available. In light of that, some of my soccer teammates were dealing in car stereos. They got their supplies from those who were fortunate enough to travel outside of Egypt regularly. They then sold those stereos to friends and acquaintances in their circles. I jumped on the opportunity as well. It was very lucrative but I had to examine my dealings in relationship to sharia law and Islam.

I saw no hypocrisy in this investment. The equipment wasn't sinful. Content determined the sin, not the technology. My father and I had stereos in our personal cars. Music may have been forbidden, but blasting the Quran from the speakers was not.

I saved enough money so when the opportunity arose, I became a silent partner in my cousin's parts supply company. My fifteen thousand Egyptian pounds investment brought quick returns. Small business was a new venture in Egypt during this period as capitalism was replacing communism.

TIME TO EQUIP MYSELF FOR BATTLE

The extra time before school began was a tremendous blessing. I used that time to consider how to best arm myself for the battle

Allah so clearly chosen for me. As a Muslim, I never had to question the legitimacy of my faith. When my father punished me for seeing a movie with my mother, I didn't ask why. I knew the Quran told him to do so. I never asked, "Why should I pray five times a day?" or "Why must I fast during Ramadan?" or "Why must I avoid music, theater, and other entertainments?" I knew the answer: Mohamed told us so.

The man on the train changed everything. Although I knew him only through my father's story, he presented me with a challenge. He represented the "other," those people who had no understanding of Islam, the Prophet, or the legitimacy of the faith. Attributing Islam's success to "the sword" was an affront to everything I knew. I began to focus on how I should I respond to men like him who were completely blind. I needed to find a way to help them see the truth.

Despite my deep knowledge of the Quran and Islamic jurisprudence, I felt for the first time I lacked the tools to fulfill this mission. My excellent English skills would be of little use if I did not have irrefutable proof to share. Saying, "You must enslave yourself to Allah," would not persuade a man who has no understanding of Allah. I could not persuade a woman who did not know Mohamed to wear the hijab because Mohamed said she must. Who was Mohamed to her?

When I was at the English School, we studied the lives of the authors whose literature we were preparing to read. The school's instructors firmly believed the best way to understand an author's deeper message was to look beyond the words on the page to the life of the writer. What experiences contributed to the message writers were communicating? What had they endured, suffered, or overcome in their lives?

The library my father and I built at our house held many of the answers I needed. I intended to take full advantage of this time out of school to assess my faith, my history, and my identity as a Muslim from a skeptic's point of view. I had to go back to the beginning to prove Islam was the one true faith, Allah the one true god, and Mohamed the final Prophet. I felt certain I could do this easily. I could not have been more wrong.

CHAPTER 12

THE PROPHET MOHAMED

O Hear me, all of you Christians. You better believe in Mohamed, the Quran and the message of Islam. You have no excuse not to, because he is exactly what has been prophesied in your sacred books. You better believe in him or otherwise I obliterate your faces and turn them towards your backs and curse you the same way I cursed the Jews before. That is a decree from me, Allah, and I, Allah, will always fulfill my decree.

—Quran 4:47

My life was built upon three related truths: Allah is the only god; Mohamed was his final Prophet; and Islam is the only true religion. In addition, I believed in all the prophets before Mohamed from Adam through Noah, Joseph, Moses, David, Solomon, and all the way to Jesus.

I also believed the true message of these prophets was distorted after their deaths. These prophets of old, I was convinced, foretold the last coming of Mohamed to perfect the message of Allah, which is Islam. I believed it was the mission of my Prophet to correct the path of those who distorted the true ancient message. I also believed it was permissible to use force, if necessary, to accomplish the holy mission of righting this wrong.

After Mohamed's death, it became the mission of each generation of Muslims to carry on and illuminate the truth until the Day of Judgment. I spoke this truth every day, and others around me echoed it. Preparing to take this message to non-believers presented a challenge like none I had ever encountered. When my father first told me of his conversation on the train, I thought he would have won any rational man over simply by introducing him to Mohamed and explaining what was at stake if he didn't accept the truth.

I didn't know it then, but that was the beginning of my quest to peel back the layers of Islam. My goal was to convert Christendom and persuade its citizens beyond any doubt that Islam was the one true faith. This "calling," I sensed, would be harder than memorizing the Quran, harder than leading a pilgrimage, harder than abstaining from worldly delights, harder than getting into medical school, much harder, in fact, than anything I had ever undertaken in my young life.

GETTING STARTED

This calling required me to study as I never studied before and to put aside all my preconceived beliefs. What I "knew" to be true was irrelevant if I could not effectively sway a godless audience. Providentially, Allah granted me time to embark on this journey by giving me a reprieve before I began medical school. I would not disappoint Allah by squandering that time. Mohamed, as the Quran says, came to guide all mankind to Allah: *"Say, O mankind, I am the Rasool (Messenger) of Allah to all of you."* In my mind the legitimacy of the prophet Mohamed was self-evident; I just needed to guide mankind to the Prophet and let them know about him.

Frankly, I was cocky enough to think I could handily master the task before me, but it was easy to be cocky when I was comfortable. My comfort did not last long. On a Thursday evening during an unusually cold February, I was in my room—the room

I was born in, my doctor father delivered me there—waiting for my dad to get home from work to prepare his Friday prayer message. It was our comfortable routine, and I never considered a time would come when it would ever be any different.

As soon as I heard his key in the lock, I ran out of my room to our regular meeting place—dad's home office. He was already sitting at his desk, surrounded by the volumes of Islamic texts I so frequently turned to for guidance.

My dad looked up and asked, "Why are you still here?"

"What do you mean?" I asked.

"You have your own house now," he replied. "We acquired it and fully furnished the place. Why haven't you moved in yet?" He was right. I did not know what I was thinking. Guys my age would have killed to have the great set-up I had, let alone the ability to get out from under a parent's constant gaze. Not me. Reluctant to leave the comfort and familiarity of home, I was dragging my feet. My excuse to my father, and to myself, was I just wanted to wait until medical school started. Then I would move. Just not today.

"Mohamed, collect your stuff and go to your new house," my dad said assertively. "If you forget something, you can get it in the morning."

I was stunned but thought I could stall a little longer. "Okay, but first let's prepare for tomorrow's message, and then I'll go." I was hoping it would be too late to leave by the time we finished, and I could sleep once more in my own room. My scheme didn't work. Dad said that since this was a different mosque with a different crowd, he would just give the same message as last Friday. With that, he dismissed me with a promise he would swing by "my house" at 3 a.m. for our walk to the mosque for morning prayer.

My father encouraged me to go enjoy my new house, but I felt as if I had just been disinherited. I shuffled off to my new house and tried to comfort myself with the thought I could always go back home. But there is truth to the saying, "You can never go home again." That cold Thursday evening in February had an air of finality about it. I was literally closing one door and opening another, beyond which, I would soon discover, were adventures, doubts, pain, darkness, lies, and finally truths.

I walked into my house and went directly to my bed. I sat there in the cold darkness, no television or any other entertainments to lift me from my solitude. All were forbidden. It was then I started planning the details of what would be more than a year of "free" time before medical school. I had nothing else to do.

First, I decided to convert one room to use as a gym to get myself in shape and improve my fitness for soccer. I'm glad I had soccer, but it really didn't have a place in my long-term plans. It did, however, provide an income and a welcome respite from endless hours of poring over historical and theological texts to fulfill my primary mission in life—becoming a doctor and an imam to Christendom.

Thankfully, the proximity of my place to my dad's incredible theological library would make it easy for me to fill the hours and days doing research. And even though my dad pushed me out of the house, I still had unlimited access to him and the top Islamic preachers. I doubted there was anyone anywhere who would undertake the task I set for myself, but I knew, beyond a doubt, I had the world's best resources to call upon.

I also had an area set aside in my house I planned to use as my own study office. It was already furnished with top-notch medical executive office furniture the previous occupant left behind. Until school started, it would serve as my Islamic studies area.

Sleep never came that first night. As the hours ticked slowly by, I managed to work out, at least to my satisfaction, the details of my personal and professional life. Then my thoughts returned to my father's encounter on the train. My dad disappointed me. I would do better. I would be fully equipped to bring Islam to the European people the way in which my Prophet, whose name I shared, required.

I would be speaking to Christians, Jews, and all manner of doubters, but history and the various proofs of Islam would be on my side. I grew so excited I finally gave up on sleep altogether and jumped out of bed. I quickly located a stack of notebooks I placed in my fancy new office and determined to use them to record the evidence of my research. Perhaps my discoveries would one day find their way into the pages of my first Islamic book. That book in turn would launch an Islamic writing career that would rival or surpass my father's.

My thoughts were interrupted by my father's knock at the door. We hurried along to the mosque for morning prayers. Once there, I took my place at the microphone and blasted the call to prayer throughout the neighborhood, my voice still showing the effects of hormonal changes. As I screeched out my chant in praise of Allah, I imagined myself soon offering up the same call to prayer in England.

Later that day, I recorded my first research note: when Mohamed delivered his message to the multitudes, they fell to their knees and believed him. Only those egoists driven by greed or jealousy rejected his legitimate message. That seemed a simple enough concept to impart. Beyond that, though, I wanted to enlighten the non-believers with a story about another man who was once a skeptic, Umar.

UMAR

Every Muslim knows the story, and in my mind, Umar's conversion powerfully affirmed my belief in Mohamed's prophethood. My father should have used this story to persuade the man on the train. He did not, though, and I decided to dig deeper to try to figure out why.

Umar was a doubter and a hostile one at that. He was a constant traveler to places like Constantinople in Turkey, Egypt, and what is now Europe. He was considered a learned man and a great student of governmental systems. He was fascinated by history and the geopolitical movements of empires. Upon returning to his home in Mecca, he heard about Mohamed, who was then an obscure man and not of great significance.

All of a sudden, however, Umar saw how Mohamed's preaching about a new religion was making him increasingly popular. Mohamed claimed, in fact, he was receiving revelations from the only true God, delivered to him by the angels. I am sure Umar encountered plenty of people who fancied themselves teachers, but Mohamed was different. Whenever Mohamed spoke, he kindled unrest among the people. Umar didn't care about what Mohamed was preaching, but then he learned about the civil unrest Mohamed was creating in their city by encouraging slaves to rebel against their masters if their masters didn't convert to Islam as they did. Not liking what he was hearing, Umar decided very quickly he would eliminate the messenger and the message by chopping off Mohamed's head.

Umar never stopped to wonder whether Mohamed was a man of means and if he might have to worry about retaliation. Mohamed did not seem worthy of concern. When Umar told others of his impromptu plan, he learned his own sister had turned to Mohamed. That revelation further stoked his anger. She was dishonoring him and their esteemed family by her actions, and he sought out his sister to punish her for following this troublemaker. Umar was so angry at her he started beating her.

As she lay bloody on the ground, she pleaded with him to just listen to her for a minute before he took her life. She then shared some key verses from the Quran with him, verses allegedly affirming the legitimacy of Mohamed. In that moment, Umar's anger cooled, and his rage yielded to a vow to follow Mohamed.

PREPARING FOR THE BATTLEFIELD

How could anyone not be inspired by that story? I was disappointed my dad, a giant of the faith, hadn't taken the same course of action as Umar's sister. My dad was weaker than a woman, and that thought shook me. My father should have overwhelmed the man on the train with the power of the Quran. I was certain anybody who heard the truth of Islam and the story of Mohamed had no choice but to submit immediately and start a new life as a Muslim.

I had to admit, though, conversion would not be quite that simple. My message had to be irrefutable. It had to help the infidel understand beyond the shadow of doubt that Mohamed was the final Prophet, the answer to questions of life and afterlife he didn't even know he was looking for. I had to think this through. My approach would need to be scientific and methodical. I needed airtight arguments before I went abroad again. Without them, I would risk the scorn of the great Islamic teachers and, more importantly, the wrath of Allah for not advancing his kingdom on earth as he commissioned all us Muslims to do.

The Quran clearly instructs Muslims to prepare well for the battlefield. The Muslims who were my betters committed themselves to jihad, the holy war. They were ready to spill their blood for his kingdom and Allah's glory. In my weak and humble mission, I hoped to resemble those true warriors.

MY STRATEGY

I decided I would the play Devil's advocate, as they say, and work through several different scenarios in my head. This was the type of critical thinking I learned at my British school. My goal was to see people embrace Islam, to forsake all their old ways, their pleasures and entertainment, and their habits. I wanted to see women dramatically change the way they dressed and the way they lived. I wanted them to leave everything behind and fully submit to Allah as true slaves to the master of the universe.

That meant embracing the idea their one role in life was to please their master and to worship him day and night. They were to be tools with no larger purpose than to help establish Allah's kingdom on earth. They had to understand the reward in this life or the one beyond was not guaranteed. They would have to work for it every day and night, hoping—and only hoping—their work would be acceptable to Allah, their master. In many cases they would only know of the outcome of their work on the Day of Judgment. If they wanted guarantees, they had to embrace jihad and fight in the cause of Allah to either victory or death.

As the Quran reminded us: *"Those who fight in the cause of Allah, who are willingly forsaking their comfort and earthly life, in order to receive the rewards in their graves, and in the hereafter in Heaven. Let it be fully known that their fights in the cause of Allah will be fully rewarded, whether they are killed or achieves victory—We surely will bestow upon them great reward"* (Quran 4:74).

ALLAH AND THE QURAN

A perfectly good starting point was with Allah. Certainly, doubters would ask for proof that Allah is the one true god, creator of heaven and earth. They would need to know Allah directly revealed the Quran to Mohamed so we would know exactly what Allah wants from us all. The Quran would be my proof for all the above. The Quran would point unbelievers to Allah. But what if they responded with more questions, like, "Why do I have to follow the Quran?" or "Who said so?" or "Who wrote it?" Those questions would certainly be fair. After all, these people would be ignorant of Allah. My natural inclination would be to respond, "Mohamed gave us the Quran as it was told to him by Allah."

STARTING WITH MOHAMED

But how could I convince skeptics Mohamed was telling the truth and he was who he claimed to be? "Allah said so" was always an acceptable proof and the final word among us Muslims, but that would not be a proof enough for doubters. I could, however, give proof of the Prophet. I would go back to Mohamed's life journey to prove he was who we Muslims said he was. Then skeptics would know the Quran was 100 percent true. I would prove Mohamed was the Prophet and the final message of god to humankind. That was my beginning. From there, all I had to do was let the Quran do its miraculous work.

Awesome! I had a plan. Mohamed was the most honest man, the most perfect man. His story was one of a true prophet, and all I had to do was go through the Islamic books and write down my irrefutable bullet points. It was all there. I just needed to highlight the key arguments. Should be a snap, I figured.

It wasn't.

Here is why. As I got started, I decided to study the Quran passage Umar's sister shared with him. I wanted to look at it from a different angle and examine how that passage changed his mind. After all, Umar was a skeptic, an angry man determined to destroy Mohamed and Islam in its infancy. Instead, he embraced Islam after hearing this passage and became one of the biggest champions of the faith, a real jihadist and a conqueror like no other in Islamic history. He followed Islam to the nines, followed every ordinance and, helped establish Allah's kingdom on the ruins of the Roman and the Persian empires, the ruins he created by his zealotry and jihad.

It was the whole of chapter twenty from the Quran, the name of which is *Taha*, meaning marvelous. That name later became one of Mohamed's ninety-nine given names. That chapter tells the story of Moses in detail, including his encounter with the pharaoh. After that the text delves into the ancient story of Adam and Eve. Toward the end of the chapter, the verses commemorate the fact the people around Mohamed did not believe in him or in his legitimacy as a prophet. They challenged him to perform any miracle or show any heavenly sign to confirm his prophethood. Allah instructed Mohamed to answer those who were challenging him by saying, *"If you are waiting on a sign or a miracle, wait as long as you want to. I am not going to do anything, but one day you all will know. And definitely when the Day of Judgment will come, you all will be severely punished for your disbelief in me."* (Quran 20: 133–135). After scrutinizing those verses, I realized there was a problem. Even though they communicated the exchange between Mohamed and his doubters, Mohamed's answer from the Quran would lead me to the same dilemma, the same vicious circle.

"The Quran is the exact word of god," I would say.

"Why?" the skeptic would answer.

"Because Mohamed told us so."

"And why should I believe Mohamed and accept that he is a legitimate prophet and superior to all other prophets?"

"Well, because the Quran told us that."

APPLYING LOGIC AND CRITICAL THINKING TO ISLAM

I spent years in a Western education system and was fairly well exposed to the reasoning and constructive debate driving minds in that system. My dreams were big. I wanted people to believe every word the Prophet Mohamed uttered. I wanted them to realize every word in the Quran was true. I wanted to convert the masses to the one true faith in Islam. If I dreamed of having any success in fulfilling these dreams, I had some heavy lifting to do. I had to use all my knowledge, all my resources, and my power to find an irrefutable argument to answer any question a skeptic could ask. I felt I was fully equipped and ready for the task. I was sure no one else could pull it off. The challenge was all mine.

My most useful tools included the stories around Mohamed's birth, his childhood, his youth, his divine encounters, and his life. I gathered a wealth of incidents and historical facts, most of which were known to us Muslims as proof of Mohamed's legitimacy. Since we already believed, we did not need this material, but it was a great source of awe and made for excellent preaching and worship sessions, especially for young Muslims. None of this, of course, was open for debate. Skepticism was not allowed. The stories mostly served to reinforce our admiration for the Prophet and our faith.

All I had to do was highlight the strongest arguments. I was sure they would overwhelm the doubters. No one would ever dare challenge such solid historic evidence. No one?

CHAPTER 13

MECCA IN HISTORY

If you reflect, meditate, and study the Quran with great depth you will come to the conclusion of how perfect it is. If it had not come from god you would have found discrepancies and contradictions.

—Quran 4:82

This is where it all began, and this is where I will start, by telling the story of the holy city, Mecca. To me, at the time, it meant something very significant that Mohamed was born in Mecca, the holiest city that ever existed. It is where Allah's house, the *Kaaba*, is located. This house is thought to be the center of the earth and features a concealed tunnel connecting the Kaaba directly to Allah's throne in heaven, thus it is the only path between man and god. It was altogether fitting then that Mecca should have been such a draw to all prophets and the birthplace of Mohamed, the seal of them all.

Mecca was and still is considered the link between Mohamed and Abraham, the patriarch of all the prophets, and it also links Mohamed to the first man, Adam. The city was the "holy land" of all the prophets and, in my belief at the time, was irrefutably special. The Quran clearly states the Kaaba was first built by the angels and then rebuilt by Adam. It washed away during Noah's flood, then sat largely ignored until Abraham and Ishmael set about rebuilding it around 1850 BC. The city, at least in the hearts and minds of every Muslim, flourished from that time forward. If this story were true, Mecca would have been one of the oldest cities in continuous existence on the face of the earth.

This background meant one very important thing—there would be much historical and religious evidence pointing to the significance of the city, its holiness, and its rightful claim to being the birthplace of the final prophet, Mohamed.

As an Egyptian, I found this evidence especially exciting. My home was the ancient land of the pharaohs, where mountains of sand and looming pyramids bear witness to civilizations long gone. There is ample evidence for other ancient cities as well such as Damascus in Syria. Excavations at Tell Ramadi on the outskirts of that city prove Damascus was inhabited as early as 8,000 to 10,000 BC, making it among the oldest continually inhabited cities in the world. The same can be said for the ancient cities of Turkey. Although not as venerable, the cities of Europe also show ample physical proof of a civilization more than three millennia old.

I started pouring over history books, archaeological records, and the works of the great and reputable historians to find mention of Mecca during the times of the prophets. I wouldn't need much—just solid evidence the city was what the Quran said it was so I could have another source to back me up other than the Quran. I quickly hit my first roadblock, a major one. I found nothing—no recorded history, no remnants, no traces of life whatsoever. The list of ancient cites is long. The cities are subdivided among the continents and subcontinents. Mecca did not appear on any of the lists. I was planning to speak to the educated masses of Europe, some who might even have been historians. For them, I needed tangible proof Mecca was one of the oldest cities on earth. I became obsessive in my quest to find something—anything—I could use. I spent every available hour looking. Why, I wondered, wasn't there any mention of Mecca in the history books?

I found records of such trivia as Egyptian Queen Hatshepsut's creation of the first zoo in history, thirty-five hundred years ago, and Chinese Emperor Wen Wang's zoo built not long after that. I learned a great deal about Egypt and China from that era, but nothing about Mecca. According to the Quran, Mecca was rebuilt by Abraham at about the same time as these zoos were created. It troubled me that records of zoos and menageries existed, but I could find no trace whatsoever of Mecca from that era.

KAAB IBN LUAAYY

Confused and disturbed, I engrossed myself in Islamic history books to find answers to my questions since I could not find them anywhere else. Kaab ibn Luaayy's name jumped out at me. He was the direct ancestor, seven generations back, of Prophet Mohamed, and he lived in Syria. His name struck me—"Kaab."

I wondered whether his name could have been the origin of the name "Kaaba." He is the first one in history to mention the Kaaba, but he did not even reference to it with the name "Kaaba." Instead, he called it the Arabic word for "The Sanctuary."

It is also very well documented he is the one who made Friday, the seventh day of the week, a special day for Arabs. Friday in Arabic is *Jumaah*, which means "congregating together." Kaab began the practice of gathering his people around "The Sanctuary" on that day to make announcements and discuss current events. I found the exact text of one of Kaab Ibn Luaayy's first speeches in which he called for regular gatherings. This took place more than five hundred years before Prophet Mohamed was even born. And yet Friday didn't become the sacred weekly day in Islam until after Mohamed immigrated to the city of Medina and started the Islamic state there upon his arrival.

QUSAI IBN KILAB

The next ancestor who intrigued me was Qusai ibn Kilab, four generations removed from the Prophet Mohamed. He also was raised and lived in Syria. When Qusai came of age he traveled south gathering his nearest kin and settling them in the Mecca Valley for the first time. Prior to that, they were dispersed all over. Very few lived in or around the Mecca Valley, a barren area with far too few water wells to attract settlers.

Qusai ruled as the first king of his new settlement. He is credited, according to most authoritative Arab historians, with either building or rebuilding the Kaaba. It was possible, I thought, that he named Kaaba in honor of his great-grandfather Kaab. Or perhaps Kaab was the one who originally built it, and Qusai just rebuilt it and kept the same name. I could find nothing to answer these questions. Nor did I find any reference to Ishmael or Abraham inspiring Qusai to build the Kaaba.

In any case, after Qusai worked on the Kaaba, he started working on planning and building the city of Mecca. He ordered the new inhabitants of the city to build their homes and businesses around the Kaaba to mark it as the center of the city.

Qusai is also known to have built, in Mecca, the first "town hall" in the history of the Arabian Peninsula. It was a spacious building known as the "House of Assembly." Qusai's intention was to have the leaders of different clans meet in this hall to discuss their social, commercial, cultural, and political affairs. Qusai's childhood and upbringing, in the vibrant metropolitan area of ancient Syria taught him a lot, about business, city planning, culture development, and growth. He was a visionary and an astute new king and governmental leader.

As king, Qusai established the governing rules for his new united kingdom in this valley, and he called the new city "Mecca." His business plan was to create a place where other clans and pilgrims would want to come to visit and trade. He bestowed the designation "pilgrim" to the visitors of his city. The label "visitor" or "traveler" did not serve his hope of recurring returns. To make the experience as memorable as possible for the visitors he wanted to add a spiritual and mystical element to the journey.

Qusai encouraged the visitors to bring the symbols and statues of their own gods with them to Mecca and resurrect those around the Kaaba. In this way the Kaaba would be a place for all gods and also a place to invite others to contemplate each visitor's god. Quickly, more than 360 gods were erected and worshiped at the Kaaba. Qusai then created laws governing the pilgrims who came to Mecca to visit the Kaaba. To entice visitors, he provided free food and water, paid for by a tax on the people of Mecca. He assigned various clans and families the responsibility for looking after the visitors during pilgrimage, taking care of the Kaaba, and keeping peace among the many tribes who started moving through and living in Mecca.

Free water and food were the major tools used to attract the visitors to the Kaaba and the new city. It should be noted Qusai was calling these visitors the Arabic equivalent of "pilgrims" one hundred fifty years before the dawn of Islam. The pilgrims would inevitably engage in commercial and bartering activities with the inhabitants of the city. This commerce helped create a flourishing and growing urban area. The only problem that might derail this ambitious plan of Qusai's was a shortage of water or food. Food and water are especially precious commodities in the barren Arabian Peninsula. Qusai depended on a few wells in the Mecca valley, and they were the reason he chose that area to build his new city.

Qusai amassed great wealth and fame from his efforts in creating Mecca. Right before he died, he transferred all his rights, powers, and the ownership of the House of Assembly to his firstborn son. He also made his son the owner and custodian of the Kaaba. Thus, he got his name "Abd El Dar." El Dar means the sanctuary.

ABD MANAF

Qusai's second son, Abd Manaf, who later became Mohamed's great-great-grandfather, vehemently contested this inheritance. The effects of this conflict continued among their descendants and affected the history of Mecca right up to Mohamed's time and even after. Abd Manaf gained some revenge for his misfortunes through the efforts of his son Hashim. Vengeance came in a very unexpected way. The main food supply at the time for Mecca was the area's stock of camels, goats, and sheep. Residents drank the milk of these animals and ate their meat. There was not much else to eat. In time, the growing population overwhelmed the availability of food and water, and the incoming pilgrims added to the problem. The result was famine.

HASHIM

Hashim came to the rescue. Using the primitive dry bread available locally, Hashim initiated the practice of putting crumbled bread in hot broth in lieu of a full meal. The privileged put a piece of meat on top. This new practice alleviated the pressure to overuse the animal stock, and this eventually led to the end of the famine. With this simple idea Hashim saved the city and its commerce. He rose to fame as "the man who fed the starved."

I was beside myself when I was reading all this history. That same meal is still a signature meal in Mecca and in all Saudi Arabia. It is the meal typically served the day after the Mount Arafat excursion during the pilgrimage. It is what the Prophet Mohamed ate, and thus Muslims all eat it even today. Of course, I usually had three big pieces of meat on top of my broth.

Having saved the city, Hashim demanded all rights given by Qusai to Abd El Dar be transferred to his clan with Hashim being the rightful new king. To commemorate the transfer, Hashim and his brothers and allies dipped their hands in a bowl of rich perfume with nutmeg powder and swore they would never abandon one another. They then rubbed their scented hands over the stone of the Kaaba in confirmation of their pact. They were named the "Alliance of the Scented Ones."

My heart was racing at this point. I wondered whether that was why "The Black Stone" was always smothered in that same perfume mix? While circling the Kaaba, Muslim pilgrims, me included, made sure we rubbed our hands on the heavily scented black stone each time we passed by the corner where that stone is still mounted. The black stone is the only landmark that still exists from the time this incident took place.

The stone may have been preserved, I thought, to mark the special spot where Mohamed's great-grandfather and his clan swore their oath. To this day, the black stone is coated with that perfume daily by a designated staff member. When, as a boy, I asked why the black stone was always sticky and smothered in perfume, I was told it was the scent of heaven.

It was not heaven that Hashim, Mohamed's great-grandfather, was seeking by forming the "Alliance of the Scented Ones." Rather, he wanted full control of the Kaaba and the kingship of the city his grandfather founded. He was seeking complete ownership of his ancestor's inheritance. His rivals, the ancestors of Abd El Dar, also swore an oath of union. They called their group "Alliance of the Confederates." A bloody war was about to erupt, but to avoid bloodshed the two groups reached a compromise. Hashim was appointed leader of the city. The members of his Alliance of the Scented Ones were assigned all of the pilgrimage's affairs. They would have full control of collecting the taxes from the citizens and supplying food and drink for the pilgrims. The Alliance of the Confederates retained the keys to the Kaaba and management of the House of Assembly.

As the newly appointed leader of the city, Hashim recognized the hardships of life in Mecca, a barren "valley without cultivation." The water problem he exploited in his rise to power was still unsolved to this point. To attract pilgrims, he needed to find a more permanent solution. An astute and a visionary leader, Hashim was a frequent traveler. He frequently invited people and tribes to visit his city. It was during these marketing trips when he realized the potential of taking part in the lucrative trade to Syria and Egypt passing through Arabia. The volume of commerce between Rome and India via the Red Sea and the Arabian Sea was huge after Rome conquered Egypt in 30 BC.

Hashim sought and obtained trading privileges from the Roman governor of Syria as well as from the Roman governor of Egypt. He then procured an edict from the Byzantine Caesar, exempting Quraish, his tribe, from duties or taxes when operating in the countries under the Byzantine domain. Caesar also wrote to the Ethiopian king to inform him Hashim and Quraish would be his partners in the trade the Ethiopian king previously dominated.

Hashim launched his new enterprise by going south to the shores of the Arabian Peninsula to meet the ships coming from

India and Asia. The goods were then transported by caravan to Syria and Egypt. But Hashim decided to make a stop in Mecca along his route in order to offer some of the goods to those who visited his city. As a result, Mecca became acknowledged as a major city in Arabia, and markets were established around the city to deal with new business. The Ethiopian king who previously dominated this business and agreed under pressure from the Romans to share his venture with Hashim and the Meccans got terribly upset. It especially disturbed him to see the rising star of the city of Mecca.

Hashim continued to be a frequent traveler and a marketer. He had wives and kids in multiple cities. One of his wives was a powerful woman and the head of her tribe in a city called Yathrib, which would be later named Medina. Hashim fathered a boy with this woman. That boy would later move to Mecca and become the grandfather of Mohamed.

On one of his trips, Hashim died in Gaza. Many years later, after Mohamed's ascent to power, the Islamic conquest of Jerusalem and Syria led to Muslim control of Gaza. This enabled the Muslims to build a mosque on the site of Hashim's grave to commemorate and honor the tomb of Mohamed's great-grandfather. That neighborhood in Gaza is named after Hashim to this day.

ABD AL-MUTTALIB

A few years after Hashim's death, his son, Abd al-Muttalib, whom he fathered in Medina, moved to Mecca to live with the rest of his extended family. Then the inevitable happened: the scattered water wells around the Mecca valley started to dry up. Abd al-Muttalib had a dream. An angel appeared to him and told him there was a well dug and used by Roman soldiers in their expeditions many years earlier when Mecca was not even a city, but just an obscure valley.

The Roman prefect of Egypt, Gaius Aelius Gallus, led the expedition to what is now Yemen in 25 BC. Under orders from Augustus, he planned to secure the southern shores of the Arabian Peninsula. On this expedition he trusted an Arab man, a

Nabataean called Syllaeus, to guide him through the barren, end-less deserts of Arabia, but the man misled him. The long expedition led the Romans through the Mecca valley. There, they dug a well abundant with water. At the time of their departure, they covered the well and buried a couple of gold artifacts and statues to mark the location. Hundreds of years passed, and no one ever came back to dig that well again and reclaim the gold.

Abd al-Muttalib dreamed he was ordered to dig at the sacrifi-cial slaughter place of the Quraysh between the two idols, Isāf and Nā'ila. The Quraysh tribe tried to stop him from digging in that spot, but his sons guarded the location. After three days of digging they found the gold artifacts. Soon after, they found an overflow-ing source of water, which Prophet Mohamed (the grandson of Adb al-Muttalib) many years later would name the famous Zamzam well. Abd al-Muttalib, to commemorate finding the well, melted the gold artifacts and turned the gold into a door for the Kaaba.

The tears flowed from my eyes, and my heart beat swiftly. If what I was reading came from Jewish authors, I would have found peace at the conclusion of my historical digging. I believed the Jews would lie to confuse Muslims about their faith and their prophet. But this was not the case. All my sources were Arabic and Islamic. I shook with fear. I could only conclude the Kaaba was actually built by one or more of Mohamed's ancestors as a shrine, a tourist attraction for visitors. People from all backgrounds used it as a retreat. They came and worshiped their own gods, whatever gods they believed in, and had time to meditate and pray. They were provided free food and water as an incentive for coming to this site.

The people of the city benefited tremendously by engaging in all kinds of transactions with travelers while they were on their retreat. In making Mecca a resting place for the traveling caravans, Hashim elevated the city to a new level of importance.

WHERE IS ABRAHAM AND ISHMAEL?

During my research about these historical events, I found no men-tion of Abraham or Ishmael or even of people claiming lineage to them. None of Mohamed's ancestors were ever documented claiming be a descendent of Ishmael. The furthest they project in their speeches is to an ancestor by the name of "Adnan." When asked about his ancestors, Prophet Mohamed never went further than Adnan, an ancestor twenty generations removed.

When the Prophet Mohamed was bragging one time about his lineage he said: "I am a descendent of Banu Nadr Bin Kinanah. If anyone suggests otherwise I will order his beheading for offending me."[9] Mohamed mentioned the great men in his lineage, but he did not mention Abraham and Ishmael. A single hadith in which Mohamed said he was a descendant of Ishmael would have helped my case considerably, but to my sorrow there was none. Prophet Mohamed fated all of his ancestors to hellfire, including his own father, because they were not Muslims. Shouldn't he have praised them as descendants of Ishmael?

One hadith tells how Prophet Mohamed was approached by a man from his tribe to ask about the fate of their common ancestors. Mohamed declared they were all in hell for eternity. He added that if the man ever passed by any of their graves, he should shout at them that the Prophet Mohamed sent him with a message, namely that they would be dragged on their faces and stomachs in hellfire for eternity. The man mustered some bravery and asked Prophet Mohamed, "Why? What did they do to deserve such fate? They didn't know any better. They did what they thought were good deeds. They aspired to be virtuous." Mohamed answered, "they never followed Allah. Nor were they ever Muslims."[10]

MORE QUESTIONS

What about all the other prophets, I wondered. What about David, Joseph, Moses, or even Jesus? Jerusalem was always part of their stories in the Quran and in the hadiths, but there was never any mention of Mecca associated with any of these prophets. Mecca had no reliable source of water, which is the only reason for a city to exist in the middle of such a desert, at least not until Mohamed's immediate grandfather had a dream and dug the well known today as Zamzam.

Frustrating me further was the Quranic chapter called *Quraish*, which was the name for Mohamed's tribe. This was the tribe Qusai established by uniting his dispersed kinsman and settling them in the newfound city of Mecca. The chapter has only four verses. The first praised Qusai for uniting and forming the Quraish tribe. The second verse praised Mohamed's great-grandfather, Hashim, for orchestrating the change that transformed his tribe from a very poor one to a settled and prosperous one.

For the first time, the words on the page jumped out at me. All of this history happened *"a few years before Mohamed's birth."* That meant Mecca could *not* have been settled by Abraham. According to the Quran, a "formal" city didn't exist prior to that time because the region was filled with nomads. Mecca was only established *"for stabilizing and unifying the Quraish"* (Quran 106:1).

Now I had to wonder how to respond to the following argument: If the Kaaba was built by Abraham and Ishmael, if the inhabitants of Mecca and Mohamed's ancestors were the descendants of Ishmael, if the city of Mecca was the dwelling place of the prophets, the Meccans should have been living in anticipation of the arrival of the final prophet, Mohamed, and they should have been the first to believe in him and support his religion.

But that was never the case. They were the first to reject Mohamed and his message. They were his fiercest enemies. They went to war to destroy him. They died and lost many of their finest men fighting him and Islam. Mohamed's conquest of Mecca was the cornerstone of the Islamic empire to come.

I would expect and totally understand why the Meccans should have been skeptical. They should have felt the need to verify Mohamed as a prophet first. Even before his arrival, though, they were building and rebuilding the Kaaba, performing pilgrimage, setting aside Friday as a holy day, observing the sacred months of the moon calendar, and honoring many other traditions that later became part of Islamic core beliefs. If they did this to follow the steps of Abraham and Ishmael, then what was the need for Mohamed's coming?

MOHAMED

This was when I decided to turn my full attention to the Prophet's birth, childhood, and life. We all were taught from a very young age about the miracles of Mohamed's birth, and I felt confident I would be able to use that information. Mohamed was born in the year of the elephant, AD 570. In that year, an army led by a mighty king from a then Christian nation, was planning to ride elephants into Mecca to crush the Kaaba and kill the people. The chapter from the Quran commemorating the incident is called "The Elephant." It explains how Allah sent birds to throw stones from hell at the Christian invaders, killing them all in defense of the Kaaba and the people of Mecca.

I loved that story. Every Muslim kid loved that story and memorized it. We all loved seeing Allah's power in action. That story was the "bang" marking Mohamed's birth, a victory ordained by Allah, a holy sign to the birth of the final prophet, Mohamed, a heavenly protection to mark the sacred city of Mecca and preserve the house of Allah, the Kaaba. Both would be at the heart of Islamic sacredness and holiness. The intervention by Allah was very much needed to pave the way to the birth of Mohamed and Islam.

To extract evidence of this event in relation to the Prophet's birth, I wanted to dig even deeper. Abraha al-Ashram was a king who believed in God and followed the Prophet Jesus prior to Mohamed's birth. Every one of his people, including his army, followed Jesus. That was at a time when Mohamed was yet to be born, and Islam did not exist. Mecca at the time was given to paganism, nakedness, and filth. The evidence about the city's condition is abundant in the Quran and in Islamic literature.

I recorded my discoveries in my notebook and was immediately, for the first time, struck with a question. Why would Allah destroy an army following his prophet Jesus on behalf of a filthy, pagan people? Why too would Allah protect the Meccans, who would later become the sworn enemies of Mohamed and Islam (Quran 2:62)?

Even if the victory was to protect the Kaaba, the Kaaba was surrounded with filth and nakedness and housed more than three hundred sixty idols. It was not even the first *quiblah*—direction of prayer—for Muslims. Jerusalem was. Mecca would not be the quiblah until fifty-six years later. Mohamed and his followers, "The Muslims," could have rebuilt the Kaaba later as Abraham was alleged to have done had it been destroyed. And most importantly, shouldn't that Christian king and his army have known from their sacred books the Kaaba was a sacred place and the house of Allah? Why would they want to abolish a sacred house built by Abraham, the father of Jesus?   Things were not adding up.

Some Muslim scholars claimed Abraha al-Ashram, though he believed in God and Jesus, followed a distorted message. What did that mean? They were, I said to myself, still *people of the book*. Prophet Mohamed said, "The Jews and the Christians and the Sabeans were all the people of the book. Before his birth they were considered legitimate people of God and would go to heaven. But the minute he was born and thereafter, their religions were null, and Islam was the only way to heaven. He then swore that if anyone of them kept their religion after his birth and didn't convert to Islam, they would be cursed by Allah and sent to hellfire for eternity."[11] Again, this made no sense.

Abraha was a zealous Christian who was well known for promoting Christianity and building many remarkable and magnificent churches like "Al–Qalis." He was also known for fighting Judaism and paganism in the Arabian Peninsula. Would that have been his real motivation for wanting to destroy the Kaaba? Was it because he saw Mecca as a filthy place full of idols? Or was it because the Meccans were infringing on his trade deal with the Romans? Or maybe both?

This was quickly becoming a tangled mess, and the notes in the margins of my notebook reflected my confusion. With each new day came a new resolve to find the missing pieces and assemble a credible, irrefutable argument. And with each new day came a handful of new frustrations. I decided to set aside Mecca and the Year of the Elephant and just look at the circumstances of Mohamed's birth. That, I figured, would provide new rhetorical weapons for my arsenal.

CHAPTER 14

ORIGINS

Mohamed is nothing but a messenger like many other messengers who came before him so if he was to die or be killed you should not turn back on your heels and desert your belief in Allah.

—Quran 3:144

Mohamed was born six months after the death of his father. He was given the name Bin Abdullah, which simply meant "son of Abdullah." He wasn't called Mohamed until years later. I knew, as a devout and learned Muslim, what a miraculous blessing he was, but I had to set all my beliefs aside and think from a skeptic's point of view. I had to reflect on the tribal culture of the day and understand how people would have viewed his birth following the death of his father.

When a man died not long after marrying and impregnating his bride, it was considered a very bad omen. The Quran teaches the people of Mecca were very superstitious and would not have looked upon Mohamed's birth favorably. Mohamed's mother, Amina, did not nurse him. The reason why is unrecorded. Some say she died while giving birth to him, but that cannot be true because her graveside is located in an area about one hundred miles from Mecca. It is said she took Mohamed to Medina to visit the gravesite of his father and uncles and died on the return trip.

Whatever the case, Mohamed's grandfather, Abd al-Muttalib, took pity on him since he, too, was an orphan, and he sought out a nursemaid for the child. Islamic texts say it was his grandfather who went to the marketplace to find someone, anyone, who would serve as nursemaid. No woman was willing to help out a child born under his circumstances, and the baby Mohamed nearly died from hunger and thirst. It was then Halima Saadia, a poor woman who lived in the wilderness, took him home to care for him.[12]

In reviewing that story, I thought it more tragic than wonderful, more disastrous than miraculous. Why was Allah's final Prophet abandoned and taken in by a poor woman? It is totally fine he was born into hardship and unfavorable circumstances, but this did nothing to prove his prophethood.

Even some Islamic scholars over the years have seen the fault with the story. They always excused the unfortunate beginnings of Mohamed by claiming he was sent into the wilderness by his family to toughen him. I could have bought that theory if it were a common practice with the male children in Mecca. Except it wasn't. I could find no other person in his city or his tribe who was sent away and fostered by a stranger in the wilderness unless the mother was dead. In normal circumstances children were not sent away. The wet-nurse was brought into the family home to nurse the child. There was no case of the child moving out of the home to be nursed in the wilderness. Not one. In his infancy, certainly, Mohamed was not adored.

At the end of weeks of research, I still had very little, and what I did have was confusing. If I did not feel confident in sharing it with others, then I wouldn't be able to go forward. I needed help, but it was not help I could ask for. Despite the fact my intent was noble, questioning the basics of the faith was considered wrong. I couldn't go to my father or my other teachers and start firing off questions for fear they would accuse me of doubting the Prophet or my faith. I would have to find a stealthy way to extract the information without them knowing what I was doing.

As a strategy, I sought out the most highly regarded imams. I engaged them in discussions, touching discreetly on some of the issues I wrestled with, but to no avail. Their answers were vague at best and provided none of the solid evidence I needed to answer the unbeliever.

One other issue troubling me about the Prophet's childhood was the sacred duty of circumcision. It is an absolute must for every Muslim male. Speaking from a medical perspective, I once asked my dad, a doctor, who would have circumcised Mohamed. He did little more than reiterate the Islamic textbooks. These claimed the angels circumcised him. Mohamed was perfect in every way.

From a medical perspective, "born circumcised" means one thing, namely, the infant boy has hypospadias. This is a condition in which the penis opens not at the tip but on the underside. Before recent medical advances, a boy born with this condition could not be circumcised. The midwife would say, instead, the angels circumcised him. I was very familiar with the condition—and those sayings—because one of my cousins had hypospadias. He almost died during the two reconstructive surgeries required as an infant to fix it. My cousin had to go through those surgeries very early because if it is not fixed it can lead to infertility or erectile dysfunction.

The Prophet, however, was supposed to be perfect in every way. Being born with a congenital anomaly wasn't exactly perfection. So there I was, once again, faced with a dilemma. Granted, those I was hoping to convert would be unaware of the Prophet's condition. It posed a significant stumbling block nonetheless. How could I say the Prophet was perfect, as the Quran teaches, when a deformity provided clear evidence of imperfection? And how could I even ask myself such a question?

This endeavor was becoming more complicated than I ever anticipated. I was troubled less by the time it was consuming than by the questions it was raising, questions I could never voice aloud without risking condemnation. I had no choice but to push ahead.

I thought perhaps the story of Mohamed's encounter as a seven-year-old boy with the Angel Gabriel would provide concrete evidence. After all, this incident stood as a testament to his prophethood in the minds of all Muslims. The Quran tells us Allah sent Gabriel to open the chest of Mohamed in order to cleanse his heart and remove all sin. This story was presented literally, not metaphorically, and it even details how Gabriel put Mohamed's heart and lungs in a bucket next to him while he was cleansing him and concluded with Gabriel sewing his chest back together after the cleansing. (Quran 94:1–8).

This story served my entire life to reveal the sinless nature of the Prophet. As a soon-to-be physician who knew something of the skepticism I would face, I quickly concluded this story, too, was flimsy. Yes, the event was miraculous, but the Prophet didn't perform the miracle. The angel did. And the event took place when Mohamed was still young, without sin, so Gabriel must have cleansed him from original sin, which is spiritual and not physical at all. Beyond that, Mohamed taught us Muslims were all born pure, without sin, and our families, caregivers, and our environment spoiled our sinless nature.[13] This story would not help me convince skeptics.

Moving forward through the events in the Prophet's life, I stopped to consider the dramatic changes that took place when he reached the age of twelve. He lived in the wilderness, away from his family, for his entire life until that point. During the Sacrilegious Wars, Mohamed finally had a chance to step up and do his duty as a vital member of his family. Having proved himself worthy, he went to his uncle Abu Talib, a caravan trader, and pleaded to let him remain with him and not be forced to return to his life in the wilderness. Mohamed wept and could not bear to be separated from him. To this Abu Talib responded, "By God I will take him with me, and we shall never part from each other."[14]

BAHIRA'S PROPHESY

Mohamed's request was granted, and he was soon traveling with his uncles on a caravan journey to Syria. The trip proved to be a turning point and is well chronicled in Islamic literature. On this first visit to Syria, Mohamed and his uncle met a monk named Bahira. Mohamed's uncles and other traders were feasting with

Bahira. Bahira took notice of the boy tending the camels and invited him into his home.

At some point, Bahira and Mohamed spoke at length, and Bahira came to see Mohamed as the one Jesus spoke of in his last days. Mohamed was the final Prophet who would come and complete the faith. Mohamed would be the "Comforter." The "Comforter" in Arabic translates "Mohamed." This was the origin of the name "Mohamed" and was the first time the name was bestowed on the Prophet.[15]

There was much that bothered me about this story, but I needed to get to the bottom of the mystery for one reason: Bahira's prophesy was recorded in the Hadiths and in Islamic history as evidence of Mohamed's legitimacy as the one spoken of by Jesus, the final prophet who would perfect the faith. Islam told me Bahira was a Christian monk. As I studied, however, I began to think this designation was incorrect. I tried to find information about Bahira in Christian history, but again I came up with nothing. I thought perhaps he might be a fortune teller. There should have been evidence of his existence somewhere in history given his central role in proclaiming Mohamed as Prophet.

I scoured the history books and found plenty of stories about men like Nostradamus, but I never uncovered a single mention of the man Bahira. It seemed odd to me a man whose words had the historical impact of Bahira's would be mentioned in no other source other than the Islamic books. I dutifully recorded all these explorations in my notes. They helped me recall the details of Mohamed's life, but they did not give me the ammunition I needed to confront skeptics. I was frustrated, to say the least, but undaunted. I was determined to prove my faith to the world, but it was becoming clearer by the day my research was going to take much longer than I imagined at the outset.

MOHAMED MARRIES KHADIJA

I advanced through Mohamed's life. Until he was twenty-five, there were no milestones recorded aside from his encounter with Bahira. I still had nothing at the ready to make an impact on skeptics. The boy from the caravan grew up to be an honest and hardworking man. He met a woman named Khadija, a widow fifteen years older than he, and they married. At the time she met Mohamed, Khadija was successfully running the business she inherited from her father.

I knew about the success of Khadija as fact. For the first time, though, I had to consider the words of the Quran in a new light. According to the Quran, women had no status until the Prophet bestowed rights upon them. But Khadija was considered the strongest, wealthiest woman in the city long before she married Mohamed. How, I wondered, did she achieve that status without having it bestowed upon her by Mohamed. Was hers a case unlike any other woman?

Once again, though, my research revealed more conflicting facts. Khadija wasn't unique. Mohamed's own grandmother, Salma Bin Amr, was the head of her tribe and the most influential person in Medina at the time of Mohamed's birth. Islamic texts were telling me one thing, and the historical record was telling me something completely different. "Allah, please show me!" I prayed, exasperated. "Please guide me to your truth!"

I decided it was time to take a different approach. I believed the truth would stand even in the face of evidence against it. I just had to find the evidence validating the truth of Islam. What better way could there be than to examine the testimony of those who were Mohamed's first followers and believers? Their stories would absolutely validate everything I held to be true.

My starting point had to be Khadija. She would have been there from the beginning. I discovered she and her family did not practice one of the region's pagan religions. Rather, they belonged to a group that believed in Jesus as a prophet and followed the Abrahamic belief of faith in one God. Hanifa is the name given to that set of beliefs which does not believe in the Trinity and traces its lineage to Abraham. Nazarene is one of those Christian groups following the Hanifa beliefs. Her cousin, Waraqua Bin Naufel, was a monk in that same religious order. There was, however, no mention of Waraqua in the Islamic texts until the

day Mohamed had his first encounter with the Angel Gabriel in
Hira Cave.

I reached an interesting conclusion. Mohamed, I knew, married
Khadija. Waraqua, the Christian monk was Khadija's mentor and
spiritual guide. This meant Waraqua and Mohamed would have
had more than fifteen years of a very close relationship. Khadija
and Mohamed had to have been involved in Waraqua's religious
order at least until Mohamed was ordained as Prophet in the cave.

THE CAVE ENCOUNTER

Mohamed was forty when he had the cave encounter. Until this
time Mohamed was always called "Bin Abdullah" and was not
recognized as a prophet despite his alleged encounter with Bahira
at the age of twelve. Aisha told us the story of the cave in one of
the most reliable hadiths about this encounter. Aisha said that after
Mohamed was confronted by the angel Gabriel in the cave,
Mohamed ran back home to Khadija very disturbed. In her effort
to make sense of Mohamed's story Khadija went to Waraqua and
said, "My husband Bin Abdullah told me about his encounter with
Gabriel and he is not a liar." To that Waraqua repeated the words
of Bahira, the "monk" who first discerned the Prophet's calling
years earlier. Waraqua again, as Bahira did before him, prophesied
Bin Abdullah was the Comforter Jesus predicted. Strangely,
though, I could find no account of Waraqua converting to Islam
following his pronouncement.

The story of the cave was one of my favorites. I remembered
how I cried in the very place the Angel Gabriel appeared to the
Prophet to commission him as messenger. But I could not recall
anything Khadija might have said about that amazing event. I read
passage after passage, and none mentioned Khadija. All of the
sources said, "Aisha said . . ." This made no sense. Aisha became
Mohamed's wife many years later. But at the time of the cave
encounter, Khadija was Mohamed's wife, and Aisha was not yet
born. I was searching for an eyewitness account and could not find
one. Anywhere.

MORE CHALLENGES

Then I discovered a few more details that challenged the accepted version of the cave story. It turns out the cave was not unknown to Mohamed when he first visited. Starting with his great-great-grandfather, it was a family tradition to go to that cave for meditation. Those ancestors of Mohamed were idol worshipers and pagans in most historical accounts. This detail would not have troubled most Muslims, but I found it unsettling. Islamic texts dramatized his choice of that particular cave and made it sound much more extraordinary than it really was. Learning about the family tradition made the cave seem less important to me.

Turning my attention back to his initial followers of the faith, I knew Khadija was the first woman to convert, and she was previously a follower of some form of Christianity. I had no idea what that meant. Another of the first converts was Abu Bakr, the first man who believed in Mohamed. I had to wonder what Abu Bakr and Khadija converted from. If, through their conversion, they provided proof Mohamed was the Prophet, I would be able to use their testimony.

Despite my limited access to Christian materials, I made a great effort to explore the different sects within Christianity at the time of Mohamed. The Quran refers to the faith of Khadija as "Nazarene." Nazarenes are respected in the Quran. Other sects of Christians are not, and the reason is simple. Christians were accused of idolatry because of their worship of three Gods—the Father, the Son, and the Holy Spirit—but the Nazarenes of that era followed only Jesus. They recognized Jesus as a unique person but not the son of God because they believed Jesus never claimed to be the son of God. They were also anticipating that God would continue sending many other prophets to guide and instruct them in their faith. Thus, they were the first to embrace Mohamed and his message. This eagerness to believe Mohamed earned them respect in the Quran (Quran 5:83–84).

Both Abu Bakr and Khadija were strong believers in the oneness of God, and this happened to be Mohamed's first message when he began to preach. I really struggled to find the difference in what they believed before the Angel Gabriel commissioned Mohamed in the cave and what they believed afterward. I could find no testimony from either to prove Mohamed was a Prophet. There was no such profession from Khadija. As to Abu Bakr, he claimed to believe because he trusted everything Mohamed said. He was, after all, his most loyal friend and confidant. This friendship was a wonderful thing, but it offered no useful confirmation of Mohamed's account.

CHAPTER 15

THE SOURCE OF THE QURAN

*He walked until he reached the spot where the sun sets
and he found out that it sets down in a spring of dark
mud. Then he walked until he reached the area where
the sun rises and he found out it is rising from an area
where the people have no shield from it whatsoever.*

—Quran 18:86–90

I was coming up with zero that would help me fulfill goal one,
namely proving Mohamed was the Prophet. I decided I had no
choice but to move ahead to another worthy and potentially fruit-
ful goal—confirming the source of the Quran. Mohamed said the
Quran was revealed to him through the Angel Gabriel. I believed,
as did others, this meant Gabriel was visiting Mohamed on a
regular basis. These meetings began with their first encounter in
the cave and should have ended with the Prophet's death twenty-
three years later. On further analysis, however, the Quran and
Mohamed confirmed he saw Gabriel only twice during those
twenty-three years: the first, the encounter in the cave; and the

second, the night journey twelve years later. That was all. But that made no sense to me. If they only met twice, I had to ask myself how Gabriel could have revealed the Quran to Mohamed.

Mohamed explained he did not personally have regular encounters with the angel, he regularly received a whisper in his ear from Gabriel who took the form of various local people. There is a hadith from Sahih Bukhari telling about a time when the Prophet was with one of his wives, Um Salama, and she noticed him talking to one of his companions. He later asked her "Do you know who that man was? She said, it was Dihya one of your friends. Later on Um Salama heard Mohamed preaching, and he told about his recent conversation with Gabriel. His wife exclaimed, "By Allah! I only saw Dihya, not Gabriel! How can that be?" In fact, there are numerous accounts in the Quran of well-known people speaking with Mohamed. Mohamed's explanation may well have answered doubters during his day, but I knew it would be useless to me in convincing modern-day skeptics.

The fact Mohamed was illiterate is widely known and not disputed. In the cave, Gabriel instructed Mohamed to read a passage three times, to which Mohamed responded he could not read. This fact had no bearing on my faith until I began to prepare my arguments for the non-believers. It seemed to me Gabriel could have miraculously cured Mohamed's illiteracy. I had no idea why that miracle did not take place then and there, especially for Allah's Prophet. Such a miracle would have offered further evidence of just how special Mohamed was.

Given Mohamed's illiteracy, I decided to check out the people who dutifully recorded the words of Allah as given to Mohamed. I knew they, more than anyone else, would provide credible first-hand accounts of Mohamed's prophethood. To start, I needed to identify the men who recorded the first verses of the Quran during those twelve years between the revelation in the cave and the time Mohamed moved to Medina. These men, whoever they were, would set the precedent for all who would follow.

A "Quran Keeper" was an individual whose job it was to memorize the passages as they were revealed to Mohamed and write them down. The list of Quran keepers for Mecca was short, and, as I discovered, untrustworthy. Some of the men listed as Quran keepers were not even born at the time they were credited with recording the Quran verses. Clearly, this information would not resolve my doubts.

Abdullah bin Abi Sarh was one of those early Quran Keepers and the closest Quran Keeper to Mohamed for a long period of time. Then the two had a falling out. After the falling out, Sarh admitted he impersonated Gabriel on many occasions to validate Mohamed's prophethood. Insisting Mohamed never actually had any encounter with Gabriel, Sarh claimed Mohamed conjured up the Quran, Sarh made up some verses, and Mohamed approved of them. His story can be found narrated by al-Nasaa 4067 and Abu-Dawood 2683. After making such bold statements, Mohamed called for Sarh's beheading, which resulted in Sarh fleeing the country for his life.

I was reaching a point of frustration. After months digging through historic accounts, the holy text, countless books in my library, and many other sources, I had nothing to show for my efforts. Once again, I began to question my abilities. I was failing, just as I initially failed to get into medical school. What was I missing? How could I find it? I was certain the fault was mine alone.

CHAPTER 16

THE NIGHT JOURNEY

Exalted is he who took his servant Mohamed during the night from the holy mosque in Mecca to the holy mosque in Jerusalem. Allah blessed the mosque in Jerusalem and its surrounding to show Mohamed the wonders and signs of heaven and hell and to meet with him and commission him as his final prophet.

—Quran 17:1

"Goal Two" crashed and burned, much as had Goal One. I had nothing solid, concrete, firsthand. I had no choice but to keep plowing ahead. I was in too deep to stop. If I could not solve this puzzle, my entire life's purpose was destined for the trash heap.

The night journey was the most significant event in the life of the Prophet and marked the day he was elevated above all of mankind, including the prophets who came before him. The night journey is essential to the faith. I believed it held concrete, irrefutable proof Mohamed was the promise of Jesus and the blessing of Abraham.

As the story was told, Mohamed was seized from his bed at the home of his first cousin and taken by Gabriel to the mosque in Jerusalem on the back of Buraq, the winged horse with the human head. At the mosque Mohamed met all the prophets. They

213

worshiped with him, and then Mohamed ascended into heaven to meet Allah. There he received the Shahada prayer—"There is no god but Allah, and Mohamed is the seal and the final of all the prophets"—and the dictate to pray five times daily.

Given the limits of Bedouin culture, the cousin's home would have been small. She should have heard the angel's knock at the door and been made aware of Mohamed's absence for a few hours. Yet, there was no record of her having seen or heard anything. Just the opposite was true. She reportedly told Mohamed upon hearing his story, "I don't know what you are talking about." She claimed to not have seen or heard a thing and urged him to keep the story to himself for fear people would think him insane.

What followed their exchange, especially given the significance of Mohamed being named *the* Prophet, had me rattled. His cousin did not convert to Islam that day. In fact, she spurned Mohamed. The Prophet asked her to leave her husband and marry him, and she flatly refused. There were many, obvious questions I dared not ask out loud. How could a woman refuse such a proposal? How could she not have been aware of the night journey given the small size of her house? And why on earth did she not convert to Islam right then and there? My analysis of the night journey was not beginning well, but perhaps, I thought, if I just delved a bit deeper I would find a firsthand source who could give the story the legitimacy I so desperately sought. I started by ruling out Mohamed's cousin. She was useless to me.

To an outsider, I'm sure, the whole story sounded fanciful. Outlandish even. But if I could put the event into a historic framework, I was certain the facts would clarify everything. I did not get far before encountering the first problem. The historical records showed there was no mosque in Jerusalem at the time of the night journey. The mosque was actually built fifty years later. Some textbooks say the mosque may have actually been King Solomon's temple, but that was also impossible. The Romans destroyed that temple five hundred years earlier, an historical event supported by numerous firsthand accounts.

The Romans left Jerusalem in ruins and reduced the Temple Mount to a trash dump. They left it in that condition to ensure the

Jews could never return and reclaim the site. When skeptics asked Mohamed what the mosque looked like, he gave them a vivid description of the mosque including the doors, windows, and writings on the walls.

His supporters verified the mosque looked just as Mohamed said because they, too, claimed to have seen it. In truth, though, those witnesses couldn't confirm what they said they were confirming. There was no mosque or temple in Jerusalem at that time. I believed beyond a shadow of a doubt Mohamed was telling the truth. But what the witnesses said they saw, they didn't see. It wasn't there. Mecca was the most holy city on earth. The Kaaba at the heart of Mecca was placed directly under heaven and connected by a secret tunnel to Allah's throne in heaven.[16] Given Mecca's prominence, I had to wonder, why did the night journey lead to Jerusalem? Why was the direction of prayer changed from Jerusalem to Mecca three years after the night journey?

Some of Mohamed's contemporaries had problems with his story. It is recorded that Mut'im said to him, "All of your affairs before today were bearable, until what you said today. I bear witness that you are a liar. We strike the flanks of the she-camels for one month to reach the holy lands (Jerusalem), then for another month to come back, and you claim that you went there in one night! By Allat, by al-Ussa'! I do not believe you." Abu Bakr, however, defended his friend: "Mut'im, what an evil thing you said to the son of your brother when you faced him thus and declared him a liar! As for me, I bear witness that he spoke the truth."

Abu Bakr, described as Mohamed's best friend in the Quran, backed him up on every occasion. He didn't need to see actual evidence. His faith was unwavering. At the time, my faith was also unwavering, but I still needed something I could take to the doubters. The inconsistencies were mounting. I was beginning to see major tenets of my faith did not show well under a spotlight. I was growing more fearful by the day. My challenge was becoming less about proving Islam to others, and more about proving Islam to myself. I could not understand why this was happening to me. I desperately wanted to reverse the momentum.

CHAPTER 17

THE JEWISH PROBLEM

Oh people of Israel, do you remember when you challenged Moses by saying "Oh Moses we will never believe you until you show us God outright." This is when a thunderbolt knocked you all dead and then Allah woke you up from the dead again so you can believe and be grateful to him.

—Quran 2:55–56

After long days and nights spanning months, I thought I would be prepared for my mission to take Islam to the battlefield. I was not. In fact, I felt further than ever from achieving my goal. I was doubting my faith. I rationalized that the doubt flowed not from a lack of evidence but from my own failure to see that evidence. To prove Mohamed's prophethood to a skeptic, it was essential I find more proof.

I was 100 percent sure Mohamed was the Prophet. I was also sure the evidence was there. If the messenger were true, his message had to be true as well. Mohamed and his message were not at fault. Nor was Allah. They could never, ever, be at fault. I was the weak link. There are over a billion Muslims in the world. For fourteen hundred years, Islam has flourished, but I was having no success finding proof of Mohamed's legitimacy. I had to ask myself whether I should quit searching and give up on my dream of spreading Islam. If I did, I was sure Allah would be angry and would punish me (Quran 9:77). I had no excuse to stop. Allah blessed me with the time and the resources. The cousins who used to make fun of my devotion were struggling with their lives, and I had already been to Europe and earned a degree from the University of London. I had my own four-bedroom home, a new car, and in a few months, I would start medical school. Everyone had already started calling me Dr. Mohamed.

But Allah, I feared, would take all of this away from me and more if I failed in my faith, if I failed in my commitment to be his soldier, if I failed to spread his message to the enemies of Islam. I just had to win them over and expand Allah's kingdom on earth. The borders of that kingdom were stagnant for many years. Now was the time to move. I had to consider the possibility I was researching the wrong events or in the wrong period. That was not to deny the importance of these early events. They were instrumental in establishing Mohamed as a prophet. The lack of confirmation, I speculated, might have been due to the fact Islam was so new and the faithful so few. In fact, during those first twelve years only one hundred twenty-five people followed Mohamed. Most of them were his own family members, and a few were slaves he promised to ransom if they believed him and followed his religion.

So, I thought of a new plan—a new beginning. I would examine a much better documented period of Mohamed's life. I would track his migration to Medina, called "Yathrib" at the time, and look into the beginning of the Islamic state. Islamic texts teach that thousands of people followed Mohamed as soon as he migrated to Medina. These followers endorsed his prophethood and established his legitimacy. I hoped examining their testimonies would give me the tools I needed.

Jews as well as Arabs inhabited Medina so I planned to examine both groups. I found the Arabs of Medina converted to Islam because Mohamed was one of their own. They soon installed him as king and renamed their city after him. As I discovered earlier, Mohamed's great-grandmother was the chief commander of the largest area tribe. Mohamed's grandfather, who raised him, was born and grew up in Medina as well. Mohamed's own father died and was buried in Medina. Mohamed was a kinsman to them all. I could not find testimony from any Medina Arab about why they converted other than for reasons of tribal politics or economic gain. Mohamed told them who he was but did nothing to prove his prophethood.

One group in particular got my attention. The Jews of Medina were the original founders of the city. How, I wondered, did Mohamed convince them of his prophethood? I decided to follow Mohamed's footsteps and learn how he convinced the Jews of his legitimacy. In doing so, I would let my Prophet and hero speak for himself.

The first chapter I memorized in the Quran was "The Baqara," which means "the Cow." It is the longest chapter in the Quran and recounts how Mohamed proved to the Jews he was the final Prophet. In that chapter, verses 40–42, Mohamed cautioned the Jews *"not to be the first people to reject his prophethood and his legitimacy."* He insisted he was the one they had been waiting for, the one who would usher in the perfect religion and provide them victory after many years of defeat.

THE JEWS CHALLENGE MOHAMED'S PROPHETHOOD

The Jews dared to ask Mohamed the one question I was anticipating from the non-believers of the West: "Why should we believe you?" I was getting excited now because I knew I would soon have the answers I needed directly from the words and deeds of the Prophet.

To convince the Jews of his prophethood, Mohamed told them about his night journey to Jerusalem and his ascent into heaven and encounter with Allah. He told them it was similar to Moses's encounter with God but better. Instead of meeting God at a burning bush, Mohamed met him at his throne in heaven. Mohamed then explained to the Jews how Moses's message was actually all about him and the Jews distorted that message over the years. He also told them the promise to Abraham was about him as well. He instructed them in how they needed to leave behind their corrupt and distorted religious practices. Instead, the Jews should follow Mohamed. Only his message was perfect and was the one legitimate way to Allah. Mohamed then warned them in the strongest terms about the ramifications of not believing him.

The response of the Jews was shocking. They challenged Mohamed. They told him they didn't believe him. They refused to follow him. Not only that, they ridiculed him. They accused him of making up fantastic stories and imitating their own rituals. The Jews argued that he was promoting the exact same religious practices he wanted them to stop. Not only was he copying their practices, they scoffed, but he was also bowing in prayer to their holy city, Jerusalem, and praying in the exact same manner.

I was dumbfounded. Upon discovering this rebuke by the Jews, I asked myself how could anyone say those things to the Prophet? Who would be so foolish? I next looked to see how Mohamed responded to the Jews' impudence. This, I was confident, would give me what I needed. After all, there could be no better source than Mohamed on how to respond to doubters. I shouldn't have wasted my time with all my other studies. I should have started with this inquiry.

I re-read the "Cow" chapter with a critical eye. I went through all the Islamic textbooks recording Mohamed's encounter with the Jews. I dug into Islamic history books to find his argument, and I knew in my heart it would be amazing. Mohamed quoted the Jewish Book of Zephaniah, which reads, "For then I, God, will change the speech of the peoples to a pure speech so that all of them shall call on the name of the Lord and serve him with one accord." He told the Jews he, Mohamed, was the one who could assure all mankind would unite and serve the Lord "with one accord." Mohamed added that his revelation, "the Quran," was in total agreement with their prophets and their stories. The Quran provided solid proof his revelations were true and not a lie.

Their response? "Our stories are known to everyone and many details of your accounts are incorrect." They went so far as to describe Mohamed as *ha-meshuggah*, a "madman," a term frequently used by their religious leaders to describe those who believed themselves to be prophets without any proof or signs from God. There were more than five Jewish tribes in Medina when Mohamed moved there. Despite the differences among them, all agreed Mohamed was not a prophet.

Mohamed moved to Medina at the invitation of his kinsmen to act as an arbitrator. His task was to calm the bloody, political unrest among the Arab tribes and between the Arab tribes and the native Jews of Medina. A few days after his arrival in Medina, Mohamed volunteered to serve as king of the city. His tribe and the other Arab tribes approved immediately. They hoped he would bring Medina's Arabs a unifying religion similar to that of Jews. The Arabs also hoped Mohamed would relieve them of what they saw as the arrogant condescension of the Jews. The Arab tribes longed for authority over their Jewish neighbors, and I was sure the Jews must have known it. Jewish opposition to Mohamed appeared to have been both religious and political.

Mohamed's response to the Jews' rejection of him was classic. He dealt with them as only a true leader, a true Prophet, should. Mohamed reminded the Jews they were in Medina because the Romans expelled them from Jerusalem. He exploited their unspoken guilt over their failures to God. He said God was punishing them for their disobedience and for rejecting the words of the prophets through the ages. Then he chastised the Jews for rejecting and scheming to kill Jesus. Mohamed concluded his condemnation by telling the Jews if they rejected him as a prophet they would forever suffer the consequences.

I loved the way Mohamed made his case to the Jews. This line of attack was definitely going into my playbook to prove his prophethood and legitimacy. I felt Allah was finally giving me the weapons I needed to carry on. I would warn Westerners of the consequences of their actions, and I would be ready to prove the legitimacy of Mohamed, the Quran, and Islam. I needed no sword to propagate the message of Allah, at least not for now.

I decided to explore how the Jews responded to this superb argument. When Mohamed moved to Medina, he introduced the five-times-a day prayer ritual, and this became the main pillar of Islam. At that time, Mohamed had Muslims pray toward

Jerusalem, the site of the night journey. He built the first mosque in Islam to parallel the Jerusalem orientation for Islamic prayers. He also built his first home and the main mosque, where he governed as king and where he lived and prayed, to reflect that same orientation.

Mohamed also noticed the Jews were fasting from food, drink, and "marital relations" from sunset to sunrise on different days. One of those days was the day before Passover in remembrance of God's saving of Moses and his people by parting the Red Sea.

JEWS CHALLENGE MOHAMED'S RITUALS

Sahih Bukhari assures us, "When the Prophet arrived at Medina, the Jews were observing the fast on 'Ashura' [10th of Muharram] and they said, 'This is the day when Moses became victorious over Pharaoh.' On that, the Prophet said to his companions, 'You [Muslims] have more right to celebrate Moses' victory than they have, so observe the fast on this day.'"[17]

That is how fasting became another pillar of Islam, but it was not very clear yet how and when to fast for Muslims. Quran 2:183 reads, *"O, you who have believed, decreed upon you is fasting as it was decreed upon those before you that you may become righteous."* A handful of Jews, indifferent to their own religion, decided to follow Mohamed and adopt Islam merely for personal reasons. The overwhelming majority of Jews, however, refuted his arguments and rejected outright his claim to having received divine revelations from God. They labeled him instead as a false prophet. According to the Jews, a genuine prophet attained the highest degree of holiness and scholarship as well as a proximity to God. He was as close to human perfection as a man could get. The Jews boldly told Mohamed that by God's standards, he fell short, way short. They pointed to his mistreatment (beheading) of the prisoners of war after Badr and his caravan raids while passing by their city. These acts made him seem more like a pirate than a prophet. And just to make sure Mohamed got their point, the Jews reminded him how his behavior stood in stark contrast even to the honor code of the Arab tribes.

As I read this, I knew the Jews' arrogance would be met with swift repercussions. I anticipated Mohamed's response would validate him as Prophet and end this character assassination. But I didn't get the response I hoped for. Instead, Mohamed ordered the murder of one old Jewish poet, Abu Afak, who organized a poetry reading to celebrate their chastisement of Mohamed. I had wanted to see Mohamed show them exactly who he was without the use of the sword. I had to concede, though, Allah's words in the Quran made clear that those who insulted him or Mohamed must be killed. The Jews so ridiculed Mohamed for insisting he was a fulfillment of Jesus's prophecy about being "the one to come." In their view, Jesus was a madman. They reminded the equally mad Mohamed that even the followers of the "madman" Jesus would not accept his claim to being a prophet, believing instead they would be filled with the *Ruach ha-Kodesh*, the spirit of Yahweh.

As a Jewish rabbi, Jesus told his acolytes about the Hebrew concept of the Holy Spirit, the one who would come and guide them after his departure. Finally, just to ensure they soundly corrected him, the Jews reminded Mohamed, "You are not Jewish, and you are not of any Jewish decent or blood. Anyone who is not a Jew cannot be a prophet to us."

It was at this point I really needed my Prophet to speak up, to shut the arrogant mouths of these Jews who failed to appreciate the greatness of the man with whom they were dealing. I dug frantically through my sources. I was sure I would find where Mohamed told the Jews he was of the lineage of Ishmael and a direct descendent of Abraham and the prophets. And what did I find? Nothing. I found nothing he might have said to silence the Jews on this question at that time or any time. He said nothing to confirm he was uniquely related to Ishmael, whom both Jews and Christians believe to be Abraham's first son. Without his affirmation, I was left with a contradiction: Arab believers always take pride in their lineage and the connection to Mohamed. Why didn't Mohamed?

The Jews still were not done with Mohamed. They told him they had no reason to believe his claims of meeting Moses and the other prophets, let alone meeting God during the night journey. "You have no witnesses. You have nothing to corroborate your story," they sneered. They also insisted many of his alleged revelations in the Quran were identical to their stories of Abraham and Moses, but many other passages in the Quran contradicted their well-preserved ancient Scriptures. The Jews claimed, in fact, much of the Quran was completely incorrect, including its stories of King Solomon, Lot, and others.

The Jews then made the statements that took me to square one. They told Mohamed they were not about to abandon their ancient holy texts, their teachings, their laws—documents they preserved and defended for millennia as they would their own lives—unless Mohamed showed some compelling proof of his prophethood.

"It is not enough to tell us we have disobeyed many of our prophets before and warn us not to do it again by rejecting you," said the Jews. "Should we believe anyone who claims to be a prophet? God warned us of false prophets, so we will not believe you until you show proof."

I was enraged by the response of these stiff-necked people. They not only failed to listen to Mohamed, they also mocked him. They dismissed Mohamed and his followers as mere imitators who prayed as the Jews prayed, faced Jerusalem as the Jews faced, fasted as the Jews fasted. Mohamed thought he could depend on these Jewish tribes to support him, but they did just the opposite.

This was upsetting. I could find nothing to show how Mohamed proved his prophethood to the Jews. He played on their guilt, but that did not prove effective either. When Moses was faced with the doubters and questioned by Pharaoh, he performed miracles and proved himself, his prophethood, and his commission from God. This was all documented in the Quran. I could not understand why Mohamed, the final Prophet, superior to all others, did not do something similar or better with the Jews.

The Quran teaches Mohamed was shocked by the Jewish response. The Jews started calling him a madman, a false prophet, and a liar, and he responded by trying to appease them. He told them he believed as they did that the Trinity was blasphemy. He told the Jews they bore no responsibility for the death of Jesus because Jesus never actually died. He told them later, when the Romans became Christian, the Romans should never have blamed the Jews for Jesus's death and continue driving them from their homeland. Mohamed told them if they followed him as prophet they would be vindicated and, unified with the Muslims, they would be formidable. Yet again, they rejected him. I could make no sense of what I was reading. Why, I asked myself, would anyone be so foolish as to reject Mohamed and his arguments?

By this time, Mohamed had been the leader of Islam for twelve years in Mecca and eighteen months in Medina. Much of what the Jewish leaders said had the appearance of the truth. Mohamed's night journey to meet Allah took him to Jerusalem. Mohamed's prayers were oriented toward Jerusalem. I could not find Mohamed's refutation of the Jewish arguments.

ALLAH MAKES SOME CHANGES

To the best of my understanding, Allah intervened to ease Mohamed's frustration, telling him to change the direction of prayers from Jerusalem to Mecca and to change some of the names of the holidays so Islam would bear less resemblance to Judaism. As Quran 2:144 reminded me: "Mohamed! I am Allah and I have certainly noticed and am fully aware of your anguish and despair. That is why I will provide you with a better *qiblah* [direction for your prayers] with which you will be very pleased. So, turn your face toward al-Masjid al-Haram in Mecca. And tell all your followers that from now on, they need to face Mecca in their prayers and supplication. Indeed, this way those Jews will know you are telling them the truth and Islam is authentic, and not just following their ancient rituals. This will also be a warning to them that Allah is fully aware of the grief they are causing you."

This was just the beginning of the steps Mohamed took to persuade the Jews. He also went through a public reconstruction of his own house and the three mosques he built in Medina, the first ever built, to reflect the radical change in prayer orientation from Jerusalem to Mecca. He hoped this would end Jewish criticism. In exploring the history of these changes, I hoped so as well. The Quran describes Mohamed's decision-making in some detail:

> *The Jews and the stooges will challenge you by saying, "What has turned them away from their original qiblah?" Mohamed, tell them that I, Allah, was planning to make you face Mecca in your prayers all along, and for all those years I was telling you to face Jerusalem just to see what would happen when I changed it to Mecca. I did that test to see and truly examine who is a believer in Mohamed as a prophet and who is not. I wanted to make evident who would follow Mohamed all the way and who would turn back on his heels. And indeed, this is all difficult for you to understand but those who have true faith will follow Mohamed no matter what and they are the true Muslims.*
>
> (Quran 2:142–143)

As I soon realized the Jews did not yield, I was heartbroken. The Jews' ridicule was so effective, in fact, many of Mohamed's followers began to doubt his prophethood and to believe he was leading them astray. Likewise, Mohamed renamed the day of fasting, changing it from Passover to *Ashura*. The Jews continued to ridicule the name change and challenged Mohamed's legitimacy. To silence the Jews and to commemorate his first major military victory, which took place during the month of Ramada, *Ramadan* became the only obligatory fasting time for Muslims. This change in rituals also helped distance Mohamed and his followers from the Jews.

For the first time, I fully educated myself about the circumstances of that era. And I came up with zero, nothing. Mohamed never convinced the Jews of his prophethood. If he could not do it, how could I do it now? The fact he changed Islamic religious fundamentals and rituals to counter Jewish criticism would actually do more to dissuade my intended audience than persuade them. In fact, the Jewish tribes around Mohamed were so convinced he was *not* a prophet that they endured exile, executions, enslavement, and annihilation at the hands of Muslims rather than admit Mohamed was a prophet and follow him.

I felt I had sinned, and my sin was large. I harbored a hope the Prophet used stronger tools to persuade non-believers, he crushed their objections into dust. To doubt his actions, or lack thereof, was sinful and disobedient and I was overwhelmed with my shame.

CHAPTER 18

THE CHRISTIAN PROBLEM

*Should anyone argue with you concerning him, after
the knowledge that has come to you, then say: "Come!
Let us call our sons and your sons, our women and
your women, our souls and your souls, then let us pray
earnestly and call down Allah's curse upon the liars."*

—Quran 3:61

I was consumed with my quest and tormented by the questions I
was raising about my faith. To help me cope, I doubled down on
my research and on my faith. I started growing my beard for the
first time in my life and spent hours home alone studying.

My mother grew concerned when I stopped responding to her
phone calls. She took every opportunity to interrogate me about
how I was spending my time. She knew I had no studies to attend
to, and my outward appearance made it clear I was becoming more
devout. She even feared I might surprise her by joining one of the
jihad cells forming at the time and head out to a holy war.

My dad, knowing me as well as he did, had no fear that jihad
was in my future. Our shared calling was *dawah*, proselytizing by
preaching Islam. It was our weapon of choice in fulfilling our duty
to spread Islam. In a way, going off to war would have been easier.

Dawah required brainpower, research, and a close examination of the tenets of the faith. It was a hard path, but Dad and I felt we were smart enough and resourceful enough to meet the challenge. Dad, in fact, was pleased with the number of books I was taking from his library and my quick turnover of material. Neither he nor my mom had any idea about the struggle in which I found myself. In fact, no one was aware of the battle raging in my mind and heart, my growing desperation to find the truth.

As much as Dad knew about my Islamic research, he had no idea about the roadblocks I was encountering. His blindness to my struggles may have been willful, but my reluctance to speak of these struggles enabled his condition. I was terrified of even voicing my doubts to myself for fear of angering Allah and Mohamed. To cope, I wrote all such doubts off as the lies of Satan, and blamed myself for not being able to see the truth.

I was a mess, and life was becoming messier as I continued to seek answers. Each day, though, I firmly resolved to start my quest anew. I absolutely had to verify the legitimacy of Mohamed's prophethood for my arguments to fall into place. The message of Islam would be proven true—eventually. I was sure of it.

It seemed to me other prophets such as Noah, Abraham, and Jesus all performed miracles that inspired those around them. I found, however, many excuses to justify Mohamed's refusal to prove anything to the Jews. After all, Allah said the Jews deserve the worst of all punishments because of their faithlessness and disobedience through the ages. It seemed to me Allah didn't want the Jews to believe. He did not want them to redeem themselves. They were headed for Allah's rightful punishments, and it was not worth the trouble to deter them.

WHAT ABOUT THE CHRISTIANS?

That was the Jews. But what about the Christians? How did Mohamed approach them? Did he reason with them? Did he prove his prophethood to them beyond any doubt? If he had, then I would have my argument. For answers, I looked to the third chapter of the Quran, "The Family of Imran." Imran was the father of

Mary, the mother of Jesus. If I were to prove this family was chosen by God and that its members represented Allah, I had to identify signs and miracles proving as much.

This third chapter documents the miracles surrounding the birth of Mary. She is the only woman mentioned by name in the Quran and is referred to as the greatest of all women in the history of humankind. The Quran says divine intervention guided her life from the time of her own birth. As a young woman, she received a message from Allah through Gabriel that God had chosen her, purified her, and preferred her above all other women. The chapter also details and commemorates the miraculous conception and the birth of Jesus.

There was more. The chapter talks about Jesus breathing life into clay birds, healing lepers and the blind, and bringing the dead back to life. Jesus had the miraculous ability to know what people had just eaten and what the future would hold for them (Quran 3:49). The Quran confirms these miracles were performed only by the will of Allah. Had Allah not willed them to occur, they would never have come to pass. Allah gave Jesus this power to convince the skeptics of his truthfulness and to show Jesus was exactly who he claimed to be. After reporting Jesus's powers, the chapter delves into Mohamed's encounter with a group of Christians in Najran and his attempt to reason with them. Mohamed hoped to convince them of his truthfulness, his legitimacy, and his undeniable prophethood.

THE CHRISTIANS OF NAJRAN

Christianity took root in Najran a century before Mohamed was born. Located 750 miles south of Medina near Yemen, Najran was the first Christian enclave in the southern part of Arabia. At the time, the Byzantine Empire held sway over Najran and appointed its bishops. After Mohamed established himself as king of Medina, he began to expand the Islamic state. He had great success amassing territories across the Arabian Peninsula and expected nothing less than submission from the Christians in Najran.

To that end, he sent a letter to the bishops and deacons of the church in Najran, offering an invitation of sorts. "I invite you to worship Allah instead of worshiping Jesus; I invite you to be in communion with Allah instead of being in communion with what Allah had created, and I warn you that if you refuse to follow the accord, then you must pay the *jizyah*; otherwise, I must declare war on you."

When the bishop of Najran received the letter, he gathered the people and read it aloud, asking for their opinion. The Najranis decided to send a delegation of sixty of their leaders and elders to Medina. They elected their senior Christian scholar and Bishop, Abu Al-Haarith, to be the head of their delegation. His charge was to inquire why Mohamed was threatening them with either extortion or war. Given that Mohamed wanted the Najranis to abandon Christianity, the bishop also hoped to discover what was the foundation for this new faith of which Mohamed claimed to be the prophet.

After their long journey to Medina, the Najranis changed from their travel clothes into church garments made of fine silk and embroidered with crosses. Dressed for the occasion, they headed to Mohamed's mosque, the seat of government. Mohamed, however, refused to see them until they changed out of their church garments and removed their gold rings.

Upon reading this account, I smiled at the brilliance of the Prophet's demand. By requiring the Christian leaders to humble themselves before they came into his presence, he stripped them of their status. They obeyed and were given an audience with Mohamed. The Najranis asked, "Why do you want us to leave our faith? What are you asking us to follow? Do you not know that we worship God?" Mohamed responded that he was inviting them to Islam, the only true religion. He explained that their faith was based on false beliefs and teachings, and that they were worshiping the cross, not God.

Quran 5:72 reminded me of the truth behind Mohamed's demand: *"Blasphemers and infidels indeed are those who say, 'Jesus, the son of Mary is God' because the Messiah himself has said, 'O, children of Israel, worship Allah, my Lord and your*

Lord.' Indeed, he who associates others with Allah, Allah has forbidden him paradise and his refuge is the hell fire; no one will help them out from that destiny." Mohamed enumerated the various Christian errors. He told the Najranis worshiping the Trinity was not worshiping God. He explained God did not have a son. He called them "a cult of blasphemous idol worshipers" for eating pork and believing in three gods.

Quran 5:73 drove this point home for me: *"They have certainly committed blasphemy, those who say, 'God is the third of three,' i.e., the trinity, because there is no God but one, Allah. And if those do not desist from what they are saying, then they will receive a very painful punishment in hell fire."* I could not imagine Christians would have an argument against what Mohamed told them. Unwilling to yield, however, the bishop asked Mohamed, "Why do you humiliate Jesus by saying that he is a slave of Allah?" To which Mohamed responded, "Yes indeed, Jesus is a slave of Allah. He is just a prophet, even though he was immaculately conceived by the will of Allah. He is still just a regular human being."

The bishop replied, "Have you ever seen a human being without a father?" As Quran 3:59 instructed me, Mohamed was quick to respond. *"Indeed, Jesus is exactly like Adam. Allah created and formed both of them from nothing but dust by the mighty power of Allah's will."* The bishop and others in the Najrani delegation did not warm to Mohamed's message. They retorted, "According to you, all of our books are wrong. How can it be that all we know and understand of Jesus is completely different from what you are telling us? Do you know that we have documented eyewitness accounts of Jesus? Are you aware that his students wrote down everything they witnessed and all that he taught them? Why shouldn't we believe their accounts?"

Mohamed responded swiftly and firmly, reciting the Quran and telling the delegation those accounts were in error. He insisted Jesus's disciples were Muslims who submitted themselves to Allah, not to Jesus Christ. He told the Najranis their books were fraudulent. He explained how Jesus actually asked his disciples, "Who of you will testify and bear witness to my faithfulness to Allah and Allah's mission for me?" As Mohamed pointed out, Jesus's disciples bore witness that Jesus was a faithful Muslim prophet. They said, *"We truly believe in Allah and we testify that we are all faithful Muslims"* (Quran 3:52–53).

The bewildered Najrani delegates asked Mohamed the same questions I was expecting to be asked by those I would try to convert. Their bishop said, "Why should we believe you? How do we know that you are a prophet and that your words are true? Why should we discard our scripture and believe the Quran? And how do we know that your words are coming from God?"

As I continued to watch the narrative unfold, I knew the proof I needed was just around the corner, just a few more paragraphs into this compelling meeting of faiths. Said Mohamed, "What further proof do you need than the words of Jesus himself, who prophesied about me, who told you in your own books to wait for my arrival, to believe in me and follow my words in bringing you all truth? This should be in your scripture!" Mohamed recited the Quran once again, *"Jesus, the son of Mary, said, 'I am the messenger of Allah to you, confirming and fulfilling what came before me in the Torah and bringing good tidings of a messenger and a prophet who will come after me, whose name is Ahamed [i.e., Mohamed]"* (Quran 61:6).

Apparently, the Christians of Najran were as stubborn as the Jews of Medina. Their response was firm. "Our belief in Jesus remains unshaken," they told Mohamed. "We will neither forsake any of our scriptures, nor acknowledge that what you are saying about Jesus is true until you prove to us that you are not lying and that you are indeed a prophet sent by God, most high."

Growing angrier by the minute, Mohamed told them he had nothing more to offer that day. He asked, however, they wait as he would soon let them know what kind of deal he intended to propose. The delegation agreed to wait and allowed him all the time he needed to answer their questions. Mohamed wanted to hide. He did not want to confront, nor answer the Christians of Najran. He immediately went to his closest allies and said, *"I hope there is a thick wall between me and the Christians of Najran—a wall that will neither permit me to see them or them to see me!"*

Quran 17:45 reinforced this point: *"Allah will place a hidden barrier between you and those who do not believe."*

Meanwhile, everyone in the city waited with great anticipation for the Prophet to show the Christian delegation the errors of their ways. After many days, Mohamed emerged one morning carrying his twin grandsons, Hassan and Husain, the children of his daughter Fatima and her husband Ali. The delegation was surprised and wondered what he intended to do. Mohamed called out to the grand bishop of Najran, the official representative of the Catholic Church in the Arabian Peninsula. Mohamed said to him the Archangel Gabriel told him the best way to resolve the issue was through *Mubahala*. Instead of dueling with weapons, the Christians and Muslims would call down heavenly curses upon one another.

Mubahala was serious business. The Christians knew each side would have to pray that harm would befall the other side. What Mohamed was proposing was frightening. In the duel, Mohamed planned to cover himself and his family members with a large black tarp. He would then swear his claims were true and he was indeed the Prophet. If he were lying, heavenly curses would rain down on his family. If he were telling the truth, the Christians would be cursed for not believing him.

The circumstances certainly posed a dilemma for the Christian delegation, but Mohamed told them, *"This is what Allah has told me to do."* He continued with a verse from the Quran, *"Then whoever argues with you after everything you have told them, say, 'Come, let us call our sons and your sons, our women and your women, ourselves and yourselves, then supplicate earnestly against each other and invoke the curse of god upon the liars among us'"* (Quran 3:61).

As I delved deeper into this historical showdown, I found myself surprised. I read, memorized, and recited those very verses countless times since my early childhood, but I never contemplated the events leading up to them. As a believing Muslim, the context had no relevance for my life. That context wouldn't mean anything to any other Muslim either. But quite suddenly, those verses were

of supreme importance. I wanted to do exactly what Mohamed
was doing. I wanted to reach out to the Christians in neighboring
countries and share my Prophet's truth.

It was exciting for me to see the words of the Quran come to
life in new ways. From childhood on, I believed Christians would
be convinced of the truth of the Quran if only they read it. I
believed too they would feel an overwhelming urge to turn from
their counterfeit religion and embrace Islam. That's what happened to Umar. Other than Mohamed, Umar was the most famous
Muslim in history. It was he who brought Islam to the East and to
the West.

Soon enough my excitement ebbed. The verses revealed when
the Prophet and the Christians entered this match game of curses
they were at a standoff. The Prophet said we were to do the same
in persuading the skeptic: "Every Muslim can and should combat
his opponent and the skeptics by this same means of Mubahala."
I cringed. Mubahala struck me as entirely impractical in the modern world. I wasn't questioning the practice. Don't misunderstand.
But I couldn't figure out for the life of me how I was going to
challenge Christians to a cursing duel in the streets of London.
Mubahala could not conceivably be of use to me. I decided to read
on. I prayed I would find a solution to my dilemma before the
story's conclusion.

At first the Christians accepted Mohamed's challenge and told
him they would be prepared to engage with him the next day.
When the designated time arrived, Mohamed brought his family
forward, covered them with a large tarp, and swore Allah's curse
on himself if he was not a prophet. But the bishop quickly intervened. "We think it is not proper to curse you. After talking the
matter out among ourselves, we have decided to withdraw from
challenging you." Mohamed told the Najranis that left them with
three choices. The first one was to accept Islam. The second was
to pay the jizyah, a poll tax whose primary purpose was—and
is—to humiliate those who knowingly rejected Islam.

If the Christians paid, they could preserve their own faith while
the Islamic State fortified itself with the income. The third option
for the Najranis was to understand if they refused the first two

options, Mohamed would declare war and eradicate every single one of them from the face of the earth.

The Christians response shocked me. They said they would not convert to Islam but conceded they had no capacity to fight Mohamed's armies. Rather, they accepted the humiliation of the jizyah to save their lives. Said their bishop, "You may order us as you like, and we shall obey you and shall make peace with you."

I was dumbfounded. I had no idea why they would make that choice. For one thing, I failed to understand how they could not have been persuaded to leave their faith. After all, nearly every Islamic scholar from the time of Mohamed until the present has insisted Mohamed's Mubahala challenge was a vital proof of the rightfulness of Islam and his prophethood.

Mohamed said, *"By him in whose hand is my soul! Surely destruction had almost descended on the people of Najran. And if they had entered into imprecation, they would have been transformed into monkeys and pigs, and there would have erupted in the valley a conflagration of fire, engulfing them all; and surely Allah would have annihilated Najran and its inhabitants, even the birds on treetops, and the year would not have ended for all the Christians of the world but they would have perished."*[18]

WHAT NOW?

My mind was racing. I closed all the books scattered across my desk and throughout my home office, turned off the lights, and walked into the living room. I was exhausted, but I anxiously paced around the room nonetheless. The questions racing through my brain were dangerous. I desperately wished there was someone with whom I could talk about my discoveries.

Mohamed said I should not ask trivial questions and express doubts about his prophethood. During his lifetime, he allowed such questions. But upon his death, the matter was settled. No further questioning was permitted. Questions reflected disbelief, and disbelief was the kiss of death.

Specific verses of the Quran came to mind, specifically Quran 5:100–102: *"O, you who have believed and are true Muslims, do not ever ask about things which, if they are shown to you, will distress you and destroy you. Other people had asked such questions before you; then they became the disbelievers and apostates."* I was alone in my apartment. I knew full well what Mohamed warned. But he was long dead, and I could not ask him anything. I said aloud, "I don't disbelieve! I want others to believe!" I tried to sleep, but I could not find even a measure of peace by closing my eyes. Every time I tried, I was transported back to my dark bedroom when I had my first encounter with Allah. I vividly recalled how it felt to await Allah's punishment from the hands of my father.

That memory, however, gave me an idea. My father cleansed himself of earthly motives before cleansing me of earthly transgressions. I hoped if I performed the purification rituals in preparation of asking Allah for his forgiveness, my anguished soul might be calmed. It was just past midnight and still hours before the call to prayer at 4 a.m. Nevertheless, I decided to walk to the mosque in the darkness.

I used my keys to enter and waited there for my father to arrive hours later. I began to pray and told Allah over and over that I had the purest of intentions. My only desire was to take the holy Quran and Islam to every corner of the planet. I told Allah I would always believe, my heart could never be pulled away from my Prophet, the Quran, and Islam. There, alone in the mosque, I prostrated myself in full submission and acknowledgment I was Allah's slave. I begged him to help me find the answers. I poured out my heart and affirmed my devotion throughout the wee hours of the morning.

So agonized was I by the fear of being considered an apostate and spending an eternity in hell, I took no notice of my physical discomfort. In Islam, there is no greater sorrow than the one I experienced. I was terrified that Allah would see how precariously close to that fatal precipice I had wandered.

My father arrived many hours later and was delighted to see me spending the night in supplications, devotions, and prayers. My piety looked so very holy to him, but he had no idea of the agony I was experiencing. All he could see was his firstborn son following his example and growing in his likeness.

It was only after the morning prayers concluded and we were walking home together that he looked me in the eye and asked if I was okay. I wanted to cry out, "No, I am not. I need help!" But I assured him all was well and continued to walk silently. Maybe that long morning spent in prayer was just what I needed to energize me for yet another round of research. Maybe I just needed to look a little deeper.

FOLLOW-UP RESEARCH

Once home, I gathered the books scattered across the room and dove back in. I had to consider once again what the Quran said about the Mubahala challenge and how it proved Mohamed's prophethood. I read those verses many times. I believed those verses. *But* I still could not understand why the Christians of Najran refused to become Muslim. The tax alone should have prompted them to convert. Their words and actions defied all my expectations. Try as I did, I had no idea what to think about this pivotal event in Islamic history.

The Najranis originally accepted Mohamed's challenge but then abruptly changed course. What happened? Further research revealed a wise old man from the Christian delegation confronted his Christian brothers. "What have you done?" the wise man asked. "How can you accept such a challenge? You know very well that Mohamed is a king. Do you think that he will allow you to get away after cursing him in front of his people and all of his followers? You have no means to either prove that he is lying or to prove that he's a prophet. Either way, he will prevail over you and will not spare any one of us!"

I thought the Christians made the right decision, but not for the reason I hoped. The words of the old wise man were true. By that time, Mohamed was already a powerful king. He had chalked up unprecedented military victories and secured vast swaths of land. Through his conquests he was on the verge of uniting the entire Arabian Peninsula under his kingship. There had never been such a powerful army. Mohamed was not a man to trifle with. For all his power, however, the Najranis refused to believe Mohamed was the prophet. Their own words and actions showed they were just protecting their own skins. They made the decision they did simply to avoid annihilation.

True, the Christians were protected by the great Byzantine Empire, but that empire was already engaged in a bloody, exhausting war with the Persians. The cumulative effect of a quarter century of almost continuous Byzantine-Persian conflict left both empires crippled. I understood why the Christians of Najran wanted to find a resolution that did not require the spilling of blood.

The Najrani course of action seemed to be the rational one. I had no experience with running an empire or fighting a war, but it seemed to me the last thing Heraclius, the emperor of Byzantium, would have wanted was to send his battered army thousands of miles south to defend the Christians from Mohamed. As a case in point, in AD 628, Heraclius sent a letter to Khosrow II of the Persians, which read, "I pursue and run after peace. I do not willingly burn Persia, but am compelled by you. Let us now throw down our arms and embrace peace. Let us quench the fire before it burns everything."

The eighty thousand *dirham* the Najranis gave Mohamed to avoid another war seemed a small price to pay. A century earlier, a Jewish king named Dhu Nowas sacked Najran and slaughtered those who would not renounce their Christian faith. The massacre was brutal, and the details were horrifying. All the priests, deacons, and nuns were thrown into a ditch filled with burning fuel. The smell of burning flesh permeated the air and was forever etched in Najrani memory. That incident had to factor into their decision to avoid warfare.

Fear of another massacre was one of many good reasons for the Christians to back away from a confrontation with Mohamed. That said, I understood clearly the Christians would have never backed down had they believed Mohamed to be who he claimed to be. They would have simply bowed to him and converted to

Islam. They didn't. They chose to submit and pay the tax. This was great for Mohamed at that time, but not so great for me in my quest for understanding.

In the ensuing treaty with the Christians of Najran, Mohamed promised in return for their paying the jizyah, they would not have to fear attack by the Muslim army. The treaty also allowed the Najranis the unfettered practice of their own faith. I didn't dwell on that too much. After all, they were steadfast in denying Mohamed's appeal. But what really bothered me was the way Mohamed worded the treaty. It read in part, "In the name of the Lord of Ibrahim, Ishaq, and Ya'qub [Abraham, Isaac, and David]." I did not understand why Mohamed failed to mention Ishmael. I thought he would have mentioned Ishmael to establish his own descent from the family of the prophets, a natural first step in proving his own claim to prophethood.

Reading the history of my faith was becoming mind-numbingly frustrating. The Jews challenged the Prophet and he answered them by changing the direction of the prayers from Jerusalem to Mecca. The Christians challenged him, and he answered them by calling down curses from heaven. He didn't succeed in persuading either group that he was who he claimed to be. The Jews chose to die rather than to follow Mohamed. The Christians chose to be extorted rather than converted. I shuddered to even think this thought, but Mohamed actually lost these battles of the mind. If I took Mohamed's arguments to the West I would certainly lose too.

I was in dangerous territory. I did my best to bury that heretical thought as deeply into my subconscious as possible, but I had to admit I was reaching the point of obsession. It was imperative I find solid ground to reaffirm everything I knew as truth, and quickly!

CHAPTER 19

ISLAM THE VICTORIOUS

You Muslims are called upon to fight and you will face mighty military powers. You must fight them hard until they submit to Allah and Islam and you will be rewarded by enormous rewards from the war spoils and Allah will reward you again in heaven. Do not turn away from that fight or Allah will punish you severely.

—Quran 48:16

For all of his success in Medina, Mohamed's path to world ascendancy can be traced to Mecca. Following years of friction, he was somehow able to convert its citizens, shedding only a minimum of blood in the process. Certainly, what happened in Mecca represented a profound turn in world history. I was hopeful the answers to my questions would be found there. What, I wondered, did Mohamed do to win the Meccans' hearts and minds? What could I learn from his victory that would help me convince the Europeans of Islam's truth?

For twenty long years, the people of Mecca were sworn enemies of the Prophet. In a shockingly short period of time, however, they submitted and became Muslims. This mass conversion was, in my mind, nothing less than a miraculous revelation of Mohamed's power. Were he not who he said he was, he could never have brought about such a turn of events. The Meccans had to have seen overwhelming evidence of his prophethood to forget the bloody conflicts of the past and follow Mohamed. One thing was certain: I would discover what that evidence was and use it going forward to fuel my mission.

In the years prior to Mecca's conversion, Mohamed accumulated a great deal of power through his alliances with regional tribes. The Arabian Peninsula was split in two, with Medina holding sway over the north and Mecca over the south. Mohamed's counterpart in Mecca was King Abu Sofian. Commissioned to convert all mankind, Mohamed was determined to unite these two kingdoms under his leadership. He accomplished this beginning with the Treaty of Hudaybiyya.

The conversion of Mecca began with something of a dream. In March 628 Mohamed envisioned he and his followers would march to Mecca and perform the umrah, an abbreviated pilgrimage. Prior to that time, the umrah had nothing to do with Islam. In fact, pilgrimages to Mecca had been part of the polytheistic traditions of the region for more than two centuries.

Mohamed told his followers he found his inspiration for the umrah not so much in a dream, as in a divine prophesy, a direct order from Allah. Allah instructed him to add the pilgrimage to the Islamic rituals. And so, he set out toward Mecca with 1,400 of his followers. On hearing the Muslims were on their way to Mecca, the king of Mecca sent his cavalry out to stop the approaching group. Envoys were sent back and forth, and ultimately, a peace treaty was signed in the area known as Hudaybiyya, hence the name.

Many issues were discussed during the meetings of the envoys, but one event in particular stood out to me, and for very good reason. When the people of Mecca denied Mohamed entry to the city, Mohamed sent a man named Othman as an emissary to start the negotiations. But the Meccans held Othman as prisoner and refused to tell Mohamed his whereabouts. They were testing Mohamed's abilities as Prophet. His followers looked to him for answers, but what he told them was Othman was dead.

Mohamed called his followers together. He asked them to pledge to fight to the death to avenge the murder of Othman. The gathering took place under a tree and is known as the "Pledge of the Tree." Each man came before Mohamed, placed his hand on top of the Prophet's, and pledged his allegiance. Some were reluctant, others enthusiastic.

Quran 48:18 explains the consequences: *"Certainly, Allah was well pleased with the believers when they swore allegiance to you under the tree, and he knew what was in their hearts, so he sent down tranquility on them and rewarded them with a near sure victory."*

To the Meccans, the pledge was a powerful demonstration of the loyalty and faith of Mohamed's followers. What was lacking, though, was a demonstration of Mohamed's abilities as a Prophet. A prophet would have known that Othman was not dead. To undermine Mohamed's claim to prophecy, the Meccans released Othman and sent along an ambassador of their own, Suhayl ibn Amr, to negotiate the terms of the treaty. As fascinating as this history was, however, it offered no proof of Mohamed's prophethood.

When the treaty was being drafted, Amr insisted Mohamed use his birth name, Bin Abdullah. Furthermore, he demanded the treaty not refer to Mohamed as a prophet or even mention Islam as a religion. Shockingly, Mohamed agreed to both conditions.

The Quran says many of Mohamed's followers were puzzled by his concessions. His son-in-law, Ali, who was drafting the treaty, was so angered by the demands of the Meccans he stopped writing. Mohamed grabbed the original draft and wrote his name in as "Bin Abdullah" after crossing out a reference to himself as prophet. By his own hand, he deleted his claim of prophethood. This action itself conflicts with the common knowledge that Mohamed was illiterate. How and when did this story change?

UMAR HAD DOUBTS!

Umar, the famed Islamic jurist, thought the treaty too conciliatory, both theologically and politically. Fully aware of Mohamed's failure to discern that Othman was alive and well, Umar did not shy from telling Mohamed his prophecy about the pilgrimage missed the mark. "That day I doubted the legitimacy of Islam and Mohamed," said Umar. He then asked Mohamed, "Are you really a prophet and messenger of God?" Mohamed responded, "Yes, I am the prophet of God."

Umar wasn't satisfied and went to Abu Bakr with the same questions. Abu Bakr backed his friend. Umar is recorded to have later said had he found a hundred men to go with him, he would have revolted against Mohamed that very day.

MOHAMED EXPLAINS HIS WAY OUT OF TROUBLE

Mohamed's justification for the failed prophecy struck me as curious. He told Umar and others who questioned him, they simply misunderstood the time frame for the fulfillment of the prophecy. He insisted he never said *when* the pilgrimage would happen—just *that* it would happen. Hundreds of Mohamed's followers left their home in Medina days before appropriately dressed for a pilgrimage. They marched. They chanted. Mohamed marched and chanted right alongside them. Had they misunderstood the time frame, then what was Mohamed doing there in their midst? These followers had to have been mightily confused.

But then again, only Allah knew the unseen and hidden. The Quran 27:65 makes this point: *"When they ask you, Mohamed, about why you didn't know, say, 'None in the heavens and earth knows the unseen except Allah. And with Allah are the keys of the unseen; none knows them except him'"* (Quran 7:188 and Quran 6:59).

In one sense, I was relieved Umar, a great champion of Islam, questioned Mohamed and the faith. If he asked those questions, then perhaps I was not guilty for asking similar ones given all I discovered. It was disturbing, though, that Umar was one of Mohamed's best friends and followers for many years. He was second only to Abu Bakr. He was a staunch supporter who lived through many of the events I have detailed thus far. He readily attested to the truthfulness of the story of Mohamed's birth, the encounter with the angel in the cave, the night journey, Mohamed's ascension into heaven to meet Allah, and his encounters with Gabriel through which the Quran was revealed.

This was the same Umar, who, upon reading the Quran, dropped to his knees in total submission to Mohamed and Islam. Mohamed even pronounced that if there were to be any prophets after him, it would be Umar. And yet even Umar had doubts about Mohamed's prophethood. When I recognized Umar was said to be reading the Quran at least fifteen years before it was actually written, my own doubts increased.

Umar's doubts came to a grand crescendo on the journey home. Taking a place in the back of the entourage, he said to himself, "O Umar! You keep asking but Mohamed did not answer any of your questions. You surely deserved to die!" Umar wasn't alone. Many of Mohamed's followers were skeptical but remained silent for fear of retaliation. Perhaps sensing their unease, Mohamed broke a long silence and proclaimed, *"I swear by Allah, this treaty is definitely a victory."*

The would-be pilgrims mumbled, "What kind of victory is it?" Mohamed rebuked them, *"That is a bad statement! Yes, this treaty is the greatest victory because now we could enter their land, back and forth freely, whether they like it or not. Islam is a de facto reality, which they have not liked up to now. In the near future, Allah will make you defeat them and gain all the benefits. Indeed, this is the greatest conquest."*

Mohamed then recited Quran 48:27: *"Truly! Allah will fulfill Mohamed's prophecy and you all will conquer Mecca. Allah and his prophet knew what ye knew not, and he granted, besides this, a speedy victory."*

THE DOUBTS PILE UP

Yes, yes, I had read it all before. But this time I couldn't control my own doubts. How, I asked myself, was this retreat a fulfillment of prophecy? At best, it seemed to be little more than an astute political gambit. In any case, the Quran reading comforted Mohamed's followers, who said, "What Allah and Mohamed say is right. This treaty is the greatest conquest. Oh, Messenger of

Allah! We did not think as you did. You definitely know Allah's orders better than us!" Umar, too, expressed his remorse. He said, "In the hopes that one day I will be forgiven, I fasted, gave alms, and performed many extra prayers."

Unfortunately, I found this episode less convincing of Mohamed's prophetic powers than his followers did. It did nothing to explain what caused the people of Mecca to embrace Islam. There had to be more to the story. Only by digging into the historical record would I find the missing links.

I was certain of one thing: prior to the treaty with Mecca, Mohamed had only converted about 150 people to Islam over a period of ten years. When he moved to Medina and became king, he accumulated roughly ten thousand followers during the next six years. But after the Treaty of Hudaybiyya, which gave Mohamed legitimacy as a recognized king, the number of followers exploded to more than one hundred thousand in a year and a half and continued to grow.

It was clear the alliance with Mecca was a brilliant political first step in expanding Mohamed's influence and power. Through his agreement with the king of Mecca, he was able to prevent the Mecca military from interceding in Mohamed's future conquests in the region.

MOHAMED RECRUITS KHALID BIN WALEED

The treaty was just the beginning. Mohamed had further designs on Mecca. Standing in his way was a fierce warrior, Khalid bin Waleed, who guarded the city of Mecca and its people. For Mohamed to succeed, he had to first convert Khalid. Born to fight, Khalid was a valuable asset to have in any battle. His brother, Walid, was not at all like Khalid. A cousin of Mohamed's sixth wife, Walid was taken prisoner by Mohamed's forces early on and quickly converted to Islam. A free follower of Mohamed, he took it upon himself to reach out to his warrior brother and encourage his conversion. Within a short time, Khalid saw the benefit of joining Mohamed and becoming the commander-in-chief of the Islamic military forces.

Khalid was not much on religion. His ancestors' religious practices never appealed to him, and even after joining Mohamed he did not commit himself to Islam's religious elements. I realized Mohamed did not win him over with talk of God. He spoke to his human nature, his desire to fight and conquer. He appealed to the warrior in the man. In that Khalid never sought out God, I could not consider his alliance with Mohamed a conversion.

Khalid was, however, a military genius and a very useful man for Mohamed to have in his court. Better still, he brought along two valuable friends when he abandoned the defense of Mecca: Amr ibn al-As, who would later conquer Egypt and Northern Africa for Islam, and Othman ibn Talha, the keeper of the key to the Kaaba.

MOHAMED ATTACKS KYBER

Less than two months after the Treaty of Hudaybiyya, Mohamed took advantage of the political confusion among the tribes and launched an attack against Kyber, the largest and most influential Jewish tribe in the Arabian Peninsula. These Jews thought Mohamed a false prophet, a dangerous, power-hungry one. They used their wealth and influence to incite other tribes to resist him.

They did not succeed. A swift series of surprise attacks enabled Mohamed to subdue them. The treaty with Mecca helped as it prevented the Meccans from offering assistance to their former ally. Mohamed's army confiscated all the enemy's weaponry. Now even better armed, he deftly used the victory to enlarge his kingdom. He appointed some of his loyal followers to remain in the region and oversee the conquered people, still another reminder he was not to be taken lightly. Refusing to convert and unwilling to die, the conquered Jews of the region paid handsomely with the jizyah, further enriching Mohamed's coffers.

MECCA SUBMITS

As furious as he was about Khalid's defection, King Abu Sufyan was powerless to do anything about it. It is recorded Khalid said, "We are the main fodder. Mohamed is victorious over the Arabs and non-Arabs." In other words, Khalid was willing to die serving in Mohamed's army. These were pretty strong words, but they did not impress his king. Said Abu Sufyan, "Even if I were the only Qurayshi alive, I would never follow him!"

Abu Sufyan came to eat those words. Mohamed asked to marry his daughter, a recently widowed Christian living in Ethiopia. She was delivered to him in Medina, and there they wed. No longer able to deny Mohamed's influence in the region, Abu Sufyan visited his daughter in Medina and entered negotiations with Mohamed. The terms of the deal came to light when Mohamed marched his army into Mecca with Khalid leading the Bedouin troops. Unlike others vanquished by Mohamed's army, the people of Mecca were given equal protection under the law. With Abu Sufyan rendered irrelevant, Mohamed took the city without resistance, and Mecca became a part of his empire.

His first act was to walk toward the Kaaba and remove all other religious icons. In fulfillment of his prophetic dream, he pledged to make the pilgrimage to Mecca the fifth pillar of the Islamic faith. For all of Mohamed's success, however, I had grave doubts about any kind of a mass conversion. If Mohamed proved his prophethood to the people of Mecca, I could see no evidence.

The treaty with Mecca, together with the decisive victory over the Jews, sent shockwaves throughout the region. Every king and military leader took notice of Mohamed. His rising Islamic kingdom was recognized as a dominant political force, and Islam was emerging as the de facto religion of the Arabian Peninsula.

Many have seen Mohamed's victory as proof of his prophethood and a sign of divine intervention. But I couldn't allow myself to see it that way, at least not at that juncture of my investigation. Perhaps when I was younger this information would have sufficed, but I was in a different place now. I needed to offer proof to a doubting, stiff-necked people, proof that Islam was the only true religion and the only path to Allah.

NO PROOF OF PROPHETHOOD

Mohamed's incredible military and political prowess was laudable, but his victories did not prove him a prophet. If they had, countless successful men throughout history could have claimed to be prophets as well. Alexander got the name "Great" because he conquered the known world. Was he a prophet? George Washington led an ill-equipped, ragtag army to defeat the mighty British Empire. He may have been the "Father" of his country, but was he a prophet? How about Vladimir Lenin and Adolf Hitler? They too rose to great power against all odds. But none of these men was a prophet, and Quran 2:49–52 explains why: *"How many times Allah has permitted a small army to overcome and become victorious over a larger army. Allah will always turn people against each other, thwarting kingdoms in the face of rising ones, because Allah will always keep the balance and prevent the human race from the total corruption of power."*

I could not understand why Mohamed sent threatening letters to kings or why he issued ultimatums offering tribal leaders a choice between submission and annihilation. After all, what did threats have to do with spreading the message of God? How was that prophet-like? Did other prophets throughout history intimidate converts into the fold?

Converting a king through coercion affects everyone in a kingdom, but subduing a people creates only followers, not believers. Followers can be persuaded to follow another, more appealing option if given the opportunity. True believers, on the other hand, will choose martyrdom over apostasy and stand by their faith even unto death.

At this point, I realized I sounded just like the man on the train. I wasn't making progress, and I was heartsick for the lack of it. Yes, Mohamed established himself as a legitimate political leader. He built alliances and eliminated foes, but there was nothing particularly spiritual about his conquests. This absence of spirituality did not seem to trouble his followers. They saw the value of proclaiming the superiority of the faith in tandem with military superiority and urged Mohamed to create a seal that would declare to others exactly who he was. The result was a signet ring forged in silver emblazoned with the words, "Mohamed, the Apostle of Allah." Three words appeared on the ring: "Allah" on top, "Apostle" in the middle, and "Mohamed" on the bottom. No duplicate was ever made.

CHAPTER 20

THE SPREAD OF ISLAM

Thawbān (may Allah be pleased with him) reported: The Messenger of Allah (may Allah's peace and blessings be upon him) said: "Allah brought the corners of the earth together for me, so I saw its eastern and western parts. The dominion of my Ummah will definitely reach as far as what was brought together for me (all parts of the world). I have been granted the two treasures, the red and the white. I asked my Lord not to destroy my Ummah due to a common drought nor to afflict them with an enemy from other than themselves who would annihilate them. My Lord said: 'O Mohamed, when I pass a decree, it is not retracted. I have granted that I will not destroy your Ummah by a common drought, nor will I release against them an enemy from other than themselves, who will annihilate them—even if the people from the surrounding regions join forces against them—until they themselves kill and capture each other.'"

—Hadith 297

My study of Mecca's submission left me frustrated and confused. I was apparently not worthy of the task I set for myself. I was beginning to doubt my commitment to the faith, to worry whether I was Muslim enough to accomplish my mission. I wondered why Allah was not opening my heart, not allowing me to see what I needed to see. Did Allah not want me to be one of his soldiers? Did he not want me in his kingdom? How, I asked myself, could the truth of Mohamed's prophethood convert the world when it could not even convince me?

My next step became clear. I needed to examine the spread of Islam. When I opened a world map on my table, I could see the Muslim world was one vast contiguous area. There were no isolated pockets of Islam, and that got me thinking. Why didn't Muslims travel across the seas to different lands and tell all nations about their faith the way Christians did?

I would have liked to think people across the globe would immediately convert if they were given the truth of Islam. Alas, the physical evidence stared me in the face, and it said otherwise. Islamic lands bordered one against another because Islam spread only through conquest. Marching armies carried the faith forward, not missionary imams. When Muslim power started to ebb in AD 750 or thereabouts, Islamic territory began to retract and has been retracting ever since.

ISLAMIZATION OF EGYPT

With a sense of dread, I knew I needed to look at my own country to see how and why it became Islamic. I always believed the conquest of Egypt was a liberation of the Egyptian people from their Christian Roman rulers. They then had the free choice of whether to become Muslim or not. Finally, the country as a whole submitted to the prophethood of Mohamed and came under the Islamic flag.

The truth was more complicated. At the time Egypt began converting to Islam, a high percentage of the people were Coptic Christians. My ancestors were probably among those Coptic people. In the way of background, the Coptic Christians split from the rest of Christendom in the fifth century over doctrinal disputes. For the next few centuries, they remained in a heated rivalry with the Byzantine Orthodox Church. The Byzantine Empire aggravated the split by using its political power to oppress the Copts, often violently.

Because of their ongoing persecution and their inability to defend themselves, the Egyptian Copts were less alarmed by the invading Muslims armies than they might have been. All they knew about the newcomers was they were monotheists like themselves. Having little political power as it was, the Copts figured they could be no worse off under Muslim rule than under Byzantine rule. They stayed largely on the sidelines as Muslim Arabs and the Byzantine defenders struggled to control the Egyptian colony.

The invading Muslims played it smart. They told the Copts they were related to them through Hagar, the mother of Ishmael, and they also believed in the oneness of god. They reminded them too how Mohamed married one of their own, Maria Qubtiyya, also known as Maria the Copt. More importantly perhaps, the Muslims promised the Copts personal freedom and religious liberty. To seal the deal, they guaranteed the return of the Coptic pope of Alexandria exiled by the Byzantines. These terms must have had a powerful appeal for the oppressed Copts.

The Egyptians followed through with their promise to side with the Muslims until they defeated the Byzantine army, and the Muslims followed through on their promise to return the Pope. Omar, the head of the Muslim state at the time, issued two documents simultaneously. One, the Treaty of 8 November 641, affirmed the defeat of the Byzantines. The second, the Pact of Omar, explained how Christians should interact with Muslims going forward.

I read over both documents carefully. The November 8 treaty dealt with the safeguarding of the churches and the security of the Christian population in Egypt. On the surface, all seemed well and good, but a parallel document, signed later between the Pope and Omar and called the "Pact of Omar," detailed various conditions.

First, the jizyah was to be paid by all *dhimmis,* meaning the protected non-Muslim subjects, mainly the Christians and Jews. Second, dhimmis were required to offer free hospitality to all Muslim soldiers for three days in their churches. Third, the dhimmis were to be loyal subjects to their Muslim rulers.

This submission led to all manner of indignities. Dhimmis were permitted to ride only on donkeys and even then to ride them side saddle. They were required to rise in the presence of Muslims. They had to wear clothing distinguishing them from Muslims. They were not to raise their voices in prayer and could hold religious processions only quietly. Their church bells were to be rung in low tones.

Only under these conditions were Egyptian Christians, most of them Copts, allowed to retain their established churches. They were not, however, allowed to restore ruined churches or build new ones. The covenant also stipulated dhimmis not have authority over Muslims in any jobs they held.

My discoveries revealed all too much. The Christians of Egypt were humiliated. The dhimmis were clearly second-class citizens. They were denied jobs, denied status, denied the right to govern their own county. The only way a dhimmi could become a full citizen was to become a Muslim. In addition to the ongoing humiliation, those who refused conversion had to pay an extra tax to live in their own country.

I always believed Muslims liberated my ancestors, and, once liberated, my ancestors embraced Islam for its beauty and truth. Instead, they were merely subjected to a different master. Free from the sporadic oppression of the Byzantine Empire, the Copts became permanently enslaved to their Muslim overlords. Everything I believed was dead wrong.

I could find no proof of Mohamed's prophethood anywhere in the historical record. A defeated people were trying desperately to mitigate their misery, and that is how Egypt became Islamic. Had I been in my ancestors' shoes, I wasn't sure whether I would have lived as a dhimmi or converted to Islam to secure the rights of full citizenship.

ONE MORE ISSUE

I had to consider one other issue: Why was Abdullah bin Sarh named the first Muslim governor of Egypt? Bin Sarh was a Quran keeper. His job was to memorize the passages of the Quran as they were revealed to Mohamed and write them down. He also frequently impersonated the Angel Gabriel when people doubted Mohamed's encounters. In fact, he went so far as to call Mohamed a liar and to say he made everything up. Later, however, he recanted everything he said and did in support of Mohamed. Yet, somehow bin Sarh ascended to the lofty position of governor.

Typically, those who said such horrible things about Mohamed could expect to be killed. According to Muslim lore, the one other man who blasphemed as bin Sarh did was executed. As the story went, the man was buried multiple times, and each time the earth expelled his body. I once considered Allah's intervention in this case a remarkable spiritual statement, but now I saw it as a warning to Muslims lest they consider straying. The message was coming across to me loud and clear—you will never rest in peace if you reject Allah and his Prophet.

These two stories added significance in that both men belonged to Mohamed's inner circle. Each was tasked to memorize the Quran, and each later admitted he impersonated Gabriel to convince Mohamed's followers of the Prophet's legitimacy. They were the first eyewitnesses to the birth of Islam, and both thought Mohamed a fraud.

CHAPTER 21

THE PILGRIMAGE PROBLEM

Indeed suffa and marwah are among the symbols of Allah so whoever makes Hajj there is no blame upon him or her for walking between them. Indeed Allah is appreciative and all knowing.

—Quran 2:158

My research was bankrupting me spiritually. I got answers, but not the answers I needed. In every instance, the evidence justified the skepticism of the man on the train and was gutting my belief system.

For fear of what I would learn, I put off examining the one thing that meant more to me than any other—the pilgrimage. The pilgrimage gave me my mountaintop experience and made me a man. It was through the pilgrimage I was bonded with my father in a way I could not have otherwise. I cried out to Allah to fortify my faith through study of the pilgrimage. Please, Allah!

Here was what I knew. After Mohamed absorbed Mecca, the pilgrimage became a pillar of the Islamic faith. I needed to take a closer look at the four features of pilgrimage: the Kaaba, the Zamzam well, the two hills, and Mt. Arafat. I then had to determine why they were not adopted until near the end of Mohamed's ministry.

KAABA

As mentioned in detail earlier, the Kaaba is the house of Allah in Mecca. Prior to Islam, there were many kaabas built throughout the Arabian Peninsula. Their purpose was to bring trade and income into each community. After his treaty with the Meccan king, Mohamed commissioned Khalid to destroy all other kaabas throughout the Arabian Peninsula. Only the one in Mecca would remain. This episode confused me. I had to question whether Mohamed conceived the pilgrimage as an exercise of faith or as a way to enhance revenue. I read the relevant verses in the Quran and noticed for the first time the Quran does not insist Muslims make the pilgrimage. It merely allows Muslims to make one. No other Islamic ritual has this level of inconsistency. Allah never required the pilgrimage. Quran 2:197 says as much. Mohamed was the one to require it.

Looking at the Kaaba with fresh eyes, I could see it did not become the center of Islam until six years prior to Mohamed's return to Mecca. In fact, Mohamed preached Islam for fifteen years before centering the new faith in Mecca. He made this move to counter the Jewish claim that the then Jerusalem-centric Islam was little more than a bad copy of Judaism. It was becoming increasingly clear to me Mohamed turned toward Mecca for no more enlightened a reason than to distance himself from Jewish theology.

ZAMZAM

As the story goes, an angel visited Mohamed's grandfather in a dream, telling him about a water source below where he slept. When the grandfather woke, he started digging and, sure enough, discovered the well. He also discovered, in the same spot, some gold statues and antiquities left behind by Roman soldiers during their expeditions in the Arabian Peninsula. The grandfather melted down the gold, built an altar, and used the gold as the door of the altar.

Until his death, he served as custodian of the city's water supply, a position inherited by his son and Mohamed's uncle, Abu Talib.

The ZamZam well was the favorite spot in Mecca for my dad and me. We used to sit and talk and pray there for hours. As treasured as was this memory, though, I had to disturb it with a question: What about Abraham, Hagar, and Ishmael? I believed, as all Muslims did, Allah ordered Abraham to leave his wife Hagar and his infant son Ishmael in a barren valley with no water and no food. Hagar ran between the two hills of Safa and Marwa desperately looking for a water source for herself and her son. She found nothing until the Angel Gabriel arrived, stuck the earth with his wing, and opened the well, an ever-flowing source of water that would not run dry until the day of resurrection. That was the reason for Mecca's foundation as a historical city. Unfortunately, my research revealed no historical signs of its existence at the time of Abraham.

THE TWO HILLS

Then there was the question of the two hills in the story, Safa and Marwa. Named for pagan gods in the pre-Islamic era, they were once used for pagan worship. Given the pagan legacy of the two hills, Mohamed's followers questioned the incorporation of the running-between-the-hills ritual into Islamic practice.

The legend says two people, Isaf and Naailah had illicit sex in this area. Evidently it was either incestuous sex or adulterous. Whichever, it was so bad an affair that god turned them each into stone. Years later when Qusai built the Kaaba, he moved those two stones to two adjacent hills on the outskirts of Mecca. Later on, people started putting their idols in the Kaaba—360 different ones. The Quresh tribe, however, was the only tribe that would circumambulate the Kaaba and then go between the hills chanting and calling on these two idols. They would say, "Here I am, submitting myself before you, Isaf," asking for his favor. After seven times around the Kaaba they would have their heads shaved. This ritual took place for hundreds of years before Mohamed's time.

When Mohamed conquered Mecca, the first thing he did was destroy all the idols except Isaf and Naailah. His journey to Mecca was the first pilgrimage, and he wanted to make its commemoration a pillar of Islam. He told his followers to continue the tradition of walking between the legendary idols of Isaf and Naailah. His followers were outraged. They told Mohamed this order was crazy. Mohamed went to Aisha for advice. As a result of his conversation with her, he came out with Quran 2:58. Mohamed then eased the troubled souls of his followers by having them destroy the two statues on top of the mountains, allegedly at Allah's command. He retained the chant however, but substituted the name Allah for Isaf! It wasn't until about three months later he came up with the story of Hagar running between the two hills. Unfortunately, the hadith explaining all this did not ease *my* troubled soul. I found myself doubting its legitimacy.

MOUNT ARAFAT

I understood Mount Arafat was where Abraham took his son Ishmael to sacrifice him, but I could find no historical record of Abraham visiting this area. Islamic teaching and history both said Abraham was living in the region that is now part of Iraq, Syria, and Jerusalem. What Islamic history did not address was how Abraham made it to Mecca, which is more than a thousand miles away from Jerusalem and even farther from Damascus or Baghdad.

Even more troubling, I was always told Mohamed descended from Ishmael. I could find no evidence, however, that Mohamed ever claimed to have been a descendant. None. On his deathbed, Mohamed commissioned his followers to take over Egypt. Even as he explained to them the Egyptian connection to Hagar, he never mentioned his own connection to her or her son Ishmael.

As I finished my research on the origins of the pilgrimage, I realized I made zero progress in my apologetic pursuit. All my agonizing, praying, researching, and beseeching Allah for help came to naught. I could not say with any degree of assurance Islam proved its worth through the legitimacy of its prophet. I found nothing to confirm Mohamed was who he said he was. I thought myself the greatest Muslim failure of all time.

CHAPTER 22

CONFUSION AND CHALLENGES

*And they will say, "Our Lord! We obeyed our leaders
and elite, but they led us astray from the 'Right' Way.
Our Lord! Give them double 'our' punishment, and
condemn them tremendously."*

—Quran 33:67–68

At the beginning of my quest I could never have believed my life
would be so utterly upended. I lack the words to describe how
thoroughly my mind and heart were tossed and tumbled. A year
earlier, I was at the top of my game. Now, I just wanted to hide in
the shadows.

I had a secret—and it was the deepest, darkest secret imagin-
able. I could hardly bear to face it myself, let alone risk revealing
it to another. I was questioning Islam, my faith, my Prophet. The
fact I could not successfully answer the questions of that damnable
man on the train crushed me. I was a dismal failure. Inadequate.
Useless.

It frustrated me to reflect on the early days of my quest. Back
then my heart was pure and my intentions beyond reproach. I felt

strong, invincible even. From that moment I worked harder than I ever worked in my life with one goal in mind: to unlock the keys to my great faith. I failed, and I could trace that failure to one thing only, my own inadequacy.

As guilty as I felt, I was caught time and again trying to convince myself I had not really floundered, in fact, I stumbled upon an unnerving truth: Mohamed was not a prophet. My failure to find evidence was beside the point. There was no evidence to be found. Alas, every time I traveled down that road, I would burst into tears, tremble in fear, recoil with horror, and return again to my deeply ingrained faith in the Prophet.

Having failed to prove myself a great Islamic scholar, I thought perhaps I could honor Allah by becoming a great doctor like my father. On the first day of medical school, however, that thought did not quiet my demons. What should have been a glorious occasion celebrating the launch of an epic life played out like a scene from a Shakespearean tragedy.

MEDICAL SCHOOL

After a sleepless night, I did not even bother to shave or dress for the occasion. Before leaving, I got a call from my father. He congratulated me for my accomplishment and asked me to stop by his home on the way to school so we could pray together for Allah's blessings. I remember protesting silently, 'Who cares? Is Allah even real? Is Mohamed a fake?' As empty as I felt inside, I did not dare share the cause of my pain. Had I, I have no doubt my dad would have felt obliged to murder me for rejecting my faith.

As the dutiful son, I did as requested. Upon arrival, my parents snapped a photo of me. The photo should have memorialized my achievement. Instead, it captured the sorry soul of a man who dared to question the truth. I tried to look the part of a bright-eyed medical student by driving my new red Mazda to school, but I feared my new classmates could see just how pathetic was the young man emerging from the vehicle.

My dad arranged for some of his colleagues to be at the medical school that day. Some of their sons were also beginning school.

The plan was to introduce us to each other and give us an immediate group of trusted friends. We all knew we were expected to continue on the paths of our fathers, to carry their legacies forward. In a sense, our admission gave us each an identity we had yet to earn, an identity burdening us with expectations.

My dad's colleagues represented multiple countries and just about every field of medicine. Hearing their stories about how they accrued great wealth and power impressed all listeners, me included. And even though my dad was not the wealthiest or most successful, he was the celebrity of the bunch. Each of the doctors attributed his great success to one thing—his devotion to the faith. Clearly no one was more devoted than my father. They recognized Dad was the best servant of Allah among them, and for that they honored him, even envied him. Then all eyes were on me. My dad was singing my praises: "This is my good and faithful son, blah, blah, blah." The words that used to fill me with such pride now made me ashamed. They were like bullets slicing through my flesh, ripping my soul to shreds. I wanted to scream.

I fought so hard to get into medical school. I had to endure humiliating days at dental school. I had to challenge my father to allow me to go to England. I had to prove to him I had what it takes to succeed. Yet, the shell of a man who stepped out of the car and made his way toward class did not have a whiff of success about him. My beard was ragged and unkempt. I had lost so much weight in my obsessive desire to find the truth that my clothes hung loosely off my body. I looked sick, tired, and weary. In my soul, that's exactly what I was. I was a dead man walking, and I could tell no one the cause of my death. Months of my life were gone, and I could never reclaim them. My only hope was to lose myself in school and try to resurrect something of my old life, the life I lived before I died, a life unburdened by doubts, failures, and fear.

Given my father's prominence as a teacher of Islam, his colleagues' sons now looked to me as his spiritual heir. I wanted to shout out loud that I could not teach them about the faith. I was not even sure I believed in Islam anymore. To say those words aloud, though, would have been suicidal. Perhaps literally. I remained silent.

I desperately needed a change of focus, and medical school provided it. I studied, made lots of friends, and validated my intuition I was meant to be a doctor. I maintained residence at my apartment, and funds kept rolling in from my business ventures. On the down side, I had to abandon my soccer sideline. Beginning a seven-year medical school commitment, time was at a premium.

Since my close friends had doctors for fathers, we all had lofty aspirations and plenty of money. We also had great freedom. We gathered each day under a certain tree on campus and formed something of a clique. We were the cool guys with bright futures and sporty cars. All my friends had girlfriends as well and regularly engaged in parties, drinking, and sex. They invited me several times to join them, but I always turned them down. Of course, they made fun of me, as I couldn't even talk about drinking and dating, but none of them came from families like mine.

To be sure, my friends did not want to talk about what I read in the Quran that day, but I wasn't so sure I wanted to talk about that either. Even so, we managed to build solid bonds with one another, and as long as I didn't take their relentless ribbing too personally, I knew we would remain friends.

Our differences, however, could not be ignored. Sometimes we carpooled. When I got into one of their cars, the most current music would inevitably be playing from the cassette deck. My friends discussed which tracks they hoped to add to their mix tapes, and I didn't have a clue about the identity of the singers or the names of songs. Feeling guilty and embarrassed, I sat silently in the backseat and willed myself into invisibility.

When they got into my car, however, they mercilessly teased me as all that came from my speakers were the words of the Quran. I felt like an idiot. I was the righteous, religious one, but I had more doubts about Islam than they did. I was expected to be like my dad, but I had no right to preach to anyone. I was just trying to hang onto my faith by going through the motions and practicing the rituals. I hoped the familiarity and repetition alone would draw me back to a place of security.

Escape! The desire to escape my reality was my guiding force. It motivated all of my actions. Every so often I felt the impulse to fight for my religion and regain my sense of assurance, but then the demons unleashed by my investigation would taunt me, and I had no choice but to retreat into my secret.

Although the life I lived was contrary to a young man's natural impulses, the lifestyles of my friends did not particularly tempt me. Still, I imagined how amazing it would be to just let loose and kiss a girl as a normal guy might. If I ever freed myself from Islam's unyielding straitjacket, I had just the girl in mind—Mona. She was a conservative girl who usually kept to herself. Her dad had a high profile in the community. I desperately wanted to talk to her. I never mustered the courage.

Escape! I went to a mosque at the school a few times. This is the mosque where Ayman Zawahiri ditched his family of doctors and joined the Muslim Brotherhood and changed from the man he was to the man he is today. I thought I could go to a place of refuge, pray, and find peace, but the imams had other ideas. They took note of my flashy car and expensive clothes and saw me as a wayward Muslim needing instruction to find the righteous path.

They were ardent, however, and desired to bring me into the fold. They even encouraged me to join the Muslim Brotherhood. Even more unsettling, they sought to teach me from the Quran. Teach *me*? They had no idea who I was or what I already knew, but they were prepared to teach *me*. I wanted peace and quiet, and they wanted to help me get my life right. The efforts of these foolish men disgusted me. They brought me verses and hadiths to condemn me, and I just wanted them to shut up. They were flies buzzing around dead meat.

The metaphor is apt. I was like dead meat, decaying toward disintegration. I used to feel confident I was pleasing Allah and the Prophet. I knew what reward awaited me at the end of the day. I was a good slave of Islam. It was easy to reject temptation. I could easily condemn others. But I had none of those convictions in my heart anymore. I had no assurance heaven existed. I could not even convince myself Allah existed. I wanted to shout, "Don't rock a boat that is already full of holes. Just leave me alone and let me go through the motions. Just let me pray!"

The only true escape from my struggle came on Fridays. I always spend the day with my uncle and my dad. There was safety in the routine, because in routine, I could just do, rather than think. The three of us got together in the morning for breakfast and coffee and discussed Dad's upcoming message at the mosque. We talked about life, politics, religion, family—our regular fare. Together we headed to the mosque where Dad was preaching. Sometimes it was his own mosque, but often he preached at other mosques throughout the city. No matter the venue, Dad always drew a crowd, as many as three thousand worshipers at the larger mosques. For just a short while each Friday, I could lose myself in the normality of the day and forget all my questions.

On those days my father would introduce me to prominent citizens and members of the Brotherhood, all of whom achieved great success in business, politics, or the Islamic movement. The evening always concluded with dinner and more conversations about the day's prayer and message.

I loved going to those mega-mosques and meeting new people. We visited one particular mosque run by the Brotherhood in Mokattam Hills, southeast of Cairo. It was there I met an important family that would influence the future of Egypt for years to come. The Sallams, two brothers and a brother-in-law, were part of a new wave of capitalism sweeping across Egypt, a refreshing change from the vestiges of the Communist legacy.

The Sallams made a lot of money manufacturing appliances. They used their wealth to purchase a large tract of land for their business. On it they built two beautiful office towers connected by a walkway. Entrance was by invitation only. My dad spoke there many times, and I attended a majority of his sessions. I enjoyed being included and could not help but feel important. Rituals, comfortable conversations, hanging out with the rich and influential—that was my normal, and I craved it. My secret tried to surface, but I figured if I kept moving, I would get through this trial, one day at a time.

Before I knew it, my first year of medical school was over, and I made a conscious decision to lean in to Islam again. This time I would answer one question: If Mohamed wasn't who he said he was, why would he have deemed himself a prophet and unleashed such a powerful religious force? I was about to figure that out.

When I finished my first year of medical school, I once again had time on my hands. And so I delved back into my quest. I meticulously reviewed everything I researched the previous year, and then, to be safe, I reviewed it all again. Still, I could find no evidence to disprove the claims of the man on the train. I could find no proof Mohamed was who he said he was.

None of this made any sense to me. It seemed clear Mohamed lied and the people around him believed the lie. But why, I wondered, did he lie in the first place and why would they believe him? I knew it was mad to entertain these thoughts. Thoughts such as these led to the death of many a man and woman over the centuries.

THE TRUTH IS FINALLY REVEALED

Quite suddenly, I had an "aha" moment. The people who followed Mohamed did so for a very specific reason. When I examined every aspect of Islam—the five pillars, the motivations, the encounters, the miracles, the followers—a startling, unifying theme emerged. The Islamic calendar didn't begin with the creation of the earth. It began with the creation of the Islamic state. Muslims were to pray five times a day so Mohamed could keep tabs on what his people were doing. Muslims were to fast during Ramadan so Mohamed could show he was not imitating the Jews but rather honoring Islam's first military victory.

But there was more. Who was promised heaven? The martyr. What better encouragement could a soldier receive than a promise of heaven? Better still, the promise included seventy-two blond and fair-skinned virgins, just like the women Mohamed desired but could only obtain by conquering faraway lands. My conclusion: Islam was more a political movement than a religion. Mohamed masked his political moves under the cover of religion. He and his followers built a state that quickly became an empire, one of the most expansive in human history. If empire building were his goal, the pillars of Islam made perfect sense. He claimed to be a prophet, and the people believed his claim, because they all had something to gain from the lie.

As a good Muslim, I believed the Islamic state was created to serve the faith and to enforce Allah's will. The evidence, however, revealed something quite the opposite. In fact, Islam was conceived as a political system. The state used "religion" as a way to enforce its will and to enslave millions of people. From the beginning, powerful men controlled Islamic law and doctrine to drive their own ambitions. Islam, I could see, was more ideology than theology and had little to do with God. This was not what I signed up for all those years ago. I wanted to be able to achieve heaven. I still did, but I realized I had been looking in the wrong places.

I felt betrayed. If the truth meant I was a servant of the Islamic state and not a servant of Allah, I was lost. Incapacitated. Surely, I thought, I could not have been the only Muslim in history to reach these conclusions.

On the edge of insanity, incapable of finding answers on my own, I decided to take the risk and talk to the one person who would keep the secret, my dad. I did not plan to challenge him, let alone confess my lack of faith. I needed him to help me, to cure me, to dig me out of the hole I dug myself into.

CHAPTER 23

THE SAFEST PERSON

Oh you who have believed, indeed, your wives and your children are your enemies, so be aware of them and stay faithful to Allah and indeed Allah is forgiving and merciful.

—Quran 64:14

I began my studies from a place of total submission to Allah. I believed the Prophet was who he said he was and the Quran and Hadith were divinely inspired. I believed Islam was superior to all other faiths and those faiths borrowed from Islam. I believed Islam's every prayer, every ritual, every law had no other purpose than to serve Allah.

I hoped and prayed my studies would confirm my beliefs and I could then throw these truths into the face of every Western skeptic I encountered.

That would not be.

Much to my great despair, what I found was Mohamed developed a faith for no greater purpose than to support his political ambitions.

The man on the train was right. It was the sword of Islam that moved men to enslave themselves. The hadiths recorded how

271

Christians and Jews in liberated lands were given a choice: convert, submit, or leave. It seemed pretty clear to me now these people weren't liberated. They were conquered. They had no real choice. They could convert or leave or live on as third-class citizens in their own country. I had a problem with this, a major one. I always assumed it was the power of my faith that moved people. Now I could see it was the power of the sword.

Mohamed had a profoundly intuitive grasp on human nature. He knew that men would do whatever they could to secure an extension of their earthly lives. He understood too, humans, as a higher creation, had a deep need for rituals and codes to live by. So he created a "religion" to meet their needs and, more importantly, fulfill his own desire for political dominance. Mohamed and the co-founders of Islam were not more moral than other conquerors throughout history—they were more clever. Mohamed succeeded where the others failed, and his ambitions did not die with him. What I was thinking was apostasy of the highest order, but I was still just vain enough to think my conclusions would be vindicated.

If Islam was not a faith designed by God, but rather an opportunistic system designed by man, I wanted no part of it. My questions centered on Mohamed. He succeeded where other would-be religious leaders failed. As far as I could see it was the application of swift and overwhelming force against non-believers that allowed him and his successors to prevail. Now understanding the role of force in Islam, I worried its force would be used against me. Who, I wondered, would give me safe haven? Who would protect me? To whom could I confide my despair? I didn't want to die. I just wanted the truth. I wanted someone to tell me and show me how I was wrong. If I confided my doubts to my mentors from Al Azhar or the Muslim Brotherhood leaders I knew or the imams at the mosques who taught me or even my uncle, I might very well be killed.

CONFRONTING MY DAD

I figured my dad was the safest person to ask for answers. He knew how strong was my faith. He alone would understand how genuine was my despair. My father would have to prove to me beyond a shadow of a doubt my conclusions were incorrect. If he couldn't do that, I was mentally prepared to walk away. In my heart, though, I longed for him to show me I was the one in error. I desperately needed affirmation that everything in which I had always believed was true and beyond reproach. My dad and I always helped each other in the past. I kept the secret of his second marriage for years so perhaps, I thought, he would keep my secret. Maybe he would understand my doubts. I had to ask.

Although I hoped Dad would relieve me of my burden, I was not sure. I worried he would lash into me as he did in that dark room many years earlier, but I was so desperate I was willing to run that risk. Our regular time to get together was Tuesdays. That was his day off. We would leave together and head to his ancestral village in the countryside. My mom thought we spent the night there. We did not. We came back to the city and spent the night with his second wife. Mom was never to know.

I thought I would talk to Dad while in the car, but I couldn't find the nerve. Nor could I find it once we got to the village. Two weeks in a row I failed to confront him. This was proving so very difficult. The words escaped me. Fear unnerved me—fear of Allah, fear of my father, fear for my life.

During this period of indecision, a shocking event reinforced my fears. One of my schoolmates from the English School witnessed a murder. His father, Farag Foda, was a writer who challenged the use of the sword in the spread of Islamic conquest. Foda's crime was no greater than my own, but a committee of clerics at Al-Azhar University took notice and accused him of blasphemy, an offense worthy of death. On June 8, 1992, two members of an Islamist group, El Gama'a El Islamya, shot Foda dead as he was leaving his house. The house was in my neighborhood, and I went to school with his son who was wounded in the shooting along with several bystanders. Foda was one of more than two hundred murders in a political-religious purge beginning in March 1992 and continuing for more than a year.

These executions sent a strong reminder to all Muslims that to challenge Islam was to buy a one-way ticket to the grave. I had no desire to proclaim to the world what I discovered. I just wanted to fade away. Keep a low profile. But there was one person I knew I had to speak to.

A month after Foda's assassination, I had that long-awaited conversation with my father. The date and setting are forever etched in my memory, July 7, 1992. It was one of the most important days in my life. We had just finished a wonderful meal at the home of my father's second wife. She and I had a cordial relationship and, in an effort to please my father, she adopted many of my mom's recipes, including the lamb she served us that evening.

Dad and I adjourned to the balcony high above the city below. It was 1992. I was twenty-two at the time. As per our custom, we began talking about Islam, and I brought up the man on the train. My uncle called him an "Orientalist," a pejorative way of describing Westerners who patronize Arabic and Islamic cultures. I explained how I had been using the Orientalist as a catalyst for my own mission.

"It seems to me, though, that Islam didn't begin in Mecca at all," I said. "It appears that it really began in Medina when Mohamed established his government. In fact, I've come to see Islam as more of a political movement than a religion." I began the conversation discussing pilgrimage. It struck me as less controversial topic than some others, an inquiry into history rather than into faith.

My dad was not an idiot. He picked up on my doubts immediately. Trying to contain himself, he turned toward me and said, "You're too social, and you are too open to others. Why do you ask?" I think he was in shock. He was trying to rationalize my behavior, blaming circumstances, medical school, the people around me. I reassured him I had good intentions. I just wanted to prepare myself to take Islam to the non-believers.

I continued to build my case, but I could see the color rising in his face and his eyes darkening. "It's really the opposite of what you have always said," I continued. "Before the Islamic State, the faith had no rules or rituals other than believing in Allah as God." I explained how everything seemed to change when Mohamed became king. I cited evidence that Islam sprang from his political ambitions, and the rules of the faith reinforced them. "Islam *is* the sword," I said with regret. "And everything else is an accessory." I said it. And then I held my breath.

"You are on the wrong path," he yelled. "Someone is influencing you!" My father was beyond angry. "Perhaps Allah is testing *me*," he added, personalizing the problem and shouting so loudly his wife rushed out to the balcony to calm him. He dismissed her curtly and continued to share his disgust with all I said to him. That evening conversation on the balcony should have been like all the others. He should have challenged me to continue growing in my faith, and I should have walked away wiser. Instead, it was the beginning of the end. I wasn't ready to accept that reality.

Not long afterward, I called and asked him to come to my apartment. I asked him to not be angry with me. He could not promise that much, but he did come. Sitting on the floor of my apartment, rummaging through my notes, I begged him for answers. "I just need you to discuss these points with me," I said, "I need you to show me with the text and historical record that I am wrong!" He said nothing. I continued, "You did not answer the man on the train, but please answer me right now." He stood and left in anger. He really could not have done any differently. There were no answers to my questions that would reunite me with Islam. He showed no kindness or compassion. He did not try to understand. To do so would have made him complicit in my sin.

THE RIFT WIDENS

Friends and relatives started sensing the tension between us. As much as it puzzled the people who knew us, I could not talk about its source. Interestingly, my dad would not talk about it either. Sitting at dinner, my mother would ask what was wrong, and we refused to tell her. By the time school started up again, we could not even fake a relationship. Visible cracks started opening, and over time they grew larger and larger. I was angry. He was angry. And we remained so for the following days, weeks, and months.

With no other option, I continued my exploration of Islam, alone. I quickly gave up any hope of my father having information

I missed, information that would pull me back into the shelter of a belief system that gave me an identity, a way of life, and a hope for eternal salvation. Although I was rapidly losing faith in everything I always believed, I still had not lost faith in the man I believed my father to be. Though our encounters were brief, tense even, I hoped somehow things could go back to the way they were.

Then, in 1994, just two years after our fateful discussion on his wife's balcony, two years of wrestling with my faith, my father did something that made me doubt him altogether. He took a third wife, a much younger woman. Worse, he never told my mom or wife number two about wife number three. Since Islam did not require such notification, there was no reason to bother.

I did not know why he married this woman. I was in no position to ask. Inexplicably, he lied on the government documents about his marital status. Nor did I know why he lied. It wasn't necessary. He just did. He claimed he had never been married, and that's what infuriated me the most. I represented hard evidence that he was married to my mom for twenty-two years. For most of those years, I was his closest confidant, his best friend. If I needed confirmation our conversation of two years prior drove us apart, I got it loud and clear with my father's dismissal of my very existence.

The image of a great man, the very picture of Islamic virtue, exploded in my face, shattered into a million ugly little pieces. He suddenly seemed small and weak. When I needed my father to be the picture of Islamic virtue, he showed me, instead, he was a flawed human being. I saw him now for what he was, just another man, as opportunistic and as self-serving as the next guy, as opportunistic and as self-serving as Mohamed, for that matter. I questioned why I ever cared about what he thought.

As disturbed as I was by my father's marriage, I felt even worse to be questioning something Allah approved. Mohamed said Allah would allow Muslim men to take four wives. My father only had three. Mohamed, on the other hand, had up to thirteen wives and many concubines. But he, as the Prophet, was allowed to do so. The Quran 33:50 says, *"O Prophet verily, we have made lawful for you, your wives . . . and those (slaves) whom your right hand possesses—whom Allah has given you—and a believing woman if she offers herself to the Prophet, and the Prophet wishes to marry her—a privilege for you only, not for the (rest of) the believers . . ."* Who was I to argue with my father or the Prophet?

I felt like I was drifting through the ocean in a boat with a thousand holes, bailing and patching to keep afloat. To survive, I would have to jump off at some point and swim to shore, having no idea in which direction to swim. My father was my compass, but that compass was smashed. I was so lost.

Now that I knew the roots of female enslavement, I had an irrepressible urge to apologize to my mother and to protect her from my father. I felt guilty, too, for concealing my father's union with his second wife. I should have thought through this urge to tell all, but I did not. I told my mom everything. I laid out the facts in vivid detail. She knew, of course. Women know these things, and a Muslim woman simply accepts them. She has no choice.

My father's influence over the years transformed my mother into a woman I no longer recognized. Instead of letting me protect her and plead her case, she became angry. The rage she should have directed at him, she turned on me. She cursed me to high heaven, and I left her home under a barrage of angry words. I should have known better. My discoveries about Islam appalled her almost as much they did my father.

There is an age-old saying, "Ignorance is bliss." In this instance, that saying could not have been more true. To this day, I believe many Muslims remain happy as long as they don't know what they don't know. I, on the other hand, had no easy out. I now knew enough about Islam to recognize the fraud at its core. I felt I had no choice. I had to act on my knowledge. But what on earth was I to do?

CHAPTER 24

A GODLESS WORLD

*And whoever turns away from Allah and Islam indeed
he will have a depressed life; miserable and poor, and
on the day of judgment he will be severely punished
and spend eternity in hellfire and this is because you
have transgressed and did not believe in the signs of
Allah.*

—Quran 20:124–127

My quest for truth alienated me from my family, consumed
years of my attention, and made me miserable beyond
description. Since my father refused to discuss anything with me,
I had no choice but to return to Mecca one more time. Surely, in
Allah's house I would find the answers I desperately sought. I
prayed Allah would share some revelation with me to dispel my
doubts and prove Mohamed's legitimacy.

The trip was to be unlike any other. This time I was a solo act.
My father and I weren't going as the dynamic duo as many times
before. Nevertheless, my role in past pilgrimages made it easier
than ever before to get the necessary documents and finalize
arrangements.

The journey was otherwise predictable. The approach to the Grand Mosque looked much as it had before, and the golden door of the Kaaba shone as brightly in the distance as in the past. Missing, though, was that sense of awe I always felt seeing the mosque. Granted, everything looked as shiny, as perfect, as beautiful as it always did, but this time the lump in my throat did not form as it had countless times before.

Instead of participating in the rituals, I opted to sit on the sidelines and observe. I thought maybe if I watched other pilgrims lose themselves in worship I would sense once again all that was holy about Islam. I hoped my observations would reveal to me some truth I overlooked.

I could not have been more mistaken. What I witnessed as an observer took my breath away, but not in the way I hoped. I saw thousands of pilgrims make their way around the Kaaba offering their prayers to Allah. But I also saw men stealthily draw knives from beneath their sacred wraps and cut the purse strings of the pilgrims walking in front of them. I saw women walk dutifully alongside their husbands only to be groped and violated by pilgrims crowding behind them. I saw all manner of vile behavior from people who were supposed to be engaged in the worship of Allah.

The pilgrims seemed not to notice the blasphemy in their midst. I couldn't blame them. On many occasions I had been down there among them without ever noticing any problems. I had to wonder, though, why Allah allowed these horrible people to defile his home. Was he not God? Was he not capable? Was he even there?

I left the Grand Mosque in despair, heartsick I had not yet received the answer I hoped for. Surely, I thought, I would find it if I ventured out to the hillside where the sacrifices were conducted. As always, the air there smelled of blood. But this time I smelled the stench of rotting flesh baking in the Saudi sun. The sacrificed meat intended for the poor was being thrown into the desert to rot. The carcasses piled up one upon another and drew flies to what was supposed to be holy. Again, I was forced to ask, "Allah, if you are here, why are you allowing this? Wasn't everything Mohamed told us a direct message from you?"

I made eight prior visits to Mecca. During every one of those visits my religious fervor clouded my vision and protected my heart, but this time, for the first time, I saw everything clearly. The bright light of truth dispelled all illusions. The pilgrimage was an exercise in fraud, a study in hypocrisy. It had nothing to do with my creator. My heart splintered there in the hot Saudi desert, and I wept. I had not been wrong. Mohamed was a false prophet. And if Allah were real, he appeared to be completely powerless. I never felt as alone as I did in that sea of people.

During my three-year search for truth, I continued to live as a faithful Muslim. I questioned, but I never missed a prayer. I never missed a fast. I went to mosque religiously. I diligently avoided sin as defined by Mohamed. Even with significant doubt, I wasn't going to risk Allah's judgment if one day I were proven wrong.

During those years, my friends in med school knew me as the religious one. In fact, they spent considerable time ribbing me about how straight-laced I was. How I couldn't look a female in the eye. How I vigilantly refused to taste a drop of alcohol. How I never let classes or recreation take precedence over my duty as a Muslim.

NO MORE FAKING IT

The tension with my father had not eased, and I saw less and less of my parents. Although two years passed since our initial blow-up, they made it unquestionably clear to me they did not want to spend time in my presence. To this day I am shocked at how quickly my father was able to turn off his feelings for a beloved son and treat me instead as a pariah.

Dad, in fact, let me know I was little more than a curse to him, a mixed-up kid who lost his way. To make sure his message hit home, he told me a story from the Quran he thought relevant. In the story, Moses is traveling on a boat with a servant of God named Khadir. Moses watches in shock as Khadir kills a boy right in front of him. When Moses asks why he did so, Khadir answers, *"His parents were believers and we feared lest he should make disobedience and ingratitude to come upon them. God will replace*

When I returned from Mecca, however, I was a changed man. I left behind those beliefs that comprised my former life. I thought them all a lie. I couldn't fake it anymore. I wouldn't fake it. Everything I did in my Muslim life was a sincere attempt to please Allah. If Allah wasn't real, I would not pretend he was. No fool, however, I was not about to tell the world I was no longer a believing Muslim. I saw what they did to Farag Foda. I was no more immune to an assassin's bullet than he was. And for all my new knowledge and seeming indifference to Islam, I retained a deep-seated fear of Allah's eternal wrath.

the child with one better in purity, affection and obedience" (Quran 18:60–82).

I was the kid on the boat. I was a challenge to my parents. Dad feared my heretical questions and actions could lead him and my mother astray. I'm sure he loved me, but he saw me as the possible source of his own destruction. In a very weird way I found this story reassuring.

But not for long. The sorrow I initially felt from his rejection quickly turned to rage. How dare he call me a curse when I was his closest confidant and apostle? How dare he lie to me, beat me into submission at age five, and then turn on me as if I were nothing to him? How dare he reject the devoted son who kissed his ring like a slave fawning over his master every time he saw him? Who did he think he was?

United in their hatred, Mom and Dad grew stronger in their relationship than ever before. My heart simultaneously ached from the enormity of my loss and burned with anger. I lost the bond with my father that had defined me for more than two decades. I lost the respect and love of my mother. I lost my identity as a Muslim and champion of the faith. I lost my soul. I was nobody. Perhaps my father was right: I was losing my mind. I thought I knew who I was. I thought I knew who I was going to be. I thought I knew what Allah expected of me. And in the end, I realized I knew nothing. I came to distrust everything I read or saw or thought. Was Allah God? Was the chair a chair? Was I actually alive? How was I to know any of this?

I remembered my mom studying philosophers like Descartes who asked similar questions. I took some comfort in this. I wasn't the only person on earth to have doubts. I wasn't alone in trying to find meaning. Others traveled a similar path. I doubted, however, whether anyone traveled precisely the same road as I. Despite its millions of adherents and centuries of existence, Islam had yet to produce, at least to the best of my knowledge, a man willing to stand up at that time and say to his fellow Muslims, "You are wrong! I have the truth!" For me to be that man perhaps I had to be possessed by demons as my father believed. How else to explain standing against my culture, my father, and my ancestors? Having the truth, though, wasn't going to keep me alive.

Without a family to lean on, I turned to friends. And I let go. I had my first beer. It was a Stella, and I liked it. I began dating and immersing myself in the local nightlife. My friends could see I was different, and they liked this new, freer Mohamed. They didn't ask any questions. They were simply happy that somewhere along the way I found at least the illusion of manhood.

My friends may have liked this new Mohamed, but I didn't. I still felt lonely, hurt, and confused. I struggled with my identity in multiple ways. I grew bitter. I questioned all of my actions. I drank more and partied harder. To escape my reality, I did everything to excess, but there was no escape. Not even in women. I quickly fell hard for this one girl. I thought of her as my girlfriend and hoped she and her family would serve as a substitute for my own. Then I learned she was cheating on me. This was a cruel new world.

At some point my dad seemed to know I had a girlfriend and a new family. When it all fell apart, he made fun of me. I hated him for it. He was a vengeful man. He told people I was messed up. He took advantage of my flaws. He looked for mistakes and used them to make me feel like I was losing my mind. On one occasion, Dad broke into my apartment and smashed all my liquor bottles in the bathtub. I went to him and threatened him: "You stay out of my life and I will stay out of yours." I no longer went home when my father was there, but even my mother made me feel unwelcome. I no longer had a place there.

MY DOWNHILL SPIRAL

My days of going to the mosque or participating in the prayers were over as well. When Ramadan rolled around over the next several years, I went home and ate to my heart's content. I was still "Muslim," but I wasn't. My new friends didn't know or care. I started hanging out at the beachside bars in Alexandria. I remember once buying a bottle of gin and drinking half of it. With the world spinning around me, I sat on the ground next to my car, closed my eyes, and thought I was going to die. At the time, death struck me as an easy way out.

I opened my eyes the next day at noon. My friends were gone. No one checked on me. They were all up on the beach. And then this one girl, hearing the call to prayer, covered her hair and started to pray. I remember thinking, "What the heck are you doing? Isn't your whole lifestyle *haram*, forbidden?"

I always believed Muslims of this sort lived each day knowing deep down they were sinners destined for hell. But the truth is they don't think that way at all. They think if they behave well enough, Islam will be forgiving, and Allah will give them grace. Of course, there is no grace in Islam. Not knowing this, they justified and rationalized and hoped for the best. The actress justified her kissing scenes. The belly dancer justified her seductive dancing. The singer justified her love songs. The drinkers and the drug users justified their easy escapes from reality.

At this point, I didn't believe Allah even existed. As I saw it, there was no one to justify their sins to. Of course, I did not share any of this. None of my friends knew what my previous life was like, and I preferred to keep it that way. They were living in a fantasy world, and I was not about to disturb it.

I couldn't blame them for living as they did. Ignorance *was* bliss. If they knew what horrors Mohamed promised people like them in the afterlife, they would not have been able to endure their lives on earth. But if there was no Islam, there was no need to rationalize anything.

Yet it was among these pathetic, broken, deceived people I found my safe place. In their company I could hide out and pretend to cling to Islam while cursing the lie. In the beginning, I had no clue what I was doing. After a while, though, I developed a reputation as a partier. Mohamed Abdullah, the party guy, traveled in very different circles than Mohamed Abdullah, the imam, but I enjoyed fame in each circle. I was the guy with the money. I was the guy who bought rounds of drinks and financed trips to exotic destinations. I was the guy who dated actresses and society women. More than anyone, I knew I would pay no penalty for my behavior. I wasn't going to have to spill my own blood in the cause of Allah to earn redemption. There was no redemption to be earned.

I was having what looked like the time of my life, but I was totally, hopelessly empty. Where once I had purpose and calling, I now had no direction at all. I did not have a clue as to who created me or why. I was reckless. I once drove three hundred miles at high speed so drunk I could not recall a single mile of that journey. I just knew I had to escape, but with each post-binge sunrise, I woke to the stark reminder that I escaped nothing at all.

This was the beginning of a years-long spiral into nothingness. Had I drunk myself to death during that period, that would have been okay with me. I hated myself. I hated my family. I hated Islam, and I could see no way out, not even suicide. The deeply entrenched fear of Allah's wrath kept me from doing something dramatic. The more I tried to distance myself from my past, the more it came back to haunt me.

The day I finished medical school, for instance, I started work at Maadi Military Hospital in Cairo. This was the same military hospital at which my father once practiced. Were I not his son, I never would have had the privilege of practicing in a hospital so prestigious so early in my career. Yet this was my *first* assignment. Where my father ended his medical career, I began mine. I was even using his old office. I found myself following in my father's footsteps all the while I was trying to run in the opposite direction.

Islam told me if I walked away from the faith, I would find failure and death at every turn. But the eyes of those around me told me I found fun and prosperity. I had it made. My success offered further proof, if more was needed, that Islam and my father had it wrong, all wrong.

CHAPTER 25

LOVE AND MARRIAGE

*Men are in charge of women, because Allah hath
made the one of them to excel the other, and because
they spend of their property. So good women are the
obedient, guarding in secret that which Allah hath
guarded. As for those from whom ye fear rebellion,
admonish them and banish them to beds apart, and
scourge them. Then if they obey you, seek not a way
against them. Lo! Allah is ever High, Exalted, Great.*

—Quran 4:34

It was at a pool party in 1995 when I met the woman who would
become my wife. I was nearing the end of my medical school
career and enjoying a day of loud music, excessive drinking, and
even a little swimming. Although an event like this would have
gotten me into major trouble in my old life, in my new life it was
just another day in the park. I had tons of people around me all
the time, girls too, lots of them. Sometimes I went out with three
girls in a day. I was the life of the party.

This new life allowed me, at last, to appreciate how beautiful
were the women around me. Dina was one such beauty. Although
she was dating a friend of mine at the time, she and I hit it off

immediately, and we spent the entire afternoon talking with one another. She was as intelligent as she was beautiful, and, better still, she was interested in me. I immediately cancelled plans with two other women I had for later in the day.

Dina was finishing up her last year in law school. She came from a family much like my mother's. They were Muslim—she did have an 11 p.m. curfew—but they were nowhere near as devout as my own, a fact my estranged father would remind me of in the future. Would he ever!

Once a diplomatic attaché, on the staff at various embassies, Dina's father traveled extensively and settled into a business as a headhunter for companies seeking employees from Egypt. Dina was the eldest of three girls. From day one, our relationship proved to be a good fit for us both. She challenged me, and we had fun together. Although at times we could butt heads rather violently, our relationship offered a nice reprieve from the pressures of work, school, and my new found hedonism.

As much as I liked Dina, I was not ready to commit to her. Everything I did as a devout Muslim involved absolute, total commitment, and that passion had only gotten me into trouble. I had zero interest in taking our relationship to the next step, namely marriage. In Islam, there is no running off to Las Vegas for a quickie wedding. The rituals surrounding marriage require total commitment from both families. I dreaded the whole process.

I told Dina on our first date I had no intention of marrying her. Independent and rebellious by nature, she accepted my declaration without argument. We were just two successful young people enjoying each other's company. No strings, no commitments, just a good time.

In my mind, my old life as a devout Muslim and dutiful son was dead. In truth, though, we all take pieces of who we were as children into adulthood. At the time I thought I could bury every relic of my old life and assume a new identity. I could not. Dina knew who my father was. Everyone did! She saw him teaching on television each evening before the news. Her bus to school went by his clinic in the heart of the city, and his name was prominent on the front of the building. I was an enigma to her with my drinking, partying, free-wheeling lifestyle. She never guessed for a moment what my childhood was like, and I certainly never offered to tell her. The old Mohamed Abdullah was dead and buried. It remains a mystery to me why she continued to be a part of my broken mess of a life. I wasn't faithful to her and never promised I would be. If my partying subsided somewhat, it was only because I had so little time for it.

As the months and years rolled by, Dina couldn't help but consider that perhaps it was time for us to think about settling down. I was reluctant to consider marriage because I had no idea what a good one was supposed to look like. My father and mother were a mess and as dysfunctional as a couple could be. My uncle Hassan was a model husband and father, but, given my experiences, I had no clue how to build a contented life centered on family and God. Uncertain and insecure, I skillfully ignored Dina's probing.

SHARIA COMES CALLING

A tragedy in Dina's family changed everything. When Dina's father, a heavy smoker, became ill, I felt the need to reach out and get to know him. He was a very kind man, and we just clicked. Although I had not hinted at marriage, I had no doubt he approved of my relationship with his daughter. It was refreshing to have a positive relationship with an older man. It helped offset the negative vibes from my father and his associates.

I had a private conversation with Dina's father the day he died in February 1998. He asked me to take care of his wife and the girls. As he knew, his death would unleash the dreaded sharia on the family in ways unimaginable to those ignorant of Muslim law.

By way of background, sharia is a fourteen hundred-year-old code that began with Mohamed. In Arabic, "sharia" means "the way" or "the constitution." Sharia was created as a set of rules for Medina, the city Mohamed governed, but it later grew to include rules for just about every feature of Muslim life down to the most basic. When the Ottoman Empire broke up in 1924, the only country to practice sharia was Saudi Arabia, but with the Islamic revival, sharia resumed its importance in Muslim households the world over.

One dictate of sharia worried me most. I refer to the dictate that unequivocally states, "When a person who has reached puberty and is sane, voluntarily apostatizes from Islam, he deserves to be killed." Despite propaganda to the contrary, sharia has not eased a bit over the years. It will never be moderated. Sharia is considered perfect, universal, and eternal. What is more, it establishes the framework for an Islamic theocracy with no separation of mosque and state. For all Muslims, even secular Muslims, Islam is not possible without sharia. It is even more encompassing than the Ten Commandments God gave Moses.

Muslims rarely recognize the evil of the law until personally faced with it. But face it they will. Sharia is the way of inheritance, everywhere, for every Muslim. All Muslims are bound by sharia in their business dealings, in inheritance matters, in marriage, and in divorce. For Dina, who always lived a secular life, the dictates of Islam didn't mean a great deal. But when her dad died, sharia affected her personally.

From her experience as a family lawyer, Dina knew what was coming. Within hours of her father's death, the uncles, as the only males in the family, came calling. They were to be the custodians of all the wealth since there were no men in Dina's immediate family. With Dina, her two sisters, and her mother still in shock, the uncles collected her father's vehicle and the money from his estate.

Dina's courage was an inspiration to me. Her world, like mine, was falling apart. Her father was dead. Her faith in Islam was being challenged. Her family wealth was being seized. Her future was unmoored because of my lack of commitment, and still she stood strong. I felt as though she needed me. I thought there had been no chance for me to marry her because of family traditions. And yet this series of events made the unprecedented possible.

I felt as if I were being awakened from a deep sleep. I knew the time had come for me to step up and be a man. That meant a commitment from me to take care of Dina and her family. To say this was an easy decision would be a lie. I struggled with my own uncertainties. But then I looked at her mom, and she seemed so completely helpless. What on earth was she to do with no estate and three daughters under her roof? Sharia stripped them of any hope for a future. Their life circumstances made them look at me as a savior. And it made me stop and look at myself.

I did not like what I saw. So I did what my conscience—what was left of it—told me was right. I helped Dina's sister complete college, and I started moving toward marriage with Dina. On one hand, I felt noble and good. On the other, I felt coerced. Before Dina and I wed, I began to wander. I wanted her, but I wanted freedom too. I asked myself, "Why are you running around on Dina? Why are you hurting this woman whom you clearly love?" I had no answers. I just had more of those seemingly unanswerable questions.

SEARCH FOR ANSWERS

In a way, sharia helped Dina understand what I had been going through. It made her see Islam was her enemy too. It helped her bear my bad behavior while she searched for the answers that would give me some peace and bring us together as a couple. To help us through this period, she began exploring websites featuring examples of positive thinking and stories of success.

Dina looked for answers from people who prospered in life. She seemed to know me better than I knew myself as I have always been fascinated by success stories. Not immediately aware of its Christian slant, Dina introduced me to one "lifestyle" website called Beliefnet. The site's uplifting messages inspired me to have hope for the future. I began to believe once again I had a reason to live.

In time, though, I started noticing Bible passages from people named Luke and Mark and others infused into the messages. I felt as though I were being deceived, seduced. The idea of me embracing Christianity struck me as absurd as did the religion itself. I grew angry and confused. I had no knowledge of Christianity and less interest. I never intended our search to challenge Islam. We just needed something positive to grasp, and the site provided it. I wanted to emulate people's success models, not adopt their faith.

I felt as if a group of religious zealots were trying to brainwash me into believing in their god, just as my father brainwashed me into believing in his. This, I wanted no part of. "Why did you show me this website?" I barked at Dina. "Do you want to see me deceived again?" I walked away from the website and walked back into my old habits: drinking, partying, hating myself, and spiraling into despair.

I was never forthcoming with Dina about my past life. As a result, she never fully understood why my emotional life was so volatile. I'm certain she spent many sleepless nights wondering what troubled the man to whom she had pledged her love. I will be the first to admit I was out of control, first with my hopeless downward spiral, and then with my relentless quest to find out who God really is.

A WEDDING NIGHTMARE

Once Dina and I committed to one another, we realized how confused we were about the way forward. Neither she nor I considered ourselves true Muslims, but neither were we anything else. The dynamic of marriage, however, is grounded in religious faith. Having none, I was unsure whether or not I should marry as a traditional Muslim would. At the time, an Egyptian had only two choices: to marry as a Muslim or marry as a Christian. Being neither, we had little recourse but to proceed with the most familiar option. I knew immediately, however, there was no way to keep my old life from casting its shadow on the wedding ceremony.

Tradition required my family and hers come together and I ask one of Dina's male relatives for her hand in marriage. I knew in my heart it was hopeless to ask my family to oblige us, but I had to try. I went to my father, told him about Dina, and asked that he and my mother accompany me to the home of Dina's uncle. As expected, my father greeted my request with a flurry of hateful comments. "I know of them from her family name," he railed. "They are not like us. They are not righteous. No, I will not permit it!"

Family is everything in Islam. A Muslim's identity and very personhood is wrapped up in the family name. Dina's family name told my father all he needed to know. Her family was not devout. My father argued at length about how Dina was not appropriate for me. He insisted I wise up and marry a pious Muslim girl.

Enraged, I spat my curses at Mom and Dad and stormed out. Did they really think I would return to Islam and live the tortured lives they did? I resolved I was done with them. Instead, I would do something unheard of. I went to Dina's uncle alone to ask for her hand. He greeted me kindly and with understanding. When I explained how Dina's father and I forged a true friendship before his death, Dina's uncle agreed to the marriage and promised to sign the marriage contract on behalf of the males in her family.

Dina and I immediately set the date for the wedding. It would take place ten days after my meeting with her uncle, on May 25, 2000. We had wasted plenty of time, and now that I agreed to marry, I wanted to get on with it. Behind the scenes, my parents were quietly hoping I would abandon my plans. My mother's sister, however, told her if she and my father attended the wedding, the gesture would help draw me back into the fold. My mother reluctantly agreed. Eventually, so did my father.

My mother told me she wanted to invite 250 people and we needed to change the date to May 26. I had already printed and mailed invitations, but I agreed to reprint and mail new ones. I wanted things to go smoothly on what should have been a very happy day. In retrospect, I have no idea why I thought I could keep peace with my family.

The first decision with which they took issue was our refusal to marry in the mosque. As a compromise, we decided to bring an imam to our wedding venue, the five-star Fairmont Hotel in Heliopolis. We invited 250 guests. My parents invited another 250. In an effort to further appease my family, I purchased a dress for my mother from the top designer in Egypt that cost a princely sum. Certainly that would make them proud, or so I thought.

Traditionally, a Muslim wedding begins with the men of the two families drawing up a marriage contract and arranging for an amount of money to be paid up front. The bride is not present for any of this. To a Westerner, it sounds a bit like I was buying Dina, but sharia requires this exchange. To keep everyone happy, I paid the bride-price to her uncle. I also gave him a gift as a sign of my goodwill and the value I placed upon his niece. The contract required her uncle to attest to her virginity. And there were other technical questions, again to assure her purity.

Finally, it came time to sign the contract. This required two witnesses, one from each family. The imam took the contract to my father to sign. That was a mistake, and I knew it as soon as he asked. Dad loudly and vehemently refused to sign and started a terrible commotion. My brother, who happily stepped into my role as favored son, also refused. Understandably, Dina's uncle felt his niece was being disrespected, and he threatened to walk out. Just as the situation was about to spin out of control, my uncle Hassan stepped up and signed for my family. I suspect he later received a stern reprimand from his younger brother, my father, but I will always be grateful to my uncle for saving the day.

Just as the dust was settling from that blow-up, my father launched a broadside against Dina and me. Instead of the customary five-minute blessing, he spoke for nearly an hour. He spewed curses on me for my behavior, chastised Dina for not wearing the hijab, and went on and on, peppering in comments throughout about how he hoped we would eventually come to our senses.

I didn't even want the traditional rituals to be a part of the wedding. Yet here was this man, my self-declared enemy, commandeering the entire wedding ceremony. He held center court at a table in the middle of the ballroom while all the wedding guests looked on, many of them aghast. It was humiliating and infuriating, and I knew then I could never forgive him.

In a true exercise of patience, I did not interfere with his tirade. When Dina finally made her appearance in the room to complete the ceremony, my heart jumped. This was the bride I had to battle my father to secure. Her dress was covered with delicate beading; her veil flowed down her back. But all I could see was her face. I questioned how I could deserve her love. She stayed by my side through many a dark day and still wanted to marry me. I was indeed a very lucky man. Although my father tried desperately to pull me back into the bondage of my past life. I would not, could not, go back to that place, to Islam, to my enslavement.

I will remember that day forever. It had the feel of an out-of-body experience. There is no other word for the dynamic but "weird," and I'm sure an outsider looking in would have found it comical. Assembled in the hotel ballroom were more than 500 people, an entire cross section of Islamic society, with almost no one interacting with anyone from outside his or her particular section.

There was a section for my devout family. To look at them, you would think they were at a funeral. There was a section for Dina's family. There was a section for all the Muslim Brotherhood members my family invited. There were doctors and medical personnel from my work. And in the very back were our rowdy, partying friends! Never had I appreciated their presence so much. Their gaiety made me immune to all the invective spewed from my father on this very, very weird day.

CHAPTER 26

GOD IS LOVE

No one has ever seen God; but if we love one another,
God lives in us and his love is made complete in us.
This is how we know that we live in him and he in us:
He has given us of his Spirit.

—1 John 4:12–13[19]

The marriage behind me, I set out to learn more about Jesus. The seeds were planted in 1998 when Dina introduced me to the Beliefnet website, and the words of Matthew, Mark, Luke, and John fermented in my brain since then. My quest for finding the meaning of life resurfaced again. Why? My earlier belief in Allah was shattered but I knew there was something else. What was it?

I began with Jesus's role in the Quran, which referred to him as *the* Messiah. The word "Messiah" in Arabic literally means, "He erased." It was unclear to me just *what* Jesus erased. Particularly confusing was a verse, Quran 3:55, which says, "O Jesus indeed, I will cease you from being alive *[mutawaffika]* and raise you to myself and purify you from those who disbelieve and make those who follow you superior to those who disbelieve until the day of resurrection."

In this verse, Allah was speaking to Jesus. To paraphrase, Allah told Jesus he would cause him to die, then lift him up, and purify him. What is undeniable is, according to the Quran, Jesus died. Yet imams the world over insist the Arabic word *mutawaffika* means "sleep." I knew it meant only one thing, "death."

The part about cleansing and purifying really jumped out at me. Jesus was cleansed after being beaten and pierced. He suffered those wounds during crucifixion. The Quran, however, insists the disbelievers put Jesus in jail and left him there. There was no crucifixion. Again, this conflicts with the Quran's earlier verse.

The Quran commanded Muslims to follow in the model of Jesus's apostles but told us nothing about what that model was. I went to sources of the Quran and found many references to the disciples (Quran 5:111–115). Since we were told to follow their model, I needed to find out what they were teaching. I did not have access to, nor want to use, a Bible, since I was taught not to trust a Bible. Chapter 36 of the Quran is called "The Heart of the Quran." Mohamed gave it that name and told us these men were holy. Verse 13 talks about two apostles, Peter and Paul, who were joined by a third person, Barnabas. Upon sharing their story of Jesus, they were rejected and almost killed, but they stood by their story in the hope they could save the lives of those who listened. Even as they were about to be stoned, they never recanted.

I next went to historical sources to find out what happened to the disciples. According to the Christian Coptic Orthodox Church of Egypt Encyclopedia, I learned the apostle Mark came to Egypt in AD 49. He knew Jesus, was mentored by him, and wrote about Jesus and his life. He also preached what would later become Christianity, which included the idea of the Trinity, and built the church of Alexandria. Like almost all the apostles, he was martyred for his faith. What hit me the most was the realization that if someone were faking a message or preaching an untruth, he would not be willing to die for the lie. Mark willingly died for his faith and belief in Jesus.

As a Muslim I was taught Jesus was a prophet with powers of a magician. I grew up to deny his death on the cross. The apostles, I was learning, knew Jesus personally. They recorded his death on the cross as well as his resurrection from the dead. So deeply did they believe Jesus was God they established churches all over the world and put the Gospel of Jesus in the hands of people far and near. The apostles believed deeply enough, in fact, almost all would die as martyrs.

Standing against the well-documented records of at least four men who knew Jesus personally was the Islamic account. This account was allegedly whispered into the ear of Mohamed, an illiterate man, six centuries after Jesus's death. This version was not even written down until after Mohamed died.

Looking back at my years of research, I realized that whenever Mohamed wanted the masses to believe something he just said, "Gabriel told me." Who could argue with that? Again, that would be me. Every word I accepted as the irrefutable word of Allah seemed shakier by the day. Each answer posed a new question.

At this uncertain time in my life these discoveries led me only into a deeper struggle with my identity. And I was angry. I knew nothing of salvation or redemption because neither was a concept in Islam. All I knew of Christianity was Jesus was the prophet of the Christians, he was a magician, and Christianity had three gods—Father, Son, and Holy Spirit—unlike the one god, Allah, in Islam.

THE BIRTH OF OUR SON

In the midst of this trial there was one undeniable blessing. Our son was conceived during our honeymoon. Dina and I dated off and on for five years before our marriage, and we were both ready to start a family. I went back to my medical work and my OB/GYN clinic. Dina went back to her legal work. And together we focused on welcoming our son into the world.

With a new baby on the way, I did what any self-respecting male would do anywhere in the world. I poured myself into work with a goal of achieving wealth and success. We already had two homes, one in the city and another at the shore, and several cars. We were able to travel extensively, and by all worldly standards, life was close to perfect.

The imperfection, however, clouded everything else. I refer to the massive void left in my soul when I pushed Islam out. Still, I was less restless than I was in the years leading up to our wedding, and the respect I received from my wife, my patients, my coworkers, and Egyptian society helped fill the void. During this time, I tried to content myself by striving for personal success if only to demonstrate my apostasy did not doom me to a life of failure.

In October of 2001, Dina delivered our son, Alex. Any new parent anywhere will tell you no words can adequately describe what it feels like to bring a child into the world. I was one such parent. I was proud, honored, and excited to be a father! To be the kind of father my son deserved, however, I knew I had to replenish my soul. I wasn't sure where to begin but I felt that now, at least, I was loved and needed. What I did as a man and father going forward mattered more than my gnawing discontent.

SEARCHING FOR JESUS

I did not want to let my son down. I did not want Alex to inherit my doubts or my sins. He deserved better. He deserved a father who could share with him a firm idea of who God was. I am convinced now that once exposed to the light of truth, humans everywhere will defy everything to seek it out. I was one such seeker. In Islam, however, my search for that light, like my reading of the Beliefnet website, was strictly *haram*, forbidden. To escape from under the shadow of that sin, I began a journey that consumes me to this day. If I were committing a sin from the Islamic perspective, I needed to understand the larger, truer perspective justifying my search.

The more digging I did, even in the Quran, I came to see the unique essence of Christianity. Finding out more about Christianity was not easy. In Egypt, I never saw a Bible or any other holy books. Information about Jesus Christ was becoming more available, but I had to look hard to find it. When I did, I was fascinated by Jesus. His message was so loving, so human, so understanding. I had a hunger for that message, yet I had one foot still in Islam.

Believing in Allah remained an insurance policy. To abandon all I knew and who I was seemed absurd, repugnant even.

That would change.

MY FATHER'S ONE MISTAKE

Alex's birth also stirred some old feelings I did not expect to resurface. I began to long for a renewed relationship with my father, a normal one. I hoped he felt the same. Once again, I decided to reach out to him and establish some sort of truce. I wanted him to know, although we parted ways, I still loved him. It was crazy, I know, but the love between a father and son defies reason. I revered the man. I admired, trusted, and believed him for most of my life. He called me names, belittled me, humiliated me, and still I loved him.

After my son's birth, I called my dad and asked him to circumcise Alex. I thought this might be a way to bring our families back together—to start anew. It was during Ramadan. Dad agreed to perform the circumcision, but nothing changed. What did I expect?

In July of 2002 I met my dad for dinner one night hoping he would change his attitude about me and my family. I was profoundly disappointed by his response. He did not return my feelings, or if he did, he refused to say so. He continued to insist I come to my senses. This was not really a surprise. There is no place for dialogue in Islam. I had to return to my old life or there would be no relationship. The chasm between us yawned as wide as ever, with both of us vowing to remain steadfast in our own convictions.

Allah is a very cruel master. He expects nothing short of complete perfection. A Muslim may spend his life opening mosques, keeping the five pillars, saying every single prayer, and earning his rewards for heaven, but in Islam, one mistake can cause a Muslim to lose everything.

I was my father's one mistake. Every Muslim knows we are placed on this planet for two reasons: to work and to worship Allah. Good works are a Muslim's reason for being. My father made it his life's purpose to store up treasures in heaven by his works here on Earth. He was a master at putting money in the bank of Allah and accumulated a goodly sum to leave behind when he died.

The Quran teaches that for every mosque a Muslim builds, he will receive a castle in heaven. My father already has a few castles waiting for him. For every school a Muslim builds, he gets more rewards still. My father has built seven. My father has used his personal wealth to pave his way to heaven, often at the expense of his own family. Islam compelled him to do just that. Short of martyrdom, there was no other way to heaven and many, many ways to hell.

Having an apostate for a son was systematically undoing all his life's work. So my father did the only thing he could do under the Islamic system to redeem himself—he tried to erase the mistake, literally. Unworried about property damage or legal consequences, he lured me into his trap and sprang it on March 29, 2003. From the first second the bomb exploded, I knew who set it and why. If my father failed to murder me, it was not for want of trying. Had I not tripped when I entered his office, I would be dead.

When the EMTs placed me on the stretcher, I could not help but cry out from the pain. My skin throbbed from the burns. My muscles contracted with the movement, and the emotional pain ate away at me from within. Just days before I felt as if I were on top of the world. I fell to the bottom, completely helpless, broken, and alone.

I looked deeply into Dina's eyes. They said so much: shock, fear, disappointment, and, yes, anger. I had to turn away. Through the fog of my brain I wondered what would happen to her and Alex if I died. Who would care for them? The crushing weight of defeat settled on my chest. My world was shattered. Islam betrayed me. I saw no way out of the dark.

THE FINAL BREAK FROM ISLAM

The men loaded me into the ambulance. Choking back her fears, Dina said, "I will follow along behind." The men rolled the gurney in and closed the doors. If there was anyone with me in the ambulance, I don't recall. All I remember was feeling alone and defeated. If my life were to end, I had nothing to show for it. What kind of a man, I thought, leaves his family so little hope? In our culture only a father or brother could step in to care for my family. That wasn't going to happen. My wife and son would have nothing and no one.

I was not too confused to ask myself one fundamental question: What kind of belief system requires a man to kill his own son to secure his place in heaven? I wanted to be loved more than anything in the world, but, in those moments, I felt completely and utterly unloved. What kind of god, I wondered, could ask so much evil of his followers? At that moment, thinking of my own son, I could see his beautiful face and smile and hear his laughter. Could I ever contemplate killing my precious boy? Were I a good Muslim, I could only answer "yes." I was not that good Muslim any longer.

From the stretcher I looked up through the windows in the roof of the ambulance, toward the sky and the streetlights twinkling at dusk. Suddenly, through the fog of my pain, I saw one thing more—the chalk on the board in the third-grade classroom of the English school I attended in Cairo that said, "God is Love." I do not know how those words penetrated the darkness. I only know they did. God always arrives at the right time!

"God is Love. God is Love," I said it again in my mind. At that moment, I was overcome with emotion and a wave of hope. Hope in *what*, I wasn't sure. I knew little of this God of love or of Christianity in general. But I knew Islam and Allah failed me and Allah was a cruel god who could never be pleased.

The Bible and the Quran contain two completely different theologies. Islam is based on the premise that to attain heaven a person must be as righteous as possible and work hard from a ritualist perspective and life aspect. If you mess up, the only way to pay the price for sin is through works. The Quran uses the prophet's examples to show how perfect he was and how we should follow his example. People who do not follow his example will pay a very hefty price for not working hard and paving their own way to heaven.

In the Bible you find a very understanding, loving God, who created us, and he understands fully our weaknesses. He knows very well that no matter what, we will fail, and we cannot reach full righteousness whatsoever. Though the stories of the prophets mentioned in the Quran are very similar, those in the Bible do not ignore their human side, their weaknesses, messing up, and how God, by his loving, caring nature, accepts their faithfulness and devoutness to him as the only reason to forgive them and to fulfill his promise to them.

Two theologies give you two different roads to the same destination, which is heaven. Both roads cannot be right. The biggest question is, Which one of those roads is going to take you to heaven? One of those two theologies has to be a lie. I finally knew which one was a lie.

I resolved from that moment I would follow the God of the Bible; even if this was a false hope, it was a hope I would hang on to. Even if I were to spend an eternity in hell for turning my back on Allah, I resolved to follow the God of love. My life would never be the same. I removed the final chain. I was no longer a slave of Allah.

EPILOGUE

On July 4, 2005, in Omaha, Nebraska, Dina, Alex, and I were baptized. The date could not possibly hold more significance. America's birthday was also our birthday! On that day, every year, we celebrate our freedom in Christ. Those years and months leading up to that most significant occasion were a whirlwind of learning, praying, and running from the past.

Once in America I soon discovered Islam was nothing like Christianity. Being raised a devout Muslim I was completely ignorant of Christianity, except for the few bits of information I received along the way. I thought it would be simple and I could learn the rituals, read the Bible, follow the rules, and I would be a Christian. I thought it was like Islam in that respect. It was so much more than that and I am so grateful for all of the people God placed beside me to teach and mentor me during the process.

Being a Christian is being born again in Jesus Christ. I had no concept of what this meant until it happened to me! I discovered my life would completely change and I would live for him and through him 24/7. I found a new Father who would never forsake me; I found the Father who would love me no matter what mistakes I make; I found confidence I would meet him in heaven; I found a Father I would die for, not one who wanted to kill me.

Indeed, our flight from Egypt proved to be nearly as harrowing as was Moses's. And that flight did not end once we reached America. The Muslim Brotherhood, we learned, has long arms and a powerful grip.

Although those born into the Church may know their faith better than I, none can value it any more than those of us who have suffered to make it our own. My embrace of Christianity proved to be every bit as measured, every bit as liberating, as my rejection of Islam. It is a glorious story, equal parts terrifying, and awe-inspiring. It is a story I look forward to sharing the rest of my life.

NOTES

1. Book 2, Hadith 0495
2. Al-Bidaayah wan-Nihaayah: 6:305,306
3. Abu Hurairah & collected in Saheeh al-Bukhari (English trans.) vol. 1, p. 356, no. 629 & Saheeh Muslim (English trans.) vol. 2, p. 493, no. 2248.
4. Ehsan Yar-Shater, ed., *The History of al-Ṭabarī, Volume IX: The Last Years of the Prophet*, trans. Ismail K. Poonawala (Albany: State University of New York Press, 1990), 112–114.
5. Sunan Abi Dawud 4252, Book 37, Hadith 13, English Translation Book 36, Hadith 4239
6. Ibn Majah in A-Mansik (Vol. 2, page 1039, no. 3112)
7. Narrated by al-Bukhaari, 4463; Muslim, 2444
8. ,aḥīḥ al-Bukhārīl-BukhṢaḥīḥ Muslim 533
9. Sunan Ibn Majah 2612 and Sahih el Gamaa 6753
10. Narrator: Abu Razin al-Aqili, Laqit bin Amer; Told by: Ibn Khuzaymah; *The Book of Tawheed*, p. 461/2.
11. Narrated by Muslim, 153
12. Sahih Ben-Haban 6441
13. Sahih Muslim 2659
14. *The History of al-Tabari* (Albany: State University of New York Press, 1988), 44.
15. The story of Mohamed's encounter with Bahira occurs in the works of the early Muslim historians Ibn Hisham (died 833 CE), Ibn Sa'd al-Baghdadi (784–855), and Muhammad ibn Jarir al-Tabari (839–923).
16. Sahih al-Bukhari 3207 and Sahih Muslim 164
17. Volume 6, Book 60, Number 202–Narrated Ibn Abbas
18. Dar Almnethor in Tafsir 39-2
19. Holy Bible, New International Version®, NIV® Copyright ©1973, 1978, 1984, 2011 by Biblica, Inc.® Used by permission. All rights reserved worldwide.